CONTESTING IMMIGRATION POLICY IN COURT

What difference does law make in immigration policy making? Since the 1970s, networks of progressive attorneys in both the United States and France have attempted to use litigation to assert rights for noncitizens. Yet judicial engagement – while numerically voluminous – remains doctrinally curtailed. This study offers new insights into the constitutive role of law in immigration policy making by focusing on the legal frames, narratives, and performances forged through action in court. Challenging the conventional wisdom that "cause litigation" has little long-term impact on policy making unless it produces broad rights-protective principles, this book shows that legal contestation can have important radiating effects on policy by reshaping how political actors approach immigration issues. Based on extensive fieldwork in the United States and France, this book explores the paths by which litigation has effected policy change in two paradigmatically different national contexts.

Leila Kawar is an assistant professor in the Legal Studies Program of the Department of Political Science at the University of Massachusetts Amherst. Her research, which has been funded by the National Science Foundation and the Council for European Studies, focuses on the intersection of legal activity with migration and citizenship. She is active in the Law and Society Association, where she served for four years as coordinator for the Citizenship and Immigration Collaborative Research Network. She is a cofounder of the Migration and Citizenship Section of the American Political Science Association.

CAMBRIDGE STUDIES IN LAW AND SOCIETY

Cambridge Studies in Law and Society aims to publish the best scholarly work on legal discourse and practice in its social and institutional contexts, combining theoretical insights and empirical research.

The fields that it covers are studies of law in action; the sociology of law; the anthropology of law; cultural studies of law, including the role of legal discourses in social formations; law and economics; law and politics; and studies of governance. The books consider all forms of legal discourse across societies, rather than being limited to lawyers' discourses alone.

The series editors come from a range of disciplines: academic law, sociolegal studies, sociology, and anthropology. All have been actively involved in teaching and writing about law in context.

Series Editors
Chris Arup *Monash University, Victoria*
Sally Engle Merry *New York University*
Susan Silbey *Massachusetts Institute of Technology*

A list of books in the series can be found at the back of this book.

Contesting Immigration Policy in Court

LEGAL ACTIVISM AND ITS RADIATING EFFECTS IN THE UNITED STATES AND FRANCE

LEILA KAWAR

University of Massachusetts Amherst

CAMBRIDGE UNIVERSITY PRESS

CAMBRIDGE
UNIVERSITY PRESS

32 Avenue of the Americas, New York NY 10013-2473, USA

Cambridge University Press is part of the University of Cambridge.

It furthers the University's mission by disseminating knowledge in the pursuit of education, learning and research at the highest international levels of excellence.

www.cambridge.org
Information on this title: www.cambridge.org/9781107415119

© Leila Kawar 2015

First published 2015
First paperback edition 2016

A catalogue record for this publication is available from the British Library

Library of Congress Cataloguing in Publication data
Kawar, Leila, 1976– author.
Contesting immigration policy in court : legal activism and its radiating effects in the United States and France / Leila Kawar.
pages   cm. – (Cambridge studies in law and society)
ISBN 978-1-107-07111-7 (hardback)
1. Emigration and immigration law–United States.   2. Emigration and immigration law–France.   3. Aliens–United States.   4. Aliens–France.   I. Title.
K3275.K39   2015
342.4408′2–dc23   2015004871

ISBN 978-1-107-07111-7 Hardback
ISBN 978-1-107-41511-9 Paperback

For Nadia Farid Baddoura

(1925–2014)

Contents

Acknowledgments

This book would not have been possible without the generous assistance of the many jurists in the United States and France who allowed me into their professional world. I cannot here thank all of the advocates, judges, and government attorneys who contributed to this project over the years – they are too many. However, I want to extend my gratitude to Dan Kesselbrenner, director of the National Immigration Project of the National Lawyers Guild, and to Lucas Guttentag, founder and former national director of the American Civil Liberties Union Immigrants' Rights Project, who took an interest in my project, made themselves available for long conversations, and allowed me use of their organizational archives in Boston and New York, respectively. In Paris, the members and staff of the Groupe d'Information et de Soutien des Immigrés graciously allowed me use of their archives, patiently answered questions, facilitated contacts for interviews, and provided valuable feedback. I am especially indebted to Professor Danièle Lochak for encouraging my research and to Jean-Eric Malabre and Serge Slama for their precious insights and friendship. Finally, I extend my thanks to the immigration specialists within U.S. and French public administration who are not named individually for reasons of confidentiality, but who spoke frankly and at length with me about their work.

I first undertook this study of immigrant rights legal activism in the context of my doctoral dissertation in the Law and Society Program at New York University. I acknowledge the support of my dissertation committee members: Christine Harrington, Christopher Mitchell, and Martin Schain. When the project was in its formative stages, Christine Harrington encouraged me to adopt a constitutive sociolegal perspective, and I am very grateful to her for pushing me in this direction. Other mentors at New York University who contributed conceptual and methodological insights to this project and deserve special thanks include Rick Abel, Paul Chevigny, David Greenberg, Lewis Kornhauser, Sally Merry, and Peter Schuck.

I am greatly indebted to those at Sciences Po Paris who provided me with an institutional home during my time in France. I particularly thank Professors Catherine Wihtol de Wenden and Bruno Latour for their graciousness and intellectual generosity. I also extend my sincere gratitude to Justice Bernard Stirn, President of the Section des Contentieux, as well as other current and former members of the Conseil d'Etat who allowed me to observe their public and private audiences.

The research for this comparative study was funded by a grant from the National Science Foundation's Law and Social Sciences Program (Grant SES-0616797); a Lurcy Trust fellowship for study in France; a Council for European Studies dissertation grant; and a Jerome Hall postdoctoral fellowship at Indiana University Maurer School of Law. A number of professional archivists deserve thanks for expertly facilitating my access to the collections of the Ford Foundation Archives, the U.S. National Archives at College Park, the Centre des Archives Contemporaines at Fontainebleau, the Centre de Recherche en Histoire Contemporaine at Sciences Po Paris, and the Bibliothèque de Documentation Internationale Contemporaine at Nanterre.

Along the way, my understanding of the legal and political stakes of immigrant rights lawyering was sharpened through conversations with a number of committed scholar-activists, especially Fran Ansley, Jennifer Gordon, Larry Kleinman, and Fred Tsao. At Bates College, my colleagues Val Carnegie, Alex Dauge-Roth, Naïma Hachad, Tina Malcolmson, Melinda Plastas, Carmen Serrano, Carole Anne Taylor, and, especially, Bill Corlett and Elizabeth Eames, offered solidarity and sustaining encouragement. My year-long fellowship at the Center for Law and Society at Indiana University Maurer School of Law offered space and freedom to write, enhanced by the collegial company of Lara Kriegel, Leandra Lederman, and Alex Lichtenstein. At Bowling Green State University, I found pluralistic and welcoming colleagues among the faculty and staff of the Political Science Department and in an Institute for Culture and Society writing group amicably convened by Scott Magelssen. I also express my sincere gratitude to reference librarian Vera Lux for her exceptional research support, as well as to Radhika Gajjala, Beatrice Guenther, Nancy Kubasek, Sridevi Menon, Andy Schocket, and many other colleagues for thought-provoking conversations about teaching and research. On multiple research trips to Paris, I was blessed with the friendship and hospitality of Carolina Sanchez Boe, François Bonnet, and Karima Mazit.

Some portions of Chapters 3, 4, and 6 were previously published in substantially different form in the following sources: *Law & Social Inquiry*, *International Migration Review*, and the *Journal of Law and Courts*. I am grateful to the journals for permitting me to draw from these works.

This book has been influenced by the thoughtful and challenging comments of a long list of friends and colleagues. Above all, I would like to recognize Rick Abel, who generously shared his wisdom and experience throughout the writing process. Allow me also to thank: Saskia Bonjour, Jonathan Goldberg-Hiller, Anil Kalhan, Anna Law, Michael McCann, Sally Merry, Johann Mori, Hiroshi Motomura, Frank Munger, Ronen Shamir, Rachel Sturman, Mariana Valverde, Stephen Wasby, and Andrea Zemgulys. At key moments, Lisa Disch, Marie Provine, Susan Sterett, and Mariah Zeisberg were particularly generous with their time, sharing suggestions for revisions and confirming that I was on the right track. I thank several anonymous reviewers for taking the time to engage with my project and for offering very helpful feedback. I also extend special thanks to Alex Huneeus, Anne Kornhauser, and Mark Massoud, who were my companions at various points during the book-writing process as well as insightful interlocutors. During the final stages of production, my dear friend Diane Chehab offered me her experienced francophone editor's eye, supplementing the excellent editorial services of Cambridge University Press.

I am deeply grateful for the moral support of my family and friends throughout this "insanely long" writing process. I could not have done it without you. Thanks especially to Giorgio, whose cooking and careful line editing accompanied this book into the world.

Abbreviations

ABA	American Bar Association
ACLU	American Civil Liberties Union
AILA	American Immigration Lawyers Association
ANAFE	Association Nationale d'Assistance aux Frontières pour les Etrangers
BIA	Board of Immigration Appeals, U.S. Department of Justice
CARDF	Central American Refugee Defense Fund
CASA	Center for Autonomous Social Action – General Brotherhood of Workers
CFDT	Confédération Française Démocratique du Travail
CGT	Confédération Générale du Travail
Cimade	La Cimade – Service Oecuménique d'Entraide de la Fédération Protestante de France
DHS	U.S. Department of Homeland Security
DOJ	U.S. Department of Justice
DPM	Direction of Population and Migrations, French Ministry of Social Affairs
ECHR	European Court of Human Rights
ECJ	European Court of Justice
EU	European Union
GISTI	Groupe d'Information et de Soutien des Travailleurs Immigrés/Groupe d'Information et de Soutien des Immigrés
INS	U.S. Immigration and Naturalization Service
LSC	Legal Services Corporation
MAJ	Mouvement d'Action Judiciaire
MALDEF	Mexican American Legal Defense and Education Fund
NCIR	National Center for Immigrants' Rights

NILC   National Immigration Law Center
SONACOTRA   Société Nationale de Construction de Logements pour les
             Travailleurs

1

What Difference Does Law Make in Immigration Policy Making?

In 1952, at the height of Cold War tensions, the U.S. Supreme Court in the case of *Harisiades v. Shaughnessy* upheld the government's efforts to deport a longtime legal permanent resident who had briefly joined the American Communist Party more than a decade earlier. In holding Peter Harisiades deportable, the Court's majority decision gave no consideration to his lack of criminal record, the length of his residence in the United States, or the possibility that he would be politically persecuted in his native Greece. "That aliens remain vulnerable to expulsion after long residence is a practice that bristles with severities," wrote the Court, "but such is the traditional power of the Nation over the alien."[1] The justices declined to interfere with the way Congress had exercised this power in the Alien Registration Act of 1940, which authorized the deportation of a legally resident alien because of membership in the Communist Party even when such membership terminated before enactment of the act. Nor was the Court willing to consider the fairness of the manner in which administrative officials had conducted Harisiades's deportation proceedings. The justices made clear that immigration policy making would be shielded from juridical interventions, or as the Court put it, "We leave the law on the subject as we find it."[2] The *Harisiades* decision was a major blow to the efforts of leftist legal networks that had organized Harisiades's defense in the hopes of securing the rights of the foreign born (Ginger 1993, 544). More broadly, for a generation of activist lawyers, the lesson of the case was that challenging immigration policy in court was essentially a hopeless cause.

Two decades later, as the 1973 oil shocks ushered in the contemporary period of immigration restrictionism, a new generation of activist lawyers sought to reopen debates over the role of law and courts in immigration policy making. Members the 1970s generation of law graduates, both in the United States and elsewhere, were galvanized by the tightening of immigration controls. In taking up the cause of immigrant defense as a form of political engagement, they dreamed of using law as a tool for social change and sought to enroll judges as allies in this project. Initially, the boundaries and goals of this project were relatively inchoate. As we will see, however, a particular form of immigration-centered advocacy gradually emerged – one that I have termed "immigrant rights legal activism" – characterized by a conscious effort to use litigation to proactively assert or develop rights for noncitizens in the domain of immigration policy making. Although these efforts frequently involve collaborations with immigration attorneys involved in more client-centered legal practice, legal activism's aspiration to intervene in national-level debates over immigration policy making sets it apart.

Previous sociolegal scholarship has not explicitly considered the constitutive relationship between immigration-centered legal activity and elite policy making. Instead, sociolegal ethnographies have shown how, at the level of local interactions, law constitutes the understandings of citizenship and justice that are formed and contested within administrative immigration hearings and immigrants' encounters with community-based legal services programs (McKinley 1997, Coutin 2000, Kelly 2012). In addition, studies of immigrant social movements have demonstrated how the language of rights can support grassroots mobilization efforts and immigrant community empowerment (Coutin 1993, Voss and Bloemraad 2011, Gleeson 2013). But what about juridically oriented activity that aims to impact immigration policy making on a national scale? What are the implications of these targeted and high-profile legal interventions? What modality of politics do they construct?

This study seeks to answer these questions by offering an in-depth examination of the emergence and development of immigrant rights legal activism within two sharply contrasting politico-legal settings, those of the United States and France. The analysis is centered around the activities of jurists who, over the past forty years, have pioneered efforts to contest immigration policies in court. As we will see, it is a project that has come to assume strikingly distinct features in each country. Focusing on the specificities of each national context, my analysis explores how immigrant rights legal activism has assembled its professional identity and how it has been taken into account by actors in the immigration policy domain. In tracing the policy-level effects of court-centered contestation, I follow in the footsteps of several generations of sociolegal scholars who have examined the "radiating effects" of action in court (Galanter 1983). Challenging the hierarchic ideal of legal positivism, the key insight of this sociolegal approach is the observation that practical engagement with law is a culturally productive process. By shifting the focus away from the official rules laid out in immigration cases and toward the *process* by which immigration policy has been contested in court, we can explore how legal engagements generate identities and meanings whose repercussions extend far beyond any single case's judicially enforced remedy or doctrinal contribution.

LEGAL CONSTRAINTS ON MIGRATION POLICY: DEFERENTIAL DOCTRINE AND CONTAINED COMPLIANCE

Legal interventions have attracted what might best be described as passing attention within the large and growing body of scholarship that examines the dynamics of immigration policy making. To the extent that court-centered activity has been discussed by scholars in this area, analysis has centered on high-profile judicial decisions that extend the set of formal rights available to noncitizens.[3] On the whole, studies of immigration policy making have associated legal interventions with the official dispositions of high-profile cases, and debate has centered on how far the legal rules and remedies produced by courts can be said to constrain the realization of legislative and administrative preferences in the domain of immigration policy.

Among the first to call attention to the adjudication of immigration policy issues as a new and significant development were liberal international relations scholars and political sociologists, who linked high-profile court decisions on immigration issues to shifting arrangements at the international level. According to one line of argument, propounded most prominently by James F. Hollifield, when national courts issue decisions that protect the rights of noncitizens, they are acting out their part in a postwar international system of embedded liberalism that ensures a commitment to free trade while demanding some level of demonstrated respect for individual rights (Hollifield 1992, Gomes 2000, Hollifield 2004). Others have suggested that it is the contemporary move toward transnationalism, visible in the "web of rights" contained in international human rights instruments and supranational treaties, that has created opportunities for judicial engagement with immigration policies by opening up legal avenues outside of the framework of national self-determination (Jacobson 1996, Jacobson and Ruffer 2003). Sociologist Yasemin Soysal likewise sees the international legal order as a source of migrant rights, though she focuses relatively less on juridical developments (Soysal 1994). In these accounts, judicial interventions are noteworthy as a break from the past, but they are best understood as instantiations of normative regimes operating across national borders.

Comparativist political science studies of immigration policy making have likewise called attention to the increased judicial role in migration governance

over time, and, in contrast to international relations scholars, they have emphasized the distinct institutional characteristics of the judiciary. This contrast is
made most emphatically by Christian Joppke, who argues that judicial decisions creating rights for noncitizens have their origins not at the international
level but rather in national constitutional principles that are extended into
the immigration policy domain. Joppke suggests that the principles enunciated in these high-profile decisions may make it difficult for policy makers to
manipulate migration channels opened up for humanitarian reasons, such as
asylum and family reunification, and may force political elites to reformulate
their overall approach to immigrant communities (Joppke 1998, 83–4). Other
comparativist studies similarly present legal decisions articulating rights for
migrants as having substantially "tempered" (Geddes 2003, 22) and "softened"
(Ellermann 2009, 169) restrictive policies. Even when few generalizable principles are enunciated and review is primarily subconstitutional, invoking and
extending judicially enunciated standards is argued to shift administrative
practices "millimeter by millimeter" (Sterett 1997, 180). Entrepreneurship by
courts in immigration issues is said to constitute the "permanent consolidation of a serious new actor" in the politics of "managed migration" (Menz
2009, 135). Indeed, in some national settings, the adjudication of immigration
has been identified as an important site for debating and developing the judiciary's broader institutional role (Soennecken 2008, Law 2010, Bonjour 2014,
Hamlin 2014).

Yet, as other studies of immigration policy making have emphasized, courts
do not always have the final say. Successful litigation may prompt governments to modify statutes to limit the substantive or jurisdictional grounds for
appealing future immigration-related decisions. Venue shopping is another
possible response to judicial decisions that place limits on how governments
can regulate migration. Virginie Guiraudon's analysis draws attention to the
way that European restrictionists have adapted to judicial interventions by
shifting the institutional context of policy making to the European level and
by moving border control operations overseas and thus beyond the jurisdiction
of national courts (Guiraudon 2000). The effect of venue shopping, according
to Guiraudon, is that different types of actors are included or excluded from
migration politics, thereby placing fewer obstacles in the way of restrictionist policy making. Focusing on the international level, Lisa Conant's analysis
similarly goes beyond the official dispositions of high-profile migrant rights
decisions to focus on the extent to which their holdings constrain subsequent
policy decisions. According to Conant, there has been a persistent tendency
of national policy makers to evade or actively resist the policy implications of
immigration case law and supporters of migrant rights have generally been

unable to break these "cycles of contained compliance" (Conant 2002, 207). Along similar lines, Martin Schain finds no appreciable impact when measuring the political significance of migrant rights decisions in forcing administrators to admit migrants they would prefer to exclude or in compelling political parties to shift their restrictionist programs (Schain 2008). According to this analysis, the overall level of migrant admissions and removals provides a comprehensive measure of how states regulate migration, and judicial interventions can be dismissed because they have hardly constrained the restrictionist tendencies of either legislators or administrative officials.

In sum, to the extent that studies of immigration policy making have considered law and legal institutions, they have tended to concentrate on the rules and remedies produced by judicial decisions in immigration matters. Debate has centered on the extent to which these official case dispositions are taken into account in migration policy determinations. In particular, studies of compliance have questioned how often formal norms actually constrain the restrictionist tendencies of policy makers. These analyses emphasize the weak coercive power of legal rules in the migration policy domain.

AN ALTERNATIVE UNDERSTANDING: LEGAL CONTESTATION AS A SITE FOR REASSEMBLING THE SOCIAL

This study takes a different approach by focusing not on the coercive power of official rules and remedies but rather on the capacity of juridical engagements with immigration to construct and reconstruct social relations, what sociolegal scholars have termed law's "constitutive" dimension (Hunt 1985). A central premise of this constructivist sociolegal approach is that the capacity of judicial decisions to constrain policy makers is only one aspect of how law contributes to reshaping political dynamics. No doubt, both legal activists and the administrative officials whose policies they challenge care about judicial decisions primarily in terms of their coercive capacity. However, the constructivist sociolegal approach urged here calls for a more capacious conceptualization of both law and its effects, one that looks beyond official case dispositions in order to explore legal contestation as a culturally productive process.

This constitutive dimension of law, overlooked by a focus on official rules and remedies, is revealed in ethnographic studies of disputing, which explore how the process of formulating claims in terms of higher order normative referents can introduce powerful new elements into the social world (Comaroff and Roberts 1981). These legal frames and narratives may reproduce established designations, metaphors, and styles of discussion. Alternatively, they may establish new categories that change the perspective through which the social world is perceived. As Lynn Mather and Barbara Yngvesson argue, it is through this "expansive rephrasing," which extends the webs of relations united under potent legal symbols, that legal change may be linked to social change (Mather and Yngvesson 1980, 279). This capacity of legal practice to construct social reality is particularly potent in immigration matters. As Kitty Calavita points out, there was no category of "immigrant" when European explorers "immigrated" to the shores of what was to become the Americas (Calavita 2010). And to the extent that we see distinct political dynamics at work in debates over "illegal immigrants" and debates over "refugees," this is due to the fact that law has created these two categories of migrants and endowed them with normative significance. Moreover, as Susan Coutin has shown through her ethnographic research, the strictures of official immigration law are rarely synonymous with everyday understandings of justice, and court-centered contestation offers one possible space for constructing alternative framings of migrants and their identities (Coutin 2011).

In addition to examining the discursive elements assembled through law, sociolegal scholars have productively explored the performative dimension of court-based interactions. Early studies adopting a constitutive sociolegal approach called attention to the distinct legal "subjectivities" engendered by law in such organizationally distinct settings as mediation procedures (Harrington and Merry 1988) and the processing of consumer protection claims (Silbey 1981). More recent work has traced the distinct "emotional valences" shaped by months and years of ongoing legal entanglements (Berrey, Hoffman, and Nielsen 2012), showing that whether people assume the role of skilled operator or humble supplicant in part depends on the specific organizational settings in which they engage the law (Ewick and Silbey 1998). What we learn from this body of work is that repeatedly engaging the law has a powerful affective influence on participants in this process, whose own local ontologies are reflexively made and remade through interactions within the space of legal institutions.

Some examples will help to illustrate how ritualized courtroom interaction can work to construct a distinct phenomenal field. In his study of a trial court in Toronto, Michael Lynch shows how participants in adversarial trial proceedings collectively produce "the judge" as a fact observable to them and to any competent watcher (Lynch 1997). Certainly, the judge is sitting in the courtroom, wearing a robe, and with formal authorization to preside over the proceedings. Yet to the extent that the courtroom continues to make sense as a place in which judges alone hold power to officially enunciate the law, it is in part because lawyers, their clients, witnesses, and courtroom staff continually orient their interactions to the judge's physical or symbolic presence. This informally patterned behavior ensures that the courtroom's local ontologies, including its hierarchy of power and authority, remain in place even when formal rules do not provide a behavioral script.

Through her fieldwork in the organizational action-setting of domestic violence control programs, anthropologist Sally Engle Merry provides another example of how routine procedures construct and hold together a phenomenal field in which legal interactions can be intelligibly accomplished and the meaning of legal institutions reinforced. Merry focuses on the way in which domestic violence court hearings and court-mandated therapeutic programs differentially position their male and female participants, thereby producing "legally engendered selves" with distinct concepts of responsibility and agency (Merry 1999). Male participants experienced the controlling side of the law and are symbolically positioned by ostensibly rehabilitative procedures as criminals behind bars. By contrast, female participants are offered a supportive environment connected to and provided by the courts, which positions them to think of themselves as endowed with rights and entitlements. As legal actors are repeatedly brought into contact with one another in these organizationally bounded experiential spaces, roles and identities that seem natural and objective are performatively constructed through the accumulation of myriad discrete signs and interactions.

Though law and society scholars have tended to focus on the experiences of ordinary citizens (and noncitizens) in courtroom settings, this does not mean that a culturally productive dimension is absent from interactions undertaken by law's trained practitioners. To the contrary, recent work by scholars of in the field of Science and Technology Studies (STS) has demonstrated that law's constitutive dimension can be explored by "studying up" as well as by "studying down." We see an important development of this mode of inquiry in constructivist STS scholar Bruno Latour's study of legal knowledge production within the particularly rarefied setting of France's highest administrative jurisdiction, the Conseil d'Etat (see Box 1). Comparing the Conseil d'Etat to a scientific laboratory, Latour investigates how the daily operations of this "factory of law" construct the necessary sense of certainty to competently render judgment in complex and difficult cases (Latour 2002). Just as laboratory scientists apply a variety of material and literary inscription devices to distill abstract claims, so too, according to Latour, do the jurists of the Conseil d'Etat rely upon devices – fact-finding methods and techniques of casuistry – to translate complex events and relationships into legal enunciations that stand up to doctrinal scrutiny. As Latour puts it, the two settings have "very different modes of reducing the world to paper" and yet both are concerned with the manipulation of these abstracted inscriptions, subjecting them "to a subtle exegesis which seeks to classify them, to criticize them, and to establish their weight and hierarchy" (Latour 2004b, 96). Without dwelling on the point, Latour notes that the dispositions of the human components of these processes are likewise reconfigured as scientists and jurists engage in the task of stitching their abstracted inscriptions into generalized knowledge.

The present study takes up Latour's invitation to study the "laboratories" of technical law from a constructivist perspective. As Latour emphasizes, expert jurists do not simply apply existing legal rules to the case at hand, but neither do they merely mediate between lived reality and preexisting structures of power. Rather, the "passage of law" should be understood as a process of ontological translation that assembles the human and nonhuman elements of the social world into webs of meaning whose precise elements cannot be known in advance and that are always subject to reassembly (Latour 2004a). Latour's unique combination of pragmatist empiricism and poststructuralist material-semiotics supplies an analytical toolkit for unpacking the "black box" of formalist lawmaking, in which legal technicians are sealed off from the sociopolitical world and where attention to official case dispositions makes it difficult to appreciate all of the other new elements forged in these laboratories of law. Just as law and society scholars elucidated the constitutive dimension of everyday dispute processes, Latour shows how *technical legal work* might also be insightfully analyzed through this lens.

Moreover, the pluralistic constructivism of Latour's approach suggests that activity in court comprises only one cluster of translations in a broader set of actor-network webs that draw political elements into the "laboratory of law" and legal elements into the "laboratory of politics." Sociolegal scholars have long recognized that the political effects of action in court are not limited to the regulatory impact of black letter law. Mark Galanter nicely encapsulates this finding when he writes that, "The product of the court is not doctrine with a mix of impurities but, instead, a whole set of messages that can be used as resources in making (or contesting) claims, bargaining (or refusing to bargain), and regulating (or resisting regulation) (Galanter 1983, 134). In other words, once we conceptualize activity in court as a site for constructing social reality – the approach adopted in both sociolegal studies of everyday disputing and constructivist studies of the laboratories of technical law – we can then look beyond the bounds of legal institutions and explore the radiating effects of legally generated frames, narratives, and performances within the broader political sphere.

One path by which these legal forms acquire a wider political salience is through their impact on social movement activity. As Michael McCann and others have demonstrated, action in court can catalyze the political mobilization of previously unpoliticized individuals while also attracting broader public support (McCann 1994, NeJaime 2011). Even when they fail to produce new doctrine, rights-based narratives may be taken up by local leaders and organizations and inspire new ways of understanding contestatory politics. At the same time, the empowering embodied experience of bringing charges and filing suits may have important effects on social movement activity. As Francesca Polletta shows in her historical study of the U.S. civil rights movement, appeals to formal procedures gave black participants the feeling "that whites were not invulnerable to challenge" (Polletta 2000, 385). Studies of legal mobilization in a comparative context have similarly emphasized the capacity of high-profile litigation to generate feelings of empowerment, forge bonds of solidarity, and support ongoing resistance even in the absence of constitutionally based judicial review (Abel 1995, Vanhala 2011, Chua 2014).

Moreover, social movements are not the only political actors whose ideas about the world are constructed through law. As scholars of judicial politics have shown, legal phrasing and staging also leaves an impact on political elites. For instance, Alec Stone Sweet's pathbreaking study first explored how repeated "dialogue" with a constitutional court sets in motion a process whereby the norms and vocabularies of constitutional law are elaborated and then absorbed into the norms and language of policy making (Stone 1992). While Stone Sweet's generalized model of the process ultimately gravitates toward an instrumentally based approach, he acknowledges that constitutional dialogues also shift the terms of debate insofar as parliamentarians come to understand themselves as having responsibilities to protect rights and to engage in balancing analyses when formulating policy (Stone Sweet 2000, 103). Judicial politics scholars have offered different assessments of how this phenomenon plays out in distinct national contexts and across diverse policy domains. Seeing the effects of engagement with law in a positive light, Stone Sweet contends that French "parliamentary life was gradually 'juridicized' and revitalized" by the Constitutional Council's interventions (Stone 1989, 31). By contrast, American public law scholar Gordon Silverstein sees the "spiraling of precedent" that accompanied the emergence of assertive judicial review in some policy areas as prompting a hardening of positions, which in turn has discouraged legislative actors from devoting energy to the difficult political work of bargaining, tradeoffs, negotiations, and persuasion (Silverstein 2009, 128–51). Regardless of whether these radiating effects are assessed positively or negatively, legally generated forms potentially exert a strong influence over policy makers, shaping how they define their sense of mission, how they understand the issues at stake, and the types of strategies they pursue.

Sociolegal scholars have not yet considered the way these dynamics play out in the immigration policy domain. This may be due in part to the fact that constitutionally based judicial review is rarely exercised to overturn immigration policies enacted at the national level. As critical legal scholar Catherine Dauvergne demonstrates in her cross-national study of immigration jurisprudence, the legal claims of individual foreign migrants tend to be "overshadowed" by a countervailing right of the sovereign nation to shut its borders (Dauvergne 2008, 27). Although lower courts may be relatively less attuned to paradigms of sovereign authority and thus relatively more hospitable to immigrant claimants than courts at the pinnacle of the judicial hierarchy, the interventions of lower court judges in immigration cases are most often confined to an incremental "error-correcting function" that shies away from any direct challenge to policy making (Law 2010, 174). Empirical studies across national contexts indicate that immigration cases "have had generally conservative endings" at all levels of the judicial hierarchy (Legomsky 1987, 224), both in terms of judges' limited willingness to offer short-term remedies and in the sense that rules laid out in judicial opinions in immigration cases have rarely compelled other state officials to explicitly increase migrant admissions or to reduce migrant expulsions. Courts have been most assertive when applying subconstitutional norms to immigration matters, but these interventions are rarely interventionist.

I suggest that the constrained nature of judicial review in immigration matters, at least in comparison to other policy domains, adds particular poignancy to calls by sociolegal scholars over the past three decades for a research agenda that conceptualizes law's power and political impact in constructivist terms. My interpretation of immigration politics in the United States and France confirms that the official case dispositions of courts in these countries have eschewed an interventionist stance on matters of national immigration policy. Nevertheless, I contend that this conception of both law and its effects is too narrow. By limiting our understanding of law to official case dispositions, and then assessing the degree to which these rules and remedies do or do not constrain the realization of restrictionist policy preferences, we neglect to consider how the process of contesting immigration policy in court may constitute the very terms of immigration politics.

Drawing on a constructivist sociolegal approach, the present study conceptualizes court-centered contestation of immigration policy as a culturally productive activity with potentially important radiating effects. In the chapters that follow, I seek to go beyond the legal positivist approach that sees law as a mode of hierarchical control. Instead of examining how legal rules and remedies invoke responses of compliance or of evasion, my goal is to explore the legal forms set in motion by the process of legal contestation. I argue that, across national settings, the process of contesting immigration policy in court can be seen to have injected a set of distinctly juridical forms into the politics of immigration. In other words, I argue that when policy makers and interest groups today address the policies and processes that bring residents of the Global South to the kitchens, beauty parlors, slaughterhouses, and tomato fields of the Global North, their debates engage – to an extent unprecedented forty years ago – with the material, discursive, and conceptual artifacts produced by repeated high-profile legal contestations.

As the following chapters will show, activity in court has made a difference in immigration policy making, but it has done so primarily by reassembling taken-for-granted concepts, categories, and relationships rather than by bringing legislators and administrators under the coercive authority of judges. Indeed, when viewed in historical and comparative perspective, the coercive capacity of law to hamper the immigration enforcement initiatives of legislators and administrative officials appears less consequent than its capacity to symbolically reshape political activity around immigration issues. As immigration questions have been stitched into the fabric of law, they have been repatterned by broader juridical design features. At the same time, the practitioners who engage themselves in these creative material reworkings have likewise been reconfigured by the project of legal activism. As we will see, the assemblages generated through the repeated practice of contesting immigration policy in court have left indirect and unforeseen traces in the sphere of national immigration policy making.

BOX 1. NOTE ON ACTOR NETWORK THEORY AND STUDIES OF
LEGAL LABORATORIES

At first glance, Bruno Latour's suggestion that the activities of creative jurists can be productively analogized to those of experimental scientists may seem far-fetched. To better understand the basis for this provocative comparison, it is helpful to unpack Latour's notion of legal laboratories – and laboratories in general – as spaces "where innovations proliferate, where group boundaries are uncertain, and when the range of entities to be taken into account fluctuates" (Latour 2005, 11). For Latour, laboratories represent domains where knowledge categories are constantly being made and remade. His "sociology of associations," more commonly known as "actor-network theory" (ANT), supplies a methodological blueprint for investigating these processes of experimentation and creative engineering.

(continued)

Rather than seeking to reify or debunk the facts produced by scientific or legal laboratories, Latour has developed a method for documenting how these taken-for-granted "black boxes" hold together in the face of unavoidable empirical complexity. His ethnographic research has explored how daily laboratory life engages experimenters (and their equipment) in a series of translations that reconfigure the messiness and complexity of the material world into "two-dimensional, superposable, combinable inscriptions" that then, and only then, can be formulated as claims intelligible within broader theoretical paradigms (Latour 1999, 29). He argues that, for a scientific claim to take on the status of a generally accepted understanding of the natural world, so that alternative descriptions and readings of the world can be ignored, the series of translations by which it was materially and discursively produced must be sufficiently verifiable to withstand vigorous scrutiny from fellow researchers. The notion of "actor networks" denotes those entities whose workability comes to be taken for granted and that, as a result, become potentially powerful components in new actor networks.

Scientific models gain their workability, in Latour's account, not only as a result of their creators' ambitions but also because objects and other humans implicated in the model's claims allow themselves to be enrolled in this manner. So too, textual inscriptions are argued to be a key component of knowledge production, insofar as they effectively efface traces of uncertainty and build the consensus necessary for acceptance. Importantly, Latour insists that not only human but also nonhuman participants in actor networks operate as mediators, "endowed with the capacity to translate what they transport, to redefine it, redeploy it, and also to betray it" (Latour 1993, 81). Sociolegal scholars have found this conceptualization of objects and inscriptions as mediators to be facilitative of new engagements with legal knowledge production (Riles 1998, 2006, Valverde 2003), and it is this object-oriented reading of Latour's work that is most widely known. Yet, as one recent and insightful commentary points out, it is also possible to approach ANT by considering what it has to say about the distinct tonality that distinguishes law from other modes of knowledge enunciation such as science or politics (McGee 2014).

The notion of legal laboratories provides a blueprint for making sense of knowledge production processes that are dynamic, heterogeneous, and contextually situated. Latour's approach – and ANT more broadly – can be understood as an empirical version of poststructuralism, with "actor networks" seen as "scaled-down versions of Michel Foucault's discourses or epistemes" (Law 2009, 145). Rather than seeking to diagnose an epochal episteme, ANT focuses on exploring particular and smaller-scale webs of relations. STS scholar John Law has suggested that the word *assemblage*, drawn from Gilles Deleuze's nomadic philosophy, is a useful term for capturing an actor network's "process of ... recursive self-assembling in which the elements put together are not fixed in shape, do not belong to a larger pre-given list but are constructed at least in part as they are entangled together" (Law 2004). Unlike the Althusserian concept of interpellation, the ANT notion of assemblage cannot be assumed to reproduce any single preexisting structure or ideology. In their review essay introducing sociolegal scholars to the ANT approach, Levi and Valverde make this point nicely, writing that, "neither human agency nor technological/cultural determinism is assumed a priori, thereby opening up a much wider set of empirical possibilities" (Levi and Valverde 2008). In other words, rather than imposing any monolithic notion of national culture or epochal discourse, the ANT approach invites us to identify empirically the specific actors, objects, and discursive constructs entwined in the concrete webs of legal associations that we choose to unpack. Latour's work demonstrates that it is through empirical examination of the imperfect and actually existing processes of legal experimentation that we can grasp the distinguishing features of law as a mode of knowledge enunciation.

REVEALING LEGAL ASSEMBLAGES THROUGH COMPARISON

If successful legal assemblages have the virtue of hiding from view alternative interpretations and readings of their components, then discerning this process of knowledge construction poses challenges for research. A comparative research strategy offers analytical leverage for uncovering and asking close questions about the concrete meaning-making processes by which the social world is imagined and that guide its activity. By pointing to surprising differences across cases as well as unexpected similarities, a comparative optic serves to "visibilize the invisible" (Knorr Cetina 1999, 22), training the analyst traveling between the compared domains in a more concrete and precise framework of seeing.

The present study explores the constitutive dimension of legal processes in two distinct settings, the United States and France, where organized efforts to contest immigration policy in court have been a feature of political life for a period of several decades. These two countries offer especially fruitful cases for comparison. Both the United States and France are immigrant-receiving states with a historically contentious politics of immigration and migration flows that reflect each country's legacy of imperialism. Both have foundational liberal political traditions that have been mobilized on behalf of immigrant communities. Most important for purposes of this study, in both countries a specialized field of immigration-centered legal activism developed at approximately the same time.[4] Yet, when placed next to one another, these U.S. and French legal contestations are striking for their differences. For instance, the cause of immigrants has been framed in the United States as a new civil rights movement, while in France it has been understood as one of the new social movements that expanded the scope of traditional leftist politics. U.S. legal activists primarily defend noncitizens from removal, while their counterparts in France not only defend noncitizens from removal but also regularly contest restrictions on immigrant admissions. In the United States, legal activism has operated through fact-centered class action lawsuits, while in France it has drawn upon the civil law system's procedures for abstract judicial review. In their differences, the juridical laboratories set in motion by immigrant rights legal activism form a commentary on each other, highlighting how legal assemblages are embedded in social life at the same time that they reconfigure social relations.

The comparative optic is particularly useful for studying the complex workings of legal expertise in modernity's text-based legal systems. Unlike ethnographies of informal dispute processes, empirical explorations of the material practices associated with formal legal institutions have primarily been conducted by scholars who are socialized, at least to some extent, in the settings they studied. There are important exceptions (Scheppele 2004, Riles 2011). Yet familiarity with the elements of one's own politico-legal culture, insofar as it limits the scope of what is assumed to be suitable for investigation, presents a formidable challenge for analysis that seeks to unpack established cultural categories (Nelken 1997). Expanding the research gaze to other contexts, particularly if it is accompanied by an approach attentive to the dangers of imposing anachronistic categories of analysis, advances knowledge by forcing researchers to confront taken-for-granted notions about their home environment. As David Nelken astutely points out, "the naiveté of the 'stranger' can open up doors," both conceptually and in practical terms (Nelken 2010, 96).

My research design incorporates a comparative optic that explicitly decenters the U.S. experience, taking seriously the task of exploring legal knowledge production without imposing the analytical categories of one national setting onto another. In particular, I aim to highlight the nationally distinct trajectories by which litigators have brought immigration issues to the courts. Comparison in this study therefore operates as a mechanism for enhanced appreciation of the rich complexity of techniques, actors, and activities set in motion by the development of immigrant rights litigation. While some commentators suggest that globalization has propelled a convergence of legal forms and practices across national contexts (Wiegand 1996, Coombe 2000, Keleman 2008), comparative studies of legal activism call into question any strong claim of convergence in this domain (Olson 1995, Morag-Levine 2003). The findings from this study of the United States and France indicate that significant differences remain in how immigration policy has been contested in court. Indeed, it is because of their particularities that the comparison of the United States and France allows us to see more deeply into how legal knowledge construction operates in each setting.

At the same time that this comparative research strategy emphasizes the particular, it also has theoretical ambition. Theory building in this study comes not from hypothesis testing, as is often the case in political science, but rather from identifying particular assemblages of actors and activities in one setting and then examining the extent to which those same assemblages can provide insights into our understanding of other settings. The goal of such a project, as Kim Scheppele writes, "is not a universal one-size-fits-all theory, or an elegant model that abstracts away from the distinctive, but instead a set of *repertoires* that can be found in real cases ... not prediction but comprehension, not explained variation but *thematization*" (Scheppele 2004, 391). Stated another way, it is the analytical strategy of iteratively moving from one setting to another and back again that builds our understanding of long-term patterns of meaning making and of webs of associations that would otherwise go unnoticed.

METHOD FOR EXPLORING THE CULTURAL LIFE OF LAW

Comparative research aiming to interpret legal practices across national contexts demands that the researcher develop a deep understanding of local contexture, which in turn requires extensive time in each research site. One reason that there are so few explicitly comparative studies of how legal activism has taken different trajectories across legal systems is that researchers do not have sufficient access to execute such a project. Particularly in the French legal context, where adjudication is carried out away from public view and where judicial decisions are characterized by an exaggerated austerity of form, examining the culturally productive role of law can be challenging.

The research for this book took place over a period of seven years. I spent four extended periods of time in France – a summer visit in 2005, a yearlong stay between August 2006 and August 2007, and return visits ranging from several weeks to several months in 2008, 2009, 2010, and 2011. The U.S. portion of the research began in the fall of 2005 and spring of 2006, when I conducted interviews with immigrant rights litigators, and continued with a focus on archival records during the summer of 2006. A fellowship during the 2011–12 academic year allowed me to significantly expand my research in U.S. public and private archives. Although it was not planned, the alternation between national research sites was crucial for facilitating deep understanding of each field of practice. Each time I found myself gravitating toward a set of analytical categories generated from the experience of one setting, I was forced to reexamine and refine my choice of terms in light of evidence gathered in the other country. Identifying a label for the activity I was observing proved particularly challenging; I knew that both countries had a history of organized litigation that operated in close proximity to national immigration policy making, yet it proved surprisingly difficult to find a suitable phrase to describe this activity. Progressive jurists in both countries identify themselves as belonging to a community of legal experts who specialize in litigating government policies that regulate immigration status. However, they use different terminology to describe their practices. U.S. immigrant rights litigators described their work as "impact litigation," "law reform," or "civil rights law," but these terms were not used by the network of specialized French jurists who identify themselves as "defending the cause of foreigners in court." I have settled on the term *immigrant rights legal activism* to denote the set of practices that are the subject of this comparative study (see Box 2).

In retrospect, this iterative research process proved to be well-suited to charting the interconnected webs of practices that have come to be identified with immigrant rights legal activism. In both France and the United States, my starting points for empirical research were my contacts within legal academia. Not only was this a setting that was relatively accessible to me, but this milieu is also institutionally central to the reproduction of each country's legal establishment, including its liberal reformist strata. Once my introductions to key actors in each national immigrant rights legal community had been facilitated, I conducted initial interviews with these individuals. In many cases, these initial contacts then generously assisted me in identifying and contacting other jurists engaged in similar work, so that a network of contacts was gradually amassed. In practice, there was a large degree of consensus among my contacts about the key players litigating immigrant rights issues on the national stage, many of whom it turned out had been active over a period of several decades. From these interviews, it became clear that immigrant rights legal activism as it exists today in the United States and France traces its genealogy back to the rise of immigrant social movements and the turn to restrictionist immigration policies in the early 1970s. Subsequent immigrant and refugee movements have brought new generations of progressive jurists into the immigrant rights legal network, but there has been a relatively high degree of organizational continuity. I carried out more than sixty in-depth personal interviews with jurists, focusing on those who pioneered the field of immigration defense in these two countries and those who remained active in the field over several decades.

Studying a field of specialized legal practice that has been in existence for more than forty years – especially one that has generated such a substantial amount of litigation – required that I pursue a research strategy capable of foregrounding those specific features that have been most significant in each of these two social worlds. The method utilized for narrowing the inquiry in each country was directly related to the underlying theoretical conceptualization of legal practices as organizationally situated and symbolically meaningful. I relied on informal dialogic interviews that focused on the shared narratives developed by those engaged in the practice of immigrant rights litigation. In short, I asked the subjects of my study to identify aspects of their practice to which they themselves attached particular significance or importance, with the goal of eliciting "snapshots of significance" that embody the field for its adherents (Geertz 1968, 2).

These snapshots of significance served to orient me in navigating the written records produced by court-centered contestations of immigration policy. In the United States, I was invited to spend time in the organizational archives of the American Civil Liberties Union (ACLU) Immigrants' Rights Project and the National Immigration Project of the National Lawyers Guild. In France, I was given permission to view the private archives of the French immigrant rights organization *Groupe d'Information et de Soutien des Immigrés* (Information and Support Group for Immigrants; GISTI). I also reviewed a number of publicly accessible archival collections, including those of the *Mouvement d'Action Judiciaire* (Mouvement for Judicial Action), the Cimade (the social services arm of the French Protestant Federation), and the *Ligue des Droits de l'Homme*, all of which had connections with immigrant rights legal activism. The periods in residence at the ACLU, the Guild's National Immigration Project, and GISTI were particularly helpful in allowing me to gain access to further depth and complexity insofar as they not only provided ample written records but also facilitated informal conversations with the staff and volunteers of these organizations. Spending time on-site also allowed me extensive access to organizational correspondence, case files, and official reports, shedding light not only on the activities of these organizations, but also on the activities of their coalition partners and external supporters.

In order to get a fuller picture of the practices engaged in bringing immigration policies before courts in each country, I sought out information about the elite benefactors and administrative interlocutors of immigrant rights legal activism. In terms of written records, the main sources of this data were the archived papers of the Ford Foundation's Rights and Social Justice Program, the single most important funder of U.S. immigrant rights legal mobilization, and the *Direction de la Population et des Migrations* (Directorate of Population and Migrations; DPM) and the *Direction des Libertés Publiques et des Affaires Juridiques* (Directorate of Public Liberties and Juridical Affairs; DPLAJ), the national administrative structures most strongly linked to French immigrant rights legal mobilization.[5] To supplement these written records, I also conducted a small number of interviews with government attorneys in the United States and France who had spent their careers within the administrative divisions responsible for defending the government against lawsuits generated by immigrant rights legal activism.

A final source of data was provided by legal documents and media coverage. Jurists leave a great deal of written traces, and because my interviewees had identified particular litigation campaigns as holding special significance, I focused on documentation and media reports related to these temporally bounded events. Legal documents proved to be a valuable source of information about both the organizational and symbolic dimensions of immigrant rights legal activism. Many legal documents are available in electronic form in the United States through the main legal search engines. In France, where legal records are not publically available, I was able to access the private holdings of the library of the Conseil d'Etat to obtain the court's official legal analysis and commentary. In terms of media coverage, the major American and French newspapers are now electronically archived; however it was necessary to rely on the newspaper clippings contained in the *dossiers de presse numérisés* (indexed news media files) at the Library of Sciences Po, Paris for French media coverage from the 1970s and 1980s.

By using a variety of research techniques and sources of evidence to supplement one another, my research strategy aimed to supply an appropriately broad foundation for analysis of the culturally productive process of contesting immigration policy in court. If comparative work is both about discovering surprising differences and unexpected similarities (Nelken 2010, 32), then a multidimensional approach combining interviews and archival sources allows the researcher to more insightfully unpack meaning-making processes than reliance on any single method alone. As Michael McCann points out, using a variety of techniques that supplement one another is analogous in some ways to the method of "triangulation" used by geological surveyors (McCann 1994, 16). Although this study does not claim to comprehensively map the terrain of immigrant rights litigation, and is better characterized as an exploratory venture into a new empirical and theoretical terrain, its combination of interpretive methods does aim to highlight the most salient features of this previously unexplored landscape.

BOX 2. NOTE ON CROSS-NATIONAL TERMINOLOGY

Successful cross-national analysis necessitates selection of an analytical term that identifies and demarcates the set of social practices in each national context that is the subject of comparison. I use the analytical term *legal activism* to identify the court-centered activity directed toward effecting change at the level of official policy making. This designation aims to demarcate a practice that is distinct from other forms of politically engaged client representation on the part of those trained in law. It refers to the activities of practitioners who see themselves simultaneously as activists and lawyers, who deploy legal expertise to achieve political ends, and whose legal strategies are informed by political goals. The term was chosen to capture this hybrid identity, while avoiding the imposition of nationally distinct political or professional categories.

In the United States, notwithstanding the eventual emergence of organized litigation on behalf of conservative causes (Epstein 1985, Teles 2008), reform-oriented litigation has historically been most closely associated with progressive political activity. American lawyers who engage in this type of practice often refer to themselves as "civil rights lawyers" or "public interest lawyers," although courts eventually came to be seen as an appropriate venue for pursuing progressive policy goals not only in the areas of civil rights and welfare rights but also in new domains such as women's rights, environmentalism, and consumer rights. Several empirical studies conducted in the late 1970s aimed to offer a contemporaneous examination of this subject (Handler 1978, Weisbrod 1978). These initial forays were followed by the development of a large and growing scholarly literature documenting the activities of organizations aiming to propel progressive policy change (Tushnet 2004, Anderson 2006, Mezey 2007).

(*continued*)

Sociolegal scholarship on "cause lawyering" has likewise sought to investigate the commitments and practices of legal professionals who seek to use law-related means to change the law, including immigration law (see Israel 2003). In its initial formulation, cause lawyering was conceptualized as an activity that brings the political commitments of attorneys into tension with their professional responsibilities (Sarat and Scheingold 1998). In response, critics suggested that a focus on professional ethics replicates the ideology of the U.S. legal profession and leaves unexamined the way in which the commitments of progressive legal actors are structured by power relations. As the cause lawyering project was expanded to include studies of civil law systems, where the role of the state is more prominent, its agenda evolved so as to better address how state power shapes legal activity, even in the U.S. context (Sarat and Scheingold 2001). The cause lawyering project was further broadened in response to scholarly interventions contending that lawyers act politically when they orient their practice primarily toward empowering clients rather than toward winning cases or influencing policies (Menkel-Meadow 1998, Shamir and Chinsky 1998) and that the performance of attorney-client interactions has political implications (White 1990). In its most recent formulations (Sarat and Scheingold 2008, Marshall and Hale 2014), the category of cause lawyer has come to encompass forms of legal practice that are not explicitly directed toward influencing policy-making debates but that nevertheless offer routes for jurists to combine their political commitments and professional responsibilities.

Without disputing the importance of client-empowering political lawyering, I have nevertheless chosen to focus on forms of practice that engage more directly with national immigration policy making. Insofar as it explicitly aims to influence official law, legal activism is thus distinct from other forms of politically engaged client representation. Legal activism is a "mode of action" whose primary concern is to secure judicial decisions that impact existing rules and procedures so as to "attain substantive policy changes through the courts" (Cichowski 2007, 17). It is this explicit focus on courts that distinguishes legal activism from other forms of activism such as lobbying tactics or direct action. While in some instances legal activism may be organized so as to closely align with the goals of a social movement organization, this is not always the case (McCann and Silverstein 1998). Indeed, as discussed in Chapter 4, over a period of several decades, immigrant rights legal activism has maintained a degree of organizational continuity even at times when there has been no cohesive and organized immigrant social movement.

In the U.S. literature, this policy-oriented legal practice has variously been referred to as "law reform" (Handler 1978) and "planned litigation" (Wasby 1995). In my assessment, however, neither of these terms proves suitable to describe policy-oriented litigation outside of the U.S. context. Practitioners in France insist that they are not reforming the law by challenging policies in court, and are rather alerting judges to improper actions taken by the government that misinterpret the law. Legal activism is also preferable to planned litigation as an analytical focus, because the feasibility of test-case litigation depends on procedural avenues that are relatively less available outside of the U.S. legal context.

Moreover, test-case litigation is only one possible technique by which legal activists can aim to influence policy making. As the subsequent chapters describe, immigrant rights legal activists in the United States have also relied on nationwide class action lawsuits to challenge existing immigration policies, while their counterparts in France have favored petitioning the Conseil d'Etat for abstract review of administrative policies that are deemed to illegally restrict the rights of noncitizens. As one recent comparative study has pointed out, activists and organizations seeking to influence policy making can utilize a number of different strategies, ranging from organizing affirmative lawsuits, to intervening as third-party participants, to purposefully committing civil disobedience in order to provide courts with opportunities to adjudicate particular issues (Vanhala 2011, 6–8). By including all types of cases aiming to influence policy making, the analytical category of "legal activism" designates a wide range of techniques with which lawyer-activists may creatively engage as they seek to deploy court-centered activity to intervene at the level of official policy making.

ORGANIZATION OF THE STUDY

The subsequent chapters place U.S. and French legal practices immediately next to one another, organizing the material into a sequence of point and counterpoint between the two settings. I deliberately selected this mode of presentation to lift up conceptual insights that emerged from the analytical strategy of moving between the two nationally distinct domains. The series of paired contrasts calls attention to the multiple frames, narratives, and performances generated by repeatedly contesting immigration policy in court and the diverse trajectories by which these legally generated forms have shaped immigration policy making in the United States and France.

Chapter 2 sets the stage by providing historical context for the emergence in the United States and France of something that would later come to be identified as immigrant rights legal activism. Focusing on the decade of the 1970s, the analysis contextualizes early legal defense efforts within the distinct political horizons and policy debates of the period. I show how, in a process that was broadly similar in both countries, young progressive-leaning lawyers and a loose assortment of grassroots immigrant social movements discovered each other and merged their efforts. Drawing on the records of the immigration-centered legal organizations that came into existence during this period, I trace the process by which this cohort of lawyers who had taken up the immigrant cause then constructed an organizational infrastructure for their new professional network.

Chapter 3 focuses on the landmark cases that first brought immigrant rights litigation onto the national political radar. The analysis traces how litigators drew upon nationally distinct jurisprudential regimes and adapted them to the immigration domain. In the United States, immigrant defenders crafted paradigms of argumentation that relied on a pluralist vision of migrants as "a minority within a minority" that deserved special judicial protection. By contrast, their French counterparts constructed legal arguments that linked good governance and social protection norms and extended them to vulnerable immigrant workers. Focusing on the legislative politics of immigration at the time that these high-profile cases were decided, the analysis then examines the radiating effects of these legal framings within the sphere of national-level politics.

Chapter 4 turns the gaze back on litigators and explores how the process of contesting policies in court initiated a long-term shift in the way that these jurists approached their own professional project. The analysis probes how, in both countries, immigrant defenders institutionalized their efforts by adapting nationally distinct models of expert legal practice and by building alliances with elites supporters. In the United States, immigrant rights legal activism found its primary source of support in the private sector and adapted itself to a law firm model. By contrast, in France, legal activists cultivated informal relationships with state elites at the same time that they publicly expressed their autonomy from both the market and the state. In both countries, legal activists assumed more juridically centered roles and identities even as these took markedly distinct forms.

Chapter 5 and 6 together explore how the institutionalization of this form of practice likewise patterned the dispositions of national administrative officials who became the subjects of frequent and routinized litigation efforts. The analysis focuses on the distinct procedural mechanisms with which immigrant rights legal activism in each country has become most closely associated in the eyes of administrative officials. While immigrant rights legal activism in the United States has immersed itself in the street-level details of administrative institutions, its French counterpart has operated at a remove from concrete policy application. In both countries, albeit in different ways, the performance of routinized legal intervention has contributed to making the politics of law an integral facet of immigration politics.

These points provide the foundation for the development of a more general argument in the concluding chapter concerning the analytical leverage provided by the comparative constructivist approach advanced in this study. This chapter summarizes the main findings of the preceding chapters and develops their implications for research regarding law and the politics of social reform. It also returns to the question at the core of this study and addresses the implications of its findings for contemporary social justice efforts focused on immigrants and immigration law.

Throughout this book, I show how analytically decentering official case dispositions allows us to follow the process of knowledge production upstream, to identify the sets of ideas and meanings from which the juridical laboratory draws its tools and materials, as well as downstream, to see precisely how the policy-making sphere is reconfigured by the radiating effects of the frames, narratives, and performances assembled in court. Taking inspiration from Latour's provocative comparison of technical law to a scientific laboratory (Latour 2002), I conceptualize the activities of legal technicians in constructivist terms, unpacking how immigrant rights legal activism has assembled its web of knowledge practices and tracing the process by which the forms of meaning constructed by these practices have been taken up in new webs of knowledge. Shifting from a framework of studying official case dispositions to a framework of examining legal assemblages allows a greater sensitivity for how engaging with law has contributed to shifting the dynamics of immigration policy making. The comparative optic is useful for lifting up these culturally productive processes and seeing them more clearly.

Of course, there are other dimensions of the intersection of immigration policy and law that might also be relevant to a constructivist analysis. Moreover, there is no pretension that the combination of patterns discussed in this study adds up to all that could be said about concerted efforts to shape immigration policies through litigation. Rather than exhaustive, the analysis is "kaleidoscopic" – "conjunctions of activities" are examined by means of "a succession of shifts in focus," as someone might turn a kaleidoscope to view various plains of operation of the two settings (Knorr Cetina 1999, 24). Drawing on material identified by my interviewees as holding particular significance, I have focused on areas that, in my own assessment, hold the greatest potential for identifying the cultural practices deployed in the process of bringing immigration questions to the law and highlighting their radiating effects in the policy-making sphere.

2

A New Area of Legal Practice

SETTING THE SCENE / *MISE-EN-SCÈNE*

Los Angeles, May 1978 – Agents of the Immigration and Naturalization Service (INS) raid the Sbicca shoe factory in the suburb of El Monte where workers are involved in a union organizing campaign. The INS officers arrive in the morning, seal off the factory exits, and question the workforce of mostly Mexican women on the factory floor. The workers are handcuffed and man-handled; some are asked only, "Are you ready for Mexico?" They are told to sign papers waiving a hearing and agreeing to immediate voluntary departure. By early afternoon, 120 women are placed on buses and are being driven to the Mexican border. Alerted to the raid by labor organizers, attorneys from the Legal Aid Foundation of Los Angeles rush to court and succeed in obtaining a temporary restraining order that ensures the workers will not be deported until they have had a full opportunity to speak with a lawyer. Upon returning to Los Angeles, the detainees are formally advised of their rights and are told that free legal services are available. Sixty-five of those arrested withdraw their requests for voluntary departure and request legal counsel.

By the summer of 1978, when the story of these events is shared with readers of the *Immigration Newsletter* published by the National Immigration Project of the National Lawyers Guild, the members of the "Sbicca Legal Defense Team" are able to report that "Interviews were had with each worker and great successes were noted at the special bail redetermination hearings ... presently the civil case is being litigated as a class action. It seeks to define the scope of INS authority to detain and arrest workers. It also concerns the serious violations of the 4th, 5th and 6th Amendments to the Constitution."[1] Several months later, the defense team celebrates subsequent successes in court and its members describe themselves as "the legal arm" of the Labor and Immigration Action Center, "a recently organized group of unionists, community activists and legal people led by union organizers."[2]

Eight years later, these reports would be republished in the *Immigration Newsletter* as part of a historical series commemorating the Guild's Fiftieth Anniversary.[3] Meanwhile, the class action initiated in the context of the Sbicca raid would eventually come to a close in 1992, when the INS agreed to a settlement negotiated with staff attorneys of the National Center for Immigrants' Rights, Inc. By this time, of course, those who had been working at the Sbicca factory in May 1978 no longer face deportation. For the nationwide settlement's thirty-month duration, however, immigration agents must provide all persons they arrest with a written advisal of legal rights, including the right to apply for political asylum and the right to consult with attorneys before postarrest interrogation and deportation.[4]

Paris, April 1976 – Agents of France's immigration police raid the Foyer Romain-Rolland, an immigrant worker dormitory managed by the semipublic National Society for Construction of Worker Housing (SONACOTRA) in the suburb of Nanterre. The foyer residents are protesting above-market rents, unsafe conditions, and colonial-style overseers, and many are also involved in protests against the government's tightening of residency renewal criteria for foreigners. At the time of the raid, the protests had lasted more than a year and had spread to more than one hundred foyers across France. Within days of the raid, seventeen members of the protesters' coordinating committee are summarily expelled from France for "disturbing the public order."

The expulsions are contested by an informal collaborative of leftist attorneys who convince the Conseil d'Etat to suspend the expulsion orders and who also represent the foyer residents in a series of courtroom battles against the SONACOTRA. The attorneys receive logistical support from the staff of the immigrant services department of the Cimade, a social services association with a venerable history of aiding displaced persons that has recently begun collaborating with a new and energetic circle of progressive young professionals. Calling themselves "the information and support group for immigrant workers" (*Groupe d'Information et de Soutien des Travailleurs Immigrés* [GISTI]), this nascent immigrant defense network publishes a series of brochures synthesizing the administrative regulations governing foreigners' access to social services and their residency in France. During this time, GISTI's jurists also begin to experiment with organizing abstract legal challenges to these administrative policies governing immigrants and immigration.

Recounting this period twenty-five years later, Assane Ba, a former leader of the residents' organizing committee who subsequently joined GISTI's office staff, would use the term "law at the service of the struggle" to explain the organizing committee's decision to relegate lawyers and other professionals to a support committee that would supply technical information without having a say over movement strategies (Grelet et al. 2001). For their part, the young civil servants among GISTI's founders would look back on their involvement twenty-five years earlier in slightly different terms. From their perspective, political activism was driven by their desire to contest the autocratic tendencies of France's right-wing governments during this period, a tendency that seemed to be particularly apparent in the domain of immigration policy. In the words of one of GISTI's founding jurists, "We decided to focus on the legal hole around immigrants, this sort of zone of non-law, as a theme with strong connotations and weak visibility that might be interesting."[5]

A TALE OF TWO MOVEMENTS

While each has its own story, the Sbicca and SONACOTRA legal campaigns draw our attention to the new type of political and legal project that was taking shape in both the United States and in France during the 1970s. This was a moment in which jurists in both countries became involved in a complex intertwining of direct action and institutional action around immigration policy. In both countries, immigration law specialists who would later come to be associated with more-institutionalized efforts to contest immigration policy making on a national scale would identify the lawsuits that emerged from these concrete local efforts as key building blocks in the development of immigration-centered legal activism.

The newly restrictionist orientation in immigration policy making, ushered in by economic downturn, set the backdrop for these mobilizations. In France, policy responses to the onset of recession were dramatic: the government abruptly suspended all foreign worker recruitment in July 1974 and took steps to encourage foreigners to return home. Restrictionism was also a feature of American policy responses to the economic downturn. The United States had already suspended its official guest worker program a decade earlier, but U.S. policy makers in the 1970s rediscovered aggressive immigration enforcement as a way of managing a "back door" immigration policy that supplied a steady stream of irregular workers from south of the border.[6] Whereas in the preceding decade, irregular migrants had largely been left alone, American politicians staged the southern border as the site of an enforcement "crisis" (Calavita 1992).

Nevertheless, if we were to take ourselves back to that moment in the 1970s when the heightening of immigration restrictionism was a new development, it might not be evident that these policies would be challenged in court. Forty years earlier, in the midst of another period of global economic crisis, irregular migrants and guest workers had been similarly squeezed by restrictionist policies.[7] However, this aggressive targeting of migrants during the 1920s and 1930s did not prompt any noticeable protest from progressive voices within the legal profession. To the contrary, as the progressive reformers of the Wickersham Commission sought to improve U.S. immigration-related administrative processes, they explicitly affirmed the underlying rationale of removing foreigners whose labor was no longer needed so as to promote "protection of American workmen."[8] Moreover, as historian Mai Ngai points out, the commission's 1931 report made no mention of the racially disparate enforcement practices of immigration officials (Ngai 2005, 81–6). Lawyers in France also remained largely silent at this time. Indeed, rather than taking up the cause of immigrants, French lawyers voted in June 1934 to forbid foreigners, even those who had naturalized, from exercising any public legal position and banned them from inscription in the private bar (Weil 2004, 28).

What was it in the 1970s that propelled the dynamic and enthusiastic legal activity – of the type seen in the Sbicca and SONACOTRA campaigns – which responded to the tightening of immigration controls? Putting this question another way, what exactly was happening when, in both the United States and France, a motley assortment of jurists and activists with a combination of liberal and leftist affiliations sought to deploy legal tools and training in the name of struggles that they variously associated with civil rights, human rights, worker rights, and immigrant rights? Was this a bottom-up mobilization to assist immigrant protest leaders who sought to lead their own struggles? Or were those involved in these campaigns primarily motivated by a desire to leave their mark on the law? Were jurists defending the cause of immigrants or were they ultimately pursuing specifically legal goals?

This chapter explores the initial encounter between members of the 1970s generation of law school graduates and the domain of immigration policy. Seen through one perspective, these early legal efforts were embedded in the enthusiasm for grassroots political engagement that characterized the politics of the 1970s in both countries. Seen through another perspective, these efforts mark the emergence in each country of distinct law-centered professional groupings, to which participants devoted substantial time and energy and which were the vehicles for both political energy and professional ambition. As participants in immigrant rights legal networks sought to make sense of what they were doing, they adopted both of these perspectives, sometimes simultaneously. I argue that we should take both of these perspectives seriously, as both represent a valid account of how movement activism and legal expertise engaged each other as part of the contestatory politics of the 1970s.

For this reason, rather than labeling these efforts as either predominantly "political" or predominantly "legal," the analysis in this chapter emphasizes the professional, political, and organizational heterogeneity that pervaded jurists' early efforts to mobilize around the theme of immigrant defense. What becomes apparent is the extent to which immigration-centered legal mobilization during this early period defies clear categorization. In what follows, I explore these processes in each country in turn and develop what might be thought of as "left-eye" and "right-eye" perspectives for understanding efforts organized by jurists in the 1970s to defend the rights of noncitizens.

U.S. LAWYERS IN THE SOCIAL MOVEMENT

Seen from one perspective, the efforts of progressive lawyers in the 1970s to defend individuals and communities caught up in immigration enforcement raids were a product of this decade's distinct contestatory politics, in which members of the legal profession were enthusiastic participants. Those who became involved in immigrant defense efforts in the 1970s were inspired by the example of legal professionals who had devoted their skills to supporting grassroots activism in other areas. For many among the cohort of American law school graduates starting their careers in the 1970s, traditional firm-based legal practice held little appeal. In their search for models of social justice lawyering, recent law school graduates could look to those a few years ahead of them who had gone to the South to assist the civil rights movement and had returned energized to apply aggressive lawyering techniques to the problem of urban poverty as well as to prison and policing practices. As historical research on this period has documented, the *Brown v. Board of Education* decision "shifted the paradigm in terms of what law could do," and there was abundant faith among the 1970s generation of law school graduates that law and lawyers could play a part in building a better society (Kalman 1996, 2). In addition, members of the 1970s generation were energized to play this role by the flourishing of contestatory politics that they saw around them. Police action against antiwar protesters brought together networks of defense lawyers and the revitalized National Lawyers Guild supplied the social and ideological glue for a new generation of political lawyers (Scheingold 1998). Flamboyant litigators such as William Kunstler, Arthur Kinoy, and Leonard Weinglass provided role models of this type of legal practice. In the words of historian Gerold Auerbach, "Democratic currents swirled through the profession," and conventional career choices commanded diminished respect among American lawyers in the 1970s (Auerbach 1976, 264).

Moreover, this was a generation of law graduates who felt confident about their careers and had little educational debt. The creation in 1967 of a national corps of legal services lawyers supplied opportunities and financial support for those exiting law schools in the 1970s to take jobs in community legal services offices where they worked as the legal wing of an ascendant welfare rights movement (Handler, Hollingsworth, and Erlanger 1978). Law communes were another alternative to traditional law firm practice that attracted those dedicated to promoting political change. Lawyers affiliated with several of these worker cooperatives and local community groups offered detailed recountings of their efforts to challenge the traditional model of legal practice (see Gabel and Harris 1982).

Those involved in defending the Sbicca workers identified themselves as members of this generation that sought to use their legal skills to promote the causes of a wide array of oppressed or excluded groups. Volunteering in legal aid programs as law students and starting their careers in community legal services offices, they discovered that some of their most needy clients were excluded from public assistance programs on account of their immigration status. Most of these young immigrant defenders identified as white and almost none had any personal experience of migration.[9] Some had only recently graduated from law school, while others had worked briefly in community-based legal assistance offices where they gained some exposure to immigration cases. They were attracted by the prospect of defending the rights of those who came from less privileged backgrounds that they themselves had not experienced personally. Their exposure to the cause of "immigrant" rights came not from their own experience of migration but rather through their encounter with grassroots mobilizations organized by migrant communities.

For attorneys and legal workers living in areas with large immigrant populations, grassroots mobilizations were not hard to find. In the West and Southwest, the burgeoning Chicano movement linked opposition to immigration enforcement with a broader set of emancipatory political goals. In the late 1960s, the movement used walk-outs and demonstrations to seek inclusion in government antipoverty programs and state educational curricula, and student activists were also involved in antiwar protests. In the 1970s, the restrictionist turn in immigration policy became a central concern for the vanguard of Mexican American college students, union organizers, and teachers who supplied the leadership for Chicano groups such as La Raza Unida Party and the Brown Berets (Chavez 2002). Immigration protests during this period fit into a broader attack on the assimilationist and restrictionist paradigm of postwar U.S. immigration policy. Movement leaders proclaimed solidarity with undocumented immigrants in a struggle against what they saw as long-standing U.S. government oppression of all people of Mexican descent. Citizenship status was irrelevant when the task, according to movement activists, was to unite the Mexican people with others struggling against imperialism.

The Los Angeles offices of the Centro de Acción Social Autónomo (CASA) served as an early center of gravity for young lawyers seeking to contribute to these mobilizations. For CASA's founders, the goal was "uniting immigrant workers with the rest of the working class in the United States who 'enjoy' citizenship" (Gutierrez 1995, 191). The organization framed the problem of underpaid laborers living in blighted barrios as a result of U.S. capitalism, labeling both immigration raids and aggressive policing as forms of repression against an ethnic Mexican working class who were "one people" regardless of immigration status (Chavez 2002, 17). Following a politically provocative solidarity visit to Cuba, CASA's leadership personally became the targets of deportation procedures (Chavez 2002, 112). Moreover, for a period of several years during the early 1970s, CASA hosted its own legal department staffed by young "Anglo" law school graduates who sought to supply the movement's legal wing by providing legal services to CASA's membership.[10]

Elsewhere in the country, immigrant communities likewise claimed political space through their mobilizations against immigration policies. In the 1970s, inspired by international human rights initiatives and by media coverage of Indochinese boat people, Haitians in New York, Boston, and South Florida organized marches and demonstrations against U.S. government support for their country's autocratic regime and to protest the oppressive treatment of Haitian asylum seekers arriving by sea in south Florida. Haitian community leaders called attention to the fact that Haitian asylum seekers, unlike Cubans, were placed in immigration detention for lengthy periods and were denied employment authorization once released from detention. Led by a small circle of exiled dissident priests known as the Haitian Fathers, activists linked protests against immigration policies to broader efforts, such as Creole literacy programs and political change in Haiti (Kahn 2013, 66–7). In 1977, when Fr. Gérard Jean-Juste assumed the leadership of a Miami-based humanitarian assistance agency, the Haitian Refugee Center was transformed into the organizational base for the Haitian community's mobilizations. Drawing inspiration from liberation theology, Haitian activists insisted on leading their own struggle and required that the newly independent center's board contain a majority of Haitian members.[11] Yet the center was not averse to leveraging legal strategies in the service of its cause, and in the late 1970s and 1980s litigation would become a major component of Haitian political mobilizations.

Welcomed by immigrant community leaders, young professional who had acquired training in law became enthusiastic supporters of these organizations even though most shared no direct link to either the Mexican American or Caribbean American experience. They were excited to offer their skills to new movements that were explicitly political and whose nascent organizations possessed few legal resources. As immigrant defender Larry Kleinman recalled, "Back then, there weren't many of us and it was legal guerilla war. We pledged ourselves to Migra resistance."[12] This cohort of young Anglo immigrant defenders participated in protest activities organized by Chicano student activists at the Peoples College of Law in Los Angeles and the Colegio Cesar Chavez in Oregon's Willamette Valley. They read CASA's political newsletter *Sin Fronteras* and attended political events related to immigration issues, such as the National Chicano-Latino Issues Conference organized by La Raza Unida Party in October 1977, leaving the conference feeling "viscerally" that they were "part of a broader movement."[13] Taking up the rhetoric of the Chicano movement, they denounced the U.S. government for exerting "increasingly greater control over the domestic economy of Mexico and other Third World nations, causing economic depression, mass unemployment and under-employment, to the detriment of working and poor people throughout the world, driving them from their homelands."[14]

Young progressive attorneys approached the defense of Haitian asylum seekers with similar zeal and likewise embraced the political struggle of this movement. The Haitian cause attracted a cadre of recent law school graduates who were drawn to the possibility of "playing an integral part of a broader political struggle" by supplying a legal arm for this new movement.[15] Adopting the rhetoric of Haitian dissident political organizations, they decried the U.S. government's support for "fascism" in Haiti and immersed themselves in learning about the country's political history and documenting the Duvalier regime's abuses.[16] In taking over the defense of Haitian refugees, young legal professionals saw themselves as "fashioning a grassroots, transnational movement strategy designed to expose the abuses of both the Duvalier government in Haiti and the INS in the United States" (Kahn 2013, 72). Legal defense work was placed in the context of supporting Haitian political mobilizations. The young attorneys leading the Haitian defense team framed their efforts as a means of assisting movement leaders in their efforts to stimulate political activism within the community.[17]

The 1970s generation of U.S. jurists who took up immigration defense work felt themselves to be participants in a "mass movement that is being built to defend the democratic rights of all undocumented people in the U.S.," a movement in which they worked hand-in-hand with social movement activists.[18] Because immigrant groups and their allies were mobilizing politically, immigration work was identified as political lawyering. And participants in these efforts understood themselves as supplying the legal arm of what they believed, with unbridled enthusiasm, to be the emergence of a major new social movement.

IMMIGRANT DEFENSE AS A NEW LEGAL MOVEMENT
IN THE UNITED STATES

At the same time that the new generation of immigrant defenders understood legal work as useful for enhancing the visibility of protests within immigrant communities, they also saw an opportunity to leave their mark on what appeared to be a new and open legal terrain. Those working with immigrant social movements to resist restrictionist policies did not need to look far for legal issues to be explored. Experience in a local legal services office provided a quick lesson in the ways that undocumented clients might potentially benefit from recently developed criminal procedure protections and welfare rights. Indeed, during the early 1970s legal services back-up centers had been involved in a number of cases seeking to extend welfare access for noncitizens.[19] Recent law school graduates working with immigrant communities followed these developments and saw much that they found encouraging.

Perhaps more importantly, from their perspective, immigration law was an area that fell outside the mandate of existing progressive legal mobilizations. Certainly, U.S. legal organizations had for some time been supporting the civil rights mobilizations of ethnic communities with a history of immigration. Most prominently, California Rural Legal Assistance played an important role in Cesar Chavez's farmworker movement (Bennett and Reynoso 1972, Gordon 2006). By the 1970s, legal offices operated by young Asian American and Chicano attorneys were also closely involved in the nascent antidiscrimination mobilizations of their communities during this period (Minami 2000, Haney-López 2003). However, these groups primarily represented permanent residents or U.S. citizens and did not devote particular attention to the needs of irregular migrants. Moreover, in the case of the farmworker movement, organizers initially viewed recent waves of backdoor migration from Mexico as a threat to their goal of improving working conditions for farmworkers.[20] In short, there was little sense that any established law reform organization was challenging policies that targeted undocumented immigrant workers, refugees, and other irregular migrants.

As for the existing private immigration bar, its membership was viewed by progressive young attorneys as bringing little imagination to this area of legal practice. The American Immigration Lawyers Association (AILA) had been founded some three decades earlier as part of an attempt to elevate the standard and reputation of the immigration bar, however in 1973 the organization, which at the time called itself the Association of Immigration and Nationality Lawyers, had less than twenty chapters and only one thousand members.[21] On the whole, private immigration lawyers tended to center their practice on providing a similar template of representation to a predominantly low-income client base, relegating them to a position of low prestige with the U.S. legal profession (Levin 2009, 400). Certainly there were exceptions, but energetic and professionally ambitious law school graduates working with immigrant social movements generally found little in common with the clique of New York–based old-timers who still dominated AILA's leadership.

The new cohort of immigrant defenders found relatively more inspiration in the surviving remnants of a previous generation of leftist lawyers who had defended foreign-born labor organizers against ideologically based deportations. This network had been particularly active, with mixed success, during the 1940s and 1950s (Ginger 1993). However, the vibrant leftist legal networks of earlier times were largely moribund by the 1970s. When the American Committee for the Protection of the Foreign Born, an organization founded in the 1930s, was recruited to defend the cause of Haitian asylum seekers in the 1970s, it was an organization kept afloat only by the indefatigable work of its aging general counsel, Ira Gollobin.[22] Young attorneys who cast themselves as pioneers of immigrant rights lawyering were inspired by the example of this older generation of radical lawyers, viewing them as valuable mentors. However, their ambitions were not limited to assuming the previous generation's ideological battles or accepting its defeats.

For progressive and professionally ambitious recent law graduates, the task that presented itself was one of organizing a legal movement that would work alongside immigration-centered political mobilizations. Although the 1970s generation of immigrant defenders had found a path to political engagement through the mobilizations of locally based groups, they continued to draw their sense of identity through contacts with similarly positioned members of their professional cohort. Moreover, their professional approach was a collaborative one; facing immigration enforcement as a common adversary contributed to their sense that there was little incentive to compete and significant reason to cooperate. In the words of immigration attorney Lory Rosenberg, "From the beginning, we were sharing all of our motions because we wanted the best thing to be applied to our clients."[23] Having discovered their cause, young immigrant defenders set about developing an organizational and technical infrastructure for their new professional community.

The first steps in developing this organizational groundwork were taken by young immigrant defenders in Los Angeles who set up an "immigration panel" within the National Lawyers Guild. The National Lawyers Guild at this time was providing a political and professional identity for recent law school graduates engaged in civil rights and welfare rights lawyering, so it seemed natural that it might do the same for immigrant rights. Immigrant

FIGURE 1. An informal gathering of immigrant defenders at the National Lawyers Guild Convention in Chicago in the summer of 1983. Clockwise from bottom left: Peter Schey, unidentified participant, Susan Gzesh, Abby Ginsburg, Marc Van der Hout, unidentified participant, and Michael Ratner from the Center for Constitutional Rights. Photo courtesy of Susan Gzesh.

defenders felt welcome within the National Lawyers Guild, more so than in other professional associations. In the words of attorney Gary Silbiger, a founder of the National Lawyers Guild's immigration panel and a participant in the CASA legal collective, "CASA was our political home, but the Guild was our legal home."[24]

Institutionalization of the new immigration-centered professional community initially proceeded slowly. The spring of 1971 saw the establishment of a monthly *Immigration Newsletter* that offered a forum for individual lawyers working with immigrant community groups. The following year, at the National Lawyers Guild's convention in Austin, the immigration panel became the National Immigration Project and its members took the first steps to establishing a nationwide professional community that would live up to their group's name. A Chicago chapter opened in 1973, followed over the next four years by chapters in New York, Boston, and Washington, D.C. The National Lawyers Guild's biannual conventions provided opportunities for project members to meet in person, and several attorneys recalled the "collegiality" of the new community of immigration defenders (see Figure 1). In 1974, the project formed a national steering committee comprised of ten members from ten cities. With the aim of encouraging others to do politically engaged immigration work so that the group "could become really national," organizers conducted "road shows" that brought them into contact with community organizations, law students, and immigration practitioners around the country.[25]

Through this nascent professional community, aspiring legal activists exchanged legal research and analysis and also shared their vision for building a movement, both political and legal, around the theme of immigrant defense. The National Immigration Project's *Immigration Defense Manual* was the product of a collective effort that culminated at an all-day meeting at the National Lawyers Guild's Seattle convention in August 1977. In a three-ring notebook of 250 pages "designed specifically to assist practitioners in the defense of non-U.S. citizens," the contributing authors offered a step-by-step guide to the legal aspects of deportation defense.[26] Immigrant defenders also found ways, with varying degrees of formality, to coordinate and systematize their practices. In 1979, attorneys in the Boston area collaborated in formulating a Freedom of Information Act (FOIA) request for information about INS "area control" enforcement operations, and then made a copy of their request as well as other sample FOIA requests available through the National Immigration Project's "Brief Bank."[27] The concrete benefits of exchanging information were made clear in the Sbicca litigation, as immigrant defenders won their initial temporary restraining order – which dramatically turned back the bus at the Mexican border – by citing case law developed by Oregon-based project members.[28] Through the professional community sustained by this network, collective knowledge could be generated, transferred, and applied to new contexts.

As the network of immigration-focused young Guild attorneys continued to expand, the same ambition that had motivated the project's formation spurred some of its members to take the first steps toward a substantially more institutionalized form of practice. In 1979, attorney Peter Schey succeeded in securing funding from the Legal Services Corporation to transform the Aliens' Rights Program, created three years earlier within the Legal Aid Foundation of Los Angeles, into a national Legal Services "back-up center." The newly renamed National Center for Immigrants' Rights had a mandate to coordinate impact lawsuits and to provide technical assistance on immigration law to local legal services offices. The goal was to "complement existing work in the immigration field" by providing specialized legal resources on a national scale.[29]

By the end of the 1970s, readers of the National Lawyers Guild's *Immigration Newsletter* would have agreed with the editor's assessment that their professional community had "coalesced and solidified," and that it was "in the vanguard of the most important immigration litigation today."[30] This initial institutionalization of immigrant rights legal activism presaged further developments in the years to come (see Chapter 4). For the moment, however, the point to appreciate is that those working to support grassroots mobilizations of immigrant communities were simultaneously engaged in the construction of a legal movement centered on specialization in immigrant defense. We can see a remarkably similar combination of lawyers and local movements in the development of immigrant rights legal activism in France during this same period.

FRENCH JURISTS IN THE SOCIAL MOVEMENT

Like their American peers, the generation of French jurists who starting their careers in the 1970s were inspired by the contestatory politics of the period. The forging of a generation of politically engaged jurists took place in France not through a decade of civil rights struggle but rather through the crucible of the dramatic events of May 1968.[31] Like other members of their generation in France, many young jurists were inspired by the idealism of this moment and the perceived excesses in the government's repressive response to the May 1968 events catalyzed a number of reactions among the loose grouping who identified as the *gauche juridique* (Vauchez and Willemez 2007). In the immediate aftermath of May 1968, politically active lawyers were most eager to undertake the "collective defense" of radical activists, but their efforts subsequently broadened into wide-ranging legal experimentation to promote social change. Moreover, as these efforts developed, they expanded to include not only members of the private bar (*avocats au barreau*) but also magistrates, legal counselors, and members of France's other law-centered professions. Young jurists were responsible for reviving the long-dormant legal department of the *Ligue des Droits de l'Homme*, which focused on assuring the defense of political dissidents (Agrikoliansky 2002). They also contributed to transforming the legal department of France's largest national labor federation, the *Confédération Française Démocratique du Travail* (CFDT), into a vital wing of the syndicalist struggle. Under the direction of Jean-Paul Murcier and assisted by Henri Leclerc, the CFDT in the 1970s developed a litigation-oriented strategy that aimed not only to protect existing rights to workplace accident compensation but also to create a new jurisprudence protecting the working conditions of nontraditional workers and guaranteeing employee participation in workplace decision making (Willemez 2003).

The perception that existing professional institutions were inaccessible, out of touch, and overwhelmingly conservative prompted recent law graduates to create their own professional associations. The *Syndicat de la Magistrature*, founded in June 1968 by magistrates at the beginning of their careers, aimed to challenge judicial hierarchy and to subject the economically powerful to the same justice faced by ordinary citizens (Applebaum 2003). Similarly, the *Syndicat des Avocats de France* was organized in the early 1970s by young lawyers committed to the provision of legal aid and who felt themselves unrepresented by the *barreau* (Michel 2004). Participants in this exciting professional transformation viewed the creation of new institutions as a first step toward reforming a justice system that was "underfunded, enclosed in an attachment to formality, subordinated to the impunity of the police, and shockingly distanced from the lives of ordinary people" (Leclerc and Blum 1970, 6).

In parallel with this rethinking of existing institutions, the 1970s generation explored alternatives to traditional legal practice. Having started their careers well-endowed in cultural and educational capital, a generation of young professionals sought to offer their skills to subordinated groups. They were particularly inspired by the new model of political engagement developed by Michel Foucault's *Groupe d'Information sur Les Prisons*, which in the early 1970s had publicized the grievances of prisoners as a first step toward mobilizing a movement for political change.[32] Invoking this example, young jurists joined medical doctors, psychiatrists, and social workers in seeking to generate a *contre-expertise*, meaning a base of knowledge for social movements aiming to subvert the discourse of power. This could be done, as they saw it, by offering social movements concrete knowledge about the most effective tactics for navigating the law and the judicial system while allowing them to direct their own struggles. In the early 1970s, the newly formed *Mouvement d'Action Judiciaire* (MAJ) offered a loose professional network for jurists seeking to express solidarity with post-1968 social movements.[33] MAJ operated as a "transversal coordination of all jurists" and its members became involved in such diverse causes as access to justice, police violence, and reform of the military justice system (Lascoumes 2009, 4–8). We see another version of this approach in the *boutiques de droit* movement of the 1970s, whose participants sought to implant themselves at the grassroots and to work collaboratively with their clients so as not to "usurp" the initiative of local social movements (Revon 1978, 52). As historian Gérard Mauger describes the post-1968 context in France: "A generation of those most highly endowed with educational, economic, and social capital began their professional careers by opening 'new fronts' in different fields of social life" (Mauger 1994). The fact that the political left in France was in disarray during the early 1970s provided an additional impetus for young professionals to find a path to political engagement through social movement activism.

In this post-1968 context, as young jurists searched for a way to insert themselves into the amorphous and evolving social movement, immigration work
offered a path to political engagement. As we saw in this chapter's introductory
section, those attracted to this area of engagement included several recent
graduates of the *Ecole Nationale d'Administration* (ENA), whose political
engagement arose from a desire to denounce what they saw as autocratic measures taken against some of their politically outspoken classmates.[34] In the fall
of 1971, searching for a theme to concretize their newfound politicization, they
had come across a recently published chronicle of daily life in France's immigrant shantytowns, or *bidonvilles*, which described how the routine interventions of police into residents' homes had created a "zone of absolute non-law"
and which presented immigrant workers as a new front in the struggle against
repressive authority.[35] Through the MAJ legal network, the ENA graduates
made contact with two other sets of aspiring immigrant defenders. The first
included members of a network of solo-practitioner lawyers and participants in
the *boutiques de droit* movement who were providing regular representation
to immigrant clients. The second was composed of social workers employed
by the Cimade's immigrant assistance programs, many of whom had connections to reformist currents within the CFDT labor federation and had been
involved in Jesuit solidarity work in the context of the struggle for Algerian
independence.[36] From this diverse collection of politically engaged immigrant
advocates emerged the association GISTI, whose first concrete activity was the
operation of a free drop-in legal consultation service on Saturday mornings at
the offices of the Cimade. The group's name reflected its founders' aspiration
to merge concrete engagements with broader political goals.[37]

What allowed GISTI's project of organizing a collective legal defense of
immigrant workers to gain practical traction was the contemporaneous emergence of widespread political mobilizations led by immigrants. Just as the
1968 movement had energized a generation of legal professionals, its echo
was felt among immigrant workers (Pitti 2006). In the late 1960s a vanguard
of student activists from France's former colonies took the first steps to organize immigrant workers politically, building on the participation of immigrant
workers in a wave of factory occupations across France during the summer
of 1968 (Siméant 1998, 178–92). The *Mouvement des Travailleurs Arabes*
emerged at the end of 1972 from the successful campaign, assisted by a number of high-profile leftist intellectuals, to defend Tunisian student activist Said
Bouziri from expulsion. Under Bouziri's direction, the movement went on
to coordinate a series of hunger strikes in the Paris region to protest administrative circulars restricting immigrant work authorizations. By 1973, activism
in the name of immigrant workers had expanded beyond Paris to the South

of France and had embraced not only opposition to restrictionist immigration policies but also the longer-term goals of improving working conditions and ending racism in the justice system.[38] Protests in the name of immigrant workers drew participants of Portuguese, North African, Mauritian, and West African background.

This mobilization on the part of France's immigrant workers was unprecedented in the diversity of nationalities who participated, and movement leaders were vocal in asserting their movement's political autonomy. They broke with the long-standing tradition of relying on communist-affiliated French labor unions to represent them and insisted on representing their own interests. Retaining control of their movement was viewed by activists as part of a broader effort at community emancipation, manifested in agitprop street theater and a range of sports and art collectives (Escafré-Dublet 2014). As part of this movement for independence and freedom of expression, immigrant activists also rebuffed the overtures of the Algerian government's *Amicale des Algériens en France* to speak on their behalf, seeing in these overtures a desire by officials in Algiers to instrumentalize their movement in the context of the conflictual diplomatic relations between Algeria and France during this period.[39]

Immigrant mobilizations borrowed liberally from the Marxist-inflected vocabulary of the French Left during this period and combined this framework with anti-imperialist rhetoric. As described in the chapter's introductory section, grievances against the semipublic SONACOTRA organization and its nationwide network of immigrant worker dormitories were heightened by the fact that residents felt they were being treated disrespectfully by racist colonial-style overseers. Leaders of the foyer struggle also had no trouble drawing links between immigration enforcement and the repression of their movement, condemning immigration enforcement actions as those of an imperialist police state (Ginesy-Galand 1984, 201). The movement attracted early support from a social justice voluntary organization, the *Collectif d'Alphabétisation*, whose work centered on literacy programs in immigrant communities but whose publications likewise adopted the radical revolutionary discourse typical of the period.[40]

GISTI's jurists were eager to manifest their solidarity with this politically committed action and their public statements adopted a Marxist-inflected rhetoric similar to that employed by the immigrant activists they were supporting. The group's earliest official publication, a practical guide to immigration law and policy published by the leftist Maspero Press, includes an opening section identifying immigrants as "disposable workers brought to fill the gaps of the capitalist economy" and describing law as "a terrain of struggle, supplying arms whose usefulness stems from the internal contradictions of capitalist societies"

(GISTI 1975, 13–14). GISTI's members emphasized that social assistance and humanitarian interventions alone would not change the condition of immigrants, and that inserting individual efforts into a collective struggle was necessary "to achieve a goal, which at the least, would establish the equality of political, economic, and social rights for all of the workers in France"(GISTI 1975, 15). The eruption of nationwide strikes and protests organized by immigrant workers, particularly the sustained mobilization of immigrant foyer residents, was a cause for excitement because it appeared to be just the type of collective struggle that would bring about fundamental social change. In a press release, GISTI called for solidarity on the part of all unions and associations with this movement so that "immigrants should not bear the entire burden, since they are protagonists in the same way as French workers."[41]

GISTI's members also fully endorsed the foyer movement's emphasis on autonomy and independence. Initial legal strategies were primarily defensive in orientation, using judicial action to stall efforts to have residents evicted from the foyers and to force the authorities to negotiate directly with the immigrant movement leaders. GISTI took pains to insist that it was "supporting immigrant workers in their combat for the recognition of their rights and their dignity" and that its legal defense efforts consisted of furnishing to members of the immigrant movement the means to defend themselves.[42] Its members organized a public statement of solidarity with the foyer movement by the main organizations of France's post-1968 juridical left, asserting that the conflict could only be resolved when the management recognized that immigrant workers were capable of negotiating their rights for themselves.[43] And GISTI declared itself "ready to participate in all common action undertaken by democratic organizations to resist attacks against foreigners."[44] If immigrant rights emerged as a cause for French lawyers, then it was in part because France's immigrant workers in the 1970s supplied them with an independent political movement to defend.

BUILDING A NEW LEGAL MOVEMENT IN FRANCE

As much as they were driven by conviction and by a commitment to supporting immigrant mobilizations, France's young progressive jurists were also attracted to the immigrant cause by the challenge of leaving their mark on the law. In the words of attorney Christian Bourguet, who throughout the 1970s provided legal representation to the leaders of the foyer struggle, legal work on immigration-related issues was exciting because there was so much law to be made and "so many things to invent."[45] A similar theme is developed by Philippe Waquet, a GISTI-affiliated attorney, who as an *avocat aux conseils* was qualified to argue the group's cases before France's highest jurisdictions. According to Waquet, the project of developing immigration law in the 1970s was professionally gratifying because it was "like a sport; it was a question of identifying ways to entice courts to get involved."[46] In other words, litigating immigration cases was a type of legal work holding abundant interest for juridical technicians.

In part, this reflected the fact that political lawyering, while it had a long and distinguished tradition in France, had rarely taken up the defense of immigrants per se. Only a decade earlier, legal defense networks established during the Algerian War had been active in providing legal representation to leaders of the independence movement and supporting the struggle to end colonial rule, but these efforts were not labeled as immigrant defense (De Felice 2002). Nor did they involve immigration law issues, because those born in Algeria or to Algerian parents were automatically classified at the time as French nationals even if, as colonial subjects, they were denied citizenship rights. Individual members of the legal networks formed during this earlier period expressed solidarity with immigrant worker movements, and MAJ founder Jean-Jacques de Felice played a key role in facilitating initial connections between GISTI's founders and prospective members. However, providing legal support to the immigrant movements of the 1970s meant engaging with legal issues that had not been addressed by the political lawyering efforts of earlier generations.

Immigration defense could also be presented as a new area of practice due to the relative isolation of immigrant workers within French society. Segregated working and living conditions and entrenched racism separated the immigrant workers of the 1970s from other workers. Even as it turned toward legally oriented strategies, the CFDT labor federation had a weak presence in the sectors in which most immigrants were working and was riven by immigration policy differences among its constituents, some of whom were not averse to the principle of border closure.[47] With labor union leadership relatively tepid on immigration policy matters, groups outside of the labor movement were encouraged to take the initiative in aligning themselves with immigrant struggles. For instance, as early as 1971, a far-left grouping of young medical professionals offered their solidarity and professional knowledge to immigrant workers protesting labor conditions in the Penarroya metal works (Pitti 2010). GISTI's role in the struggles of France's immigrants in the 1970s would follow a similar model, while emphasizing the combination of solidarity with legal expertise.

For GISTI's network of immigrant defenders, the first step toward forging this combination of solidarity and legal knowledge consisted of systematically acquiring and organizing legal documents, so that the state of the law governing immigrants could actually be discerned. France's postwar governance of immigration and immigrants had been carried out largely through administrative regulation, and few of the relevant circulars were publically available. It was not uncommon for immigrant defenders to be presented in court with administrative regulations whose existence was previously unknown. Conversely, it was difficult to formulate legal arguments on behalf of a client with few written guidelines at hand. Thus, when GISTI registered itself as an association, it listed as its primary organizational aim: "to bring together all information on the legal, economic, and social situation of foreigners and immigrants."[48] The group established a repository for unpublished tribunal decisions, expert opinions submitted to appeals courts, and immigration-related administrative circulars. Simply collecting existing state regulations was thus seen as a first step toward reducing the scope of administrative "nonlaw." GISTI's first pamphlet, titled "The Regulation of Foyers," appeared in June 1972 and in the following three years the group produced ten other brochures and a book, all of which aimed to furnish practical information on immigration rules and policy practices (GISTI 1975, 118–19).

Developing a new legal movement also involved building a sense of community among individual jurists active in defending undocumented workers and other irregular migrants. While there were no competing institutions with which to contend, this also meant that legal defense efforts were starting from a baseline of complete lack of coordination. Having officially registered their association in 1973, the pressing task for GISTI's secretariat was to assemble a list of defense lawyers who were sympathetic to the immigrant cause. Gradually, this network of correspondents came to include small groups beyond the Paris area. By the end of the 1973, a chapter had formed in Lyon, which reported in a letter to the Paris secretariat that its members were committed to the goal of "mutual sharing of information and reflection on the particular problems of migrants with an eye towards developing clear documentation on the state of the law."[49] Two years later, jurists from GISTI and MAJ organized a "Colloquium on Immigration" in Montpellier that aimed to "coordinate the different committees of support that have appeared in the course of these recent struggles by autonomous immigrant movements."[50] As immigration issues acquired a higher political profile over the course of the decade, GISTI was able to further expand its network of immigrant defenders to include lawyers associated with France's labor movement.

As membership in GISTI's immigrant defense network expanded, additional steps were taken to organize activities and coordinate among participants. For example, in 1976, GISTI circulated to its affiliated attorneys a sliding scale of recommended fees for those who accepted "collective or exemplary" cases that had been referred through its legal consultation service. Private practitioners willing to contribute their services were asked to indicate their areas of specialty and the number of these special cases they felt able to undertake on GISTI's behalf.[51] The group also launched an appeal to its correspondents for donations to a newly established fund to defray court costs of these collective or exemplary cases.

GISTI also sought to regularize the finances of its small secretariat. The group had found an organizational home for its first six years within the offices of the Cimade, where André Legouy simultaneously served as a paid staff director for the Cimade's migrant service and also played the role of GISTI's organizational coordinator. After leaving the Cimade in 1978, Legouy continued to play a central role as GISTI's first permanent staff member, although the move to its own offices required that the group secure independent sources of funding.[52] In the end, it was a donation from one of the Cimade's philanthropic supporters, the *Comité Catholique contre la Faim et pour le Développement*, that allowed GISTI to open its own offices and develop relatively more formalized organizational structures.

Like their American counterparts, GISTI's jurists sought to develop the infrastructure for their legal movement by making available a collection of increasingly sophisticated legal publications to the group's affiliated lawyers and correspondents. In 1978, GISTI published a practice guide on "Legal Avenues for Individual Defense and Appeals against Removal Measures," which outlined the appeals process, provided citations to cases, and offered practical advice on litigation strategy before administrative tribunals.[53] Among the documents made available at nominal cost to GISTI members and correspondents were the recently issued decisions of lower courts as well as the expert opinions drafted by judicial advisors to the Conseil d'Etat and the Cour de Cassation. The new legal movement for the first time assumed a European dimension in 1979, when GISTI was invited to send representatives to a European conference centered on the theme of legal defense of foreigners.[54] At the same time that GISTI declared its commitment to supporting the leaders of the foyer movement in their struggle, the group could also celebrate its increasingly well-established reputation as "an association of jurists and social workers who have given themselves the essential task of exploring the domain of the rights of immigrant workers."[55]

CONCLUSION

As the preceding discussion has documented, the origins of contemporary political lawyering on behalf of the immigrant "cause" lie in the contentious politics and turn to restrictionism that began during the 1970s. Although American and French immigrant defenders had virtually no contact with their trans-Atlantic counterparts as they became involved with immigration issues, what becomes apparent are the remarkably similarities across these two national contexts. At the beginning of the decade, few jurists saw immigration work as a political or legal project. By the end of the 1970s, exciting, innovative, and creative legal work could be found in abundance in both countries.

But what was all of this legal activity actually about? Seen from one perspective, immigration defense work in the 1970s constituted the "legal arm" of immigrant-led social movements aiming to shift the balance of power in concrete and tangible ways. We might understand it as a form of movement lawyering whose participants deployed legal tools in the service of struggles for social change. There is ample evidence in each country to support this view. In both the United States and France, young law graduates sought out connections with immigrant-led social movements and enthusiastically adopted the terms of their struggle. Moreover, as we see in their publications, these lawyers explicitly proclaimed their allegiance to a vision of politics that viewed mobilizations organized by subordinated groups as the primary engine of long-term social change.

Seen from another perspective, immigrant defenders in the 1970s were engaged in a movement that was primarily legal in nature. Participants in these networks devoted substantial time and energy to building organizations whose primary membership base consisted of politically engaged jurists like themselves. Moreover, their engagements were propelled in no small degree by a desire to use litigation to develop new and generalizable principles at the level of doctrine. Indeed, these processes of constructing legal institutions and legal knowledge reinforced each other. As scholars have shown in their studies of legal movements in other domains, collaboration is often an engine of legal knowledge production, while sharing of information reinforces solidarity within informal professional networks (Abel 1985, Galanter 1990).

Both of these visions of early immigrant rights lawyering represent a valid account of this domain during the 1970s. It was a period in which innovations proliferated, group boundaries were uncertain, and the range of protagonists was in flux. This fluidity was possible because the new area of practice, even as it approached intelligibility for its internal participants, was as yet unconnected to established professional structures. In a context in which experimentation proliferated and routinized protocols were scarce, members of the 1970s generation of law school graduates were free to interpret their efforts simultaneously in terms of technical competency and in terms of a commitment to social justice. No single model predominated because the terms of evaluation were subject to debate.

As we will see, the boundaries of this new area of practice would become substantially more defined in the decades to come. Routinized contact with the juridical world's forms and structures would gradually construct the boundaries of something in each country that would be recognizable – to practitioners and observers alike – as immigrant rights legal activism. It is this series of reconfigurations that is the subject of the following chapters.

3

Formalization of Immigrant Rights

For many among the generation of jurists that took up immigrant defense in the 1970s, the project of assisting locally based immigrant movements and the project of creating new precedent in the area of immigration law were not mutually exclusive. Both seemed achievable through lawsuits challenging the newly restrictionist turn in national immigration policy making. The primary difficulty, for these aspiring legal activists, was that legal precedent around immigration questions appeared to be in a state of deep-freeze. While the grassroots political movements with which jurists came in contact were framing immigrant identity in new and creative ways, immigration law seemed stuck in outmoded categorizations.

The outlook was particularly daunting in the United States, where doctrinal construction, enunciated by the Supreme Court at the end of the nineteenth century, declared that Congress had received all sovereign power to regulate the entry of aliens and that choices in this area would not be subjected to other constitutional limitations.[1] French immigrant defenders did not have to contend with such an explicit doctrinal obstacle, but they nonetheless encountered an implicit juridical association of immigration with national security. In a series of postwar cases, the Conseil d'Etat had made it clear that it would be unwilling to exercise review over expulsions carried out in the name of public order, adopting this position even when the notion of "public order" was interpreted particularly broadly by administrative officials.[2] Challenging immigration policy at the national level was a difficult task when courts in both the United States and France had developed long-standing precedent associating these matters with sovereignty and national security.

Members of the cohort of recent law school graduates who took up the cause of immigrant defense in the 1970s were certainly aware of these negative precedents.[3] At the same time, aspiring legal activists in both countries were optimistic about the prospects of leveraging juridical technologies that had been unavailable during prior periods of immigration restrictionism. Courts in both the United States and France were asserting and deepening innovative new avenues for judicial review during this period. For those who hoped to effect policy change through legal channels, the task was to identify ways of legally associating immigration matters with these expansionary new avenues while legally dissociating them from the realm of sovereign discretion.

This chapter explores the creative work involved in disassembling old legal associations for immigration policy and assembling new ones. My analysis emphasizes that this activity did not simply apply to immigration cases a mechanical operating code already established in other areas of law, but rather translated immigration matters into forms that then could be taken up by juridical frameworks associated with assertive review. In other words, while contemporaneous jurisprudential regimes in both countries offered a set of devices with the potential to transform immigration law through case-by-case adjudication, judges needed to do the hard work of discerning whether these devices were or were not applicable to the cases before them.[4] Furthermore, it was not only appellate judges but also other participants in the legal process who engaged in the creative process of "imposing established categories for classifying events and relationships … or developing a framework which challenges established categories" (Mather and Yngvesson 1980, 775). In the process of legal contestation, litigators have at their disposal a heterogeneous set of devices to filter the complexity of the material world so as to render it legally intelligible. When it is successful, this process of translation produces new assemblages of events, relationships, and doctrinal concepts (what jurists would call the case "holding") that appear as logical extensions of existing law.

It is through such a process of translation, I argue, that aspiring legal activists starting in the late 1970s began to transform the grievances of noncitizens targeted by immigration restrictionism into legally cognizable claims. The comparison between the United States and France highlights the substantial differences in the set of legal devices engaged in each setting. As we will see, the heterogeneous set of devices within the Warren Court's jurisprudential regime for civil rights adjudication offered opportunities for individuals to acquire expansive rights protections if they could show that they belonged to groups that had faced historical discrimination. By contrast, the jurisprudential regime of contemporary French administrative law placed little emphasis on the characteristics of those claiming rights. Instead, this set of devices predicated the expansion of individual rights on associating a challenged policy with administrative autocracy. To the extent that legal arguments for vulnerable migrants were convincing, it was because litigators successfully extended a set of legal devices from other areas of the law into the immigration policy domain.

Taking each country in turn, this chapter first outlines the jurisprudential regimes that aspiring legal activists faced as they sought to convince courts on the basis of logic and precedent to expand rights for migrants targeted by immigration restrictionism. It then traces the creative process of meaning-making through which these sets of devices were applied in cases challenging restrictionist policies, with the aim of connecting immigration to the rights-based normative referents of domestic legality as opposed to those of foreign policy. Finally, the discussion of each national setting explores how the radiating effects of these legally generated associations in turn shaped political activity around immigration policy making outside of the courts.

WARREN COURT CIVIL RIGHTS JURISPRUDENCE

Recent contributions to the scholarship on American Political Development provide a starting point for understanding the jurisprudential regime that U.S. immigrant defenders drew upon as they explored ways to work around negative precedent. As these studies remind us, the doctrines and standards of Warren Court civil rights jurisprudence were formulated by judges closely attuned to the Kennedy-Johnson liberalism of the mid- and late 1960s, a regime that promoted professionalized reform as a corrective to the sort of traditionalism for which Jim Crow served as an exemplar (Tushnet 2006, 121–7). Moreover, the expansion of this jurisprudential regime was made possible by assertive use by Presidents Kennedy and Johnson of their judicial appointment powers so that by the mid-1960s the federal judiciary was filled with judges predisposed to applying this civil rights framework (Gillman 2006).

Although it emerged from a specific political and historical context, the Warren Court civil rights jurisprudence was still a distinctly legal technology insofar as it included a set of devices for evaluating concrete events and relationships through general legal categories. Perhaps the most important of these devices was the association of different levels of judicial review with different areas of policy making. Operating within the broad paradigm established during the New Deal period, the Warren Court followed the Roosevelt Court in jettisoning formalist notions of property rights so as to adhere to the basic premise that the protective legislative programs of the interventionist welfare state would be "presumed constitutional" so long as they were reasonably aimed at "some broader, systemic regulatory purpose" (Kersch 2006, 179). At the same time, in a footnote to a 1938 Supreme Court decision, the federal judiciary reserved its authority to conduct a more searching form of review in three kinds of situations: when a law violates a provision of the Constitution on its face, when it restricts the political process, or when it implicates "prejudice against discrete and insular minorities."[5] The third portion of this formulation, associating race-based legislative distinctions with heightened review, gained particular salience in civil rights cases, most prominently in the Supreme Court's 1954 decision in *Brown v. Board of Education* ending *de jure* segregation in public schools.[6] According to the new approach, when state laws explicitly mandated racial segregation, the Supreme Court was free to subject them to its strictest form of constitutional scrutiny.

A second prominent legal device in the Warren Court's civil rights jurisprudence, one that built upon the rule associating race-based distinctions with searching judicial review, was the flexible interpretive approach applied to the question of how "discrete and insular minorities" would be identified. Although the resonance of this legal category for its adherents was inseparable from the symbolic potency of the civil rights movement, judicial interpretation subsequently enabled other racial minorities besides African Americans to be brought within its reach. By 1970, Mexican Americans and Asian Americans had been classified by federal courts as identifiable ethnic minorities within the protection of *Brown*.[7] In combination with the broad application across civil rights cases of searching judicial review, the Warren Court's loosely metaphorical approach to the category of "discrete and insular minority" allowed judges to assertively scrutinize government actions alleged to discriminate against groups whose situation could be plausibly compared to that of African Americans.

A third legal device incorporated into the Warren Court civil rights jurisprudence in its later stages consisted of a technique directing judicial correctives toward discriminatory outcomes even in the absence of clearly invidious lawmaking motivations. The Supreme Court held that the constitutional norm of equal protection required the government to act purposefully to eliminate all vestiges of racial segregation even when the racial imbalance at issue was not produced by any current policy but was the result of a legacy of state-imposed segregation.[8] District courts were instructed to design remedies that would produce schools of like quality, facilities, and staff, and were free to use numerical ratios reflecting the racial composition of the population as a starting point for achieving a completely unified, unitary, nondiscriminatory school system. Government administrators were given the burden of showing that policies producing racially disproportionate effects were not the result of present or past discrimination on their part.[9]

While the Warren Court civil rights jurisprudence continued to expand its scope and the depth of its remedies, its potential applicability to the country's growing population of irregular migrants remained an open question. Even as it applied an assertive civil rights jurisprudence in other area of policy making, the Supreme Court reaffirmed the doctrine that immigration was a matter of foreign affairs in which judicial control should be minimal. As late as the mid-1970s, in *Matthews v. Diaz* (1976), the Court cited the plenary power doctrine when refusing to apply a raised standard of constitutional review to a federal statute providing noncitizens with less favorable access to Medicare benefits.[10]

Nevertheless, for immigrant defenders of a more optimistic bent, the conceptual repertoire of U.S. constitutional law continued to offer possibilities for extending Warren Court civil rights jurisprudence into immigration matters. The decision in *Matthews v. Diaz*, while it reviewed federal immigration policy using a deferential standard, nevertheless signaled an openness in principle to balancing the public interests served by prejudicial immigration laws against the individual constitutional rights of noncitizens – even those without regular immigration status. Moreover, several years earlier in *Graham v. Richardson* (1971), the Court had signaled a willingness to extend a more exacting form of constitutional review to immigration-related laws enacted by state rather than federal lawmakers. The new generation of immigrant defenders saw the application of an elevated constitutional standard to state laws withdrawing noncitizens' social assistance benefits as a sign that appellate judges might revisit and revise some of the negative precedent preventing the expansion of immigrant rights.

IMMIGRANT RIGHTS AS CIVIL RIGHTS, PART I – THE TEXAS SCHOOLS CASES

The first concerted litigation effort to apply this jurisprudential regime to immigration issues challenged a state law that on its face discriminated on the basis of immigration status. In 1975, Texas's State Legislature amended Section 2301 of its educational code so as to cease reimbursing local school districts for the costs of educating undocumented children in free public schools. Individual school districts responded to the legislation in different ways, with some initially continuing to enroll undocumented children free of charge, but most school districts eventually either prevented undocumented children from enrolling in public schools or imposed fees on undocumented children to attend public school. Some private groups set up "alternative schools" of inferior educational quality that enrolled undocumented children free of charge. Most undocumented children whose parents could not afford public school tuition stayed at home instead of going to school.

The Mexican American Legal Defense and Education Fund (MALDEF) was the first group to organize a litigation response to the Texas law. Created in 1968 with support from the Ford Foundation, MALDEF had successfully applied civil rights jurisprudence to the domain of education policies, convincing federal courts to place Mexican Americans in the category of "discrete and insular minority" (San Miguel 1987). Given the Texas law's obvious connection to education rights, MALDEF legal director Peter Roos was eager to organize a legal challenge on behalf of undocumented children. Concentrating on a single school district had the benefit of ensuring that MALDEF's 1977 test case, *Plyler v. Doe*, would be heard in the courtroom of Judge William Wayne Justice, a federal judge who had established a reputation for assertive application of Warren Court civil rights jurisprudence. As Michael Olivas documents in his history of the litigation, MALDEF's attorneys saw *Plyler* as the Mexican American *Brown v. Board of Education*, a federal-court vehicle to consolidate previous modest victories in many small state-court cases (Olivas 2005, 201).

At the same time, legal services lawyers from the newly formed National Center for Immigrants' Rights (NCIR) were also eager to become involved in challenging the Texas law. As participants in the National Lawyers Guild's immigrant defender network, they saw the Texas law's connection not only to education rights but also to immigrant rights. NCIR's Los Angeles–based director, attorney Peter Schey, secured the role of coordinating a team of local Texas attorneys who, unwilling to wait for the outcome of MALDEF's test case, had filed separate challenges in each of the state's federal judicial districts so as to accelerate the process of allowing all undocumented children to return to school. In 1979, these cases were combined into a single consolidated action, *In re Alien Children Education Litigation*, in the Houston Federal District Court that would address statewide issues.

Focusing on the law's implications for Mexican American educational access, MALDEF's arguments drew heavily upon the categories of Warren Court civil rights jurisprudence. In framing the facts and the legal issues, they sought to convince the courts that the 1975 legislation amounted to an attempt by Texas's legislators to undo the gains of civil rights proponents. The primary thrust of these arguments was that the purportedly racially neutral legislation was in fact saturated with racism. They emphasized that most of the costs of bilingual education are borne by the federal government, thus the state's claim that the cost of bilingual education was a major rationale for the legislation targeting undocumented children was simply camouflaging invidious purposes. The legislation was framed as a reactionary response by Texas legislators against the decade-long effort of Mexican Americans and their supporters to include Mexicans in civil rights desegregation programs. By arguing that "the public schools provide virtually the only opportunity that many of these children will have to interact with the majority society,"[11] MALDEF's lawyers effectively cast their clients within a race-based mold and softened the distinction between "alienage" and "lineage." They highlighted the testimony of one state witness, who had not only conflated Mexican children with undocumented children, but who had also stated that these children have "lower educational capabilities," arguing that the court should infer from the word *capability* that the state educational official held suspect views about inherent racial differences.[12] The plaintiff children were a prime example of "a discrete and insular minority requiring heightened judicial solicitude because they have been subjected to a history of purposeful unequal treatment."[13]

The legal services attorneys of NCIR likewise relied on legal devices taken from Warren Court civil rights jurisprudence to frame the facts and issues in their case when it went to trial in the spring of 1980 in the Houston courtroom of Judge Woodrow Seals. Schey's legal team aimed to convince the court that the challenged statute should be closely scrutinized because it penalized innocent children, whom it categorized on the basis of alienage. To dissociate the schoolchildren from transitory "illegal aliens," a category evoking a jurisprudential regime of sovereign border control authority, the legal team insisted at trial on using the term *undocumented schoolchildren* rather than *illegal aliens* and presented testimony from child witnesses who had been excluded from school by the Texas law because they did not have documents but who had come to reunite with parents who were settled in the United States as legal residents.[14] Reconfigured through this device, undocumented schoolchildren could be seen, not as illegal aliens, but as part of a permanent settler group. Moreover, these settled immigrants needed special constitutional protection, it was argued, because they were part of the most vulnerable segment, "a minority within a minority,"[15] of the state's entire Mexican-origin population. The plaintiffs' arguments drew explicit comparison between the situation in Texas and racism directed against African Americans, suggesting that, "Not very long ago, it was felt that 'slaves should be maintained in a position of subordination in order that the optimum of discipline and work could be achieved' ... Texas perhaps holds the same view."[16] If local officials were allowed to exclude a particularly vulnerable group on the basis of immigration status, it was argued, the country would drift into a new type of caste system reminiscent of slavery or Jim Crow. These arguments, like those developed by MALDEF attorneys, applied jurisprudential devices drawn from Warren Court civil rights decisions, but they expended relatively greater effort on laying the groundwork for this conceptual reframing by first disassembling the category of illegal alien.

Though they varied in their emphasis, these associations of "undocumented schoolchildren" with the legally cognizable category of "discrete and insular minority" resonated with the lower court judges who heard the cases. A longtime proponent of Warren Court civil rights jurisprudence, Judge Justice had no trouble accepting the civil rights framing of immigrants in its entirely. He declared in his decision overturning the statute that undocumented immigrants were being used as "scapegoats" to divert the attention of the Mexican American community away from demands for full integration and a fair share of the state's total educational resources. The state had wanted to exclude all Mexicans, he suggested, but it was legally prevented from doing so by civil rights precedent and so it attempted to "shave off a little around the edges."[17] Judge Frank Johnson of the Fifth Circuit Court of Appeals affirmed this decision, reasoning that excluding undocumented children from constitutional protection would expose them to future discrimination more extreme than the Texas law.[18] To the delight of Schey's legal team, the more conservative Judge Seals likewise found for the plaintiffs in the consolidated case, reasoning that the educational needs of the children statutorily excluded were not different from the needs of children not excluded and that "[t]he classification used is wholly irrelevant to the achievement of the State's objective."[19]

The Supreme Court was more circumspect in accepting the entirety of the civil rights framing of undocumented immigrants. The various challenges to the Texas law reached the Court in the fall of 1981 at a single hearing, and briefs were submitted from both sets of lawyers. Rather than creating new general principles, as both Roos's and Schey's legal teams had hoped, the decision affirming the unconstitutionality of the Texas law was narrowly tailored to the circumstances of the case. When it issued its decision in the summer of 1982, the Supreme Court majority affirmed that the Texas law was unconstitutional but rejected the rigorous "strict scrutiny" analysis and refused to give validation to the claim that education was a fundamental right.[20] At the same time that it concluded that the Texas law's adverse effects outweighed its benefits, the Court made it clear that its decision was narrowly tailored to the circumstances of the case and should not necessarily be read as supporting a broader extension of rights to undocumented migrant adults. Indeed, the opinion was criticized by the dissenting justices for being based on a desired policy outcome – overturning Texas's law – rather than on general principles.[21]

In practice, the policy ambitions of Justice Brennan's majority opinion reached more broadly than criticizing Texas's law. A careful reading of the opinion reminds us of what those at the time understood more quickly, namely that the thrust of the opinion was aimed at addressing the federal government's immigration policies. Directed implicitly toward a national policy-making audience, the majority opinion asserted that the combination of lax federal enforcement and Texas's statutory discrimination created a lethal combination that threatened to create a "permanent caste of undocumented resident aliens ... an underclass that presents most difficult problems for a Nation that prides itself on principles of equality under law."[22] Although the decision overturned a state statutory provision, the majority opinion was clearly directed toward federal policy discussions, citing approvingly a presidential proposal to legalize a large proportion of undocumented immigrants, "who have become, in effect, members of the community." The opinion ensured that undocumented children in Texas could remain in public schools. Even as it shied away from extending all of the protections of the Warren Court's civil rights jurisprudential regime to undocumented adults, the decision implicitly accepted the framing of immigrant children as the most vulnerable members of a racialized minority, declaring that "depriving the children of any disfavored group of an education, [would] foreclose the means by which that group might raise the level of esteem in which it is held by the majority."[23] Though it avoided saying so explicitly, it seemed to endorse a general amnesty for undocumented immigrants.

IMMIGRANT RIGHTS AS CIVIL RIGHTS, PART II – THE HAITIAN REFUGEE CASES

At the same time as the Texas schools cases were progressing through the courts, a second important litigation campaign was also making strides toward extending the jurisprudential regime of Warren Court civil rights jurisprudence to immigration issues. While the arguments in the *Plyler* case had addressed border control only indirectly, this second set of cases challenged the policies of the Immigration and Nationalization Service (INS) directed against Haitians arriving by sea on the coast of South Florida. The Haitian litigation thus engaged more explicitly with national-level issues.

The legal process unfolded against the background of a restrictionist immigration policy shift whose effects were exacerbated by political upheaval in a neighboring state. As large numbers of Haitians fled the autocratic Duvalier regime and sought asylum in the United States during the 1970s, they encountered an asylum process that was poorly institutionalized and that allowed substantial room for discretion.[24] Although Haitians were eligible to apply for asylum through this process, in practice they were treated much less favorably than Cuban asylum applicants and almost none of their asylum claims were granted (Loescher and Scanlan 1986, 74–84). By the late 1970s, the situation for Haitian asylum seekers had become even less favorable due to the restrictionist turn in immigration policy making. In July 1978, the INS's newly created "Haitian Program" instructed agency officials in south Florida to cease requiring immigration judges to suspend deportation proceedings for asylum seekers and to cease the practice of allowing aliens ten days to prepare applications to withhold deportation.

As with the *Plyler* litigation, the legal team that assembled to challenge the "Haitian Program" brought together a set of attorneys with diverse institutional affiliations. Haitian asylum seekers had initially attracted the support of a loose cluster of New York–based lawyers affiliated with leftist attorney Leonard Boudin's National Emergency Civil Liberties Committee. By 1978, when the "Haitian Program" was implemented, however, Haitian defense efforts were largely turned over to members of the new generation of immigrant defenders. Recent law school graduate Ira Kurzban, who had studied with Boudin and had become active in immigrant defender networks upon moving to south Florida, became counsel to the Haitian Refugee Center, a former church-funded group that had recently been transformed into the organizing base for the growing politicization of the Haitian community.[25] Within a short period of time, Kurzban was joined by Peter Schey, fresh from the litigation in the Texas school cases, and by Dale ("Rick") Swartz, another young lawyer who had participated in some of his D.C. firm's *pro bono* work and who had been hired by the Washington Lawyers' Committee for Civil Rights Under Law to organize its new Alien Rights Law Project. On behalf of the Haitian Refugee Center, they secured a temporary restraining order in May 1979 ensuring that none of the approximately five thousand Haitian asylum seekers impacted by the government's new program would be removed. They then organized a team of litigators who sought to put the INS program on trial.

Aiming to convince the federal district court that unauthorized Haitian migrants should have access to the equal protection component of the Fifth Amendment against discriminatory immigration control practices, the legal team in *Haitian Refugee Center v. Civiletti* sought to separate the Haitian's claims from unreviewable "political questions" and to cast them instead as actions brought by a "discrete and insular minority." Throughout the exhaustive trial in the fall of 1979 and spring of 1980, the Haitian legal team repeatedly emphasized the racialized identity of Haitian asylum seekers, arguing that the underlying reason why Haitians had been subjected to intentional discrimination was that they were part of "the first substantial flight of black refugees" to the United States.[26] Further support for the view that Haitians were the victims of discrimination on the basis of their race was secured through testimony from the Director of Catholic Charities for the Archdiocese of Miami, who stated that, in his twenty-four years of experience the treatment of Haitians "differs from that of any other immigrant group."[27]

By gesturing at familiar features of landmark civil rights cases, the plaintiffs' arguments in *Haitian Refugee Center v. Civiletti* effectively communicated to the district court judge that INS practices should be evaluated using a Warren Court civil rights framework. The first sentence of Judge James Lawrence King's decision highlighted the racialized framing of the case by stating, "This case involves thousands of black Haitian nationals."[28] Judge King held that the government had violated the essence of constitutional due process when it created a right to petition for asylum and then made the exercise of that right impossible for Haitians. The government was ordered to submit a nondiscriminatory and procedurally fair plan for orderly reprocessing of plaintiffs' asylum applications.

Litigation continued, however, after the newly elected Reagan Administration in September 1981 enacted an aggressively control-oriented set of policies. The new approach included policies of extraterritorial interdiction, screening, and repatriation, but it also revived prior policies of perfunctory screenings and increased use of detention. These changes meant that all unadmitted noncitizens without *prima facie* claims for asylum would now be detained in a network of detention facilities around the country. These new and unpublished Reagan Administration asylum policies were challenged by a newly reconstituted legal team led by Kurzban in *Louis v. Nelson*, a class action brought in June 1981 on behalf of all unadmitted Haitians who had arrived on U.S. territory. They succeeded in obtaining a temporary restraining order in September 1981 to prevent the INS from holding any further hearings until asylum seekers were represented by counsel. At the trial in April 1982, Kurzban's litigation team deployed techniques that had been successful two years earlier in configuring black Haitian refugees as victims of discrimination. In particular, so as to counter the government's argument that detention and parole of unauthorized migrants was a political matter over which federal courts have no jurisdiction, Kurzban and his team invited testimonies and produced statistical evidence highlighting differences in how detention policies were applied to Haitians as compared to other similarly unauthorized migrants.[29]

District Court Judge Eugene Spellman was clearly moved by what he heard at trial, beginning his decision with a poetic epithet that ended with the words "sometimes you weep."[30] His decision made quick work of the government's argument that denial of parole to unauthorized migrants was a political matter, even as he ultimately concluded that there was not yet sufficient evidence to justify a remedy on the grounds of group-based discrimination. The following year, after Kurzban's team had appealed, a panel of 11th Circuit judges saw things their way and felt compelled to conclude that Haitians were the victims of discrimination on the basis of evidence presented at trial that the INS office in downtown Miami had posted sign directed "Haitians to the rear" while Cubans were directed to the standard assistance channels.[31] One year later, on appeal by the government, a subsequent *en banc* decision of the 11th Circuit held that unadmitted aliens had a statutory right to a hearing but that they enjoyed no constitutionally based protection against discrimination.[32]

When the case was appealed to the Supreme Court, Kurzban's team presented arguments that framed Haitian asylum seekers in even more explicitly racial terms. Referring to the 11th Circuit's deleterious reading of the equal protection rights of excludable aliens, advocates for the Haitians asserted that, "Not since the *Dred Scott* decision has this or any other court ever held that a class of persons is wholly immune from constitutional protection."[33] Drawing an implicit metaphor to the treatment of slaves, the brief described detained Haitians as have been "shipped [by the INS] like cattle, to remote areas of America."[34] Citing the Supreme Court's school desegregation cases, the attorneys suggested that an explicit extension of equal protection rights in this case would be a logical progression from Congress's 1965 immigration reforms that had "eliminated the vestiges of invidious racial or nationality based discrimination in the immigration statutes" by eliminating the national-origins system.[35] Just as in the Texas school litigation, rights were constructed through racialization, and race-based discrimination was framed as the primary obstacle to the realization of immigrant rights.

When it eventually decided the case in 1985, the Supreme Court backed away from extending equal protection rights to excludable aliens, although it did reverse some of the damage done by the 11th Circuit's decision. The Court declined to rule on the issue of whether plenary power barred the plaintiffs from raising a constitutional equal protection claim. Instead, applying a subconstitutional analysis arguably informed indirectly by mainstream equal protection analysis (Motomura 1990, 591–2), the Court interpreted existing immigration statutes and administrative regulations as prohibiting the INS from discriminating on the basis of race or nationality.[36] Immigration control was not so clearly a matter of pure national sovereignty, according to the Court, as to be excluded from judicial supervision. At the same time, the judicial remedy offered to the plaintiffs was formally based only on standards of administrative legality (the District Court was instructed to review the exercise of discretion by low-level INS officials to ensure that it was consistent with regulations that had been interpreted by the Court as containing no mandate for discrimination). This was disappointing to immigrant defenders who had hoped to secure an explicit doctrinal extension of Warren Court civil rights jurisprudence. Yet as we will see, even as appellate courts remained hard to convince, other audiences were swayed by the reconfiguration of immigration issues achieved in these early litigation campaigns.

IMMIGRANT RIGHTS LEGAL NARRATIVES OUTSIDE OF AMERICAN COURTS

To understand the political significance of these experiments in legal translation, we need to expand our gaze beyond the courtroom and explore how all of this frenetic legal meaning-making was perceived by a broader set of political actors. Even as their work was distinguished by its uniquely juridical approach, immigrant defenders were not the only ones to position irregular migrants within a broader civil rights paradigm. Hispanic interest groups, most notably the League of United Latin-American Citizens and MALDEF, had spent most of the 1970s attempting to gather a legislative coalition around a civil rights approach to immigration control. However, these groups faced an uphill battle during the Carter presidency as they sought to convince key Democratic constituencies to support a large-scale legalization program for irregular migrants.

The problem was not that immigration per se could not be framed in civil rights terms. A decade earlier, the "Hart-Celler" Immigration Act, which ended national-origin discrimination in immigrant admissions from Europe and Asia, had been heralded by its congressional sponsors as an extension of the civil rights legislative agenda (Skrentny 2002, 37–54).[37] The difference was that debates over the Hart-Celler bill had hardly considered migrant labor flows from Latin America, which were now increasingly irregular due to the termination of the *bracero* guest-worker program one year prior to the Immigration Act's enactment (Zolberg 2006, 344). Rather than a civil rights frame, it was an economic frame that guided Congress's response to migration flows across the southern border, reflected in the passage of a per-country cap in 1976 that limited legal immigration from Mexico by half.

Key groups within the Democratic Party balked at a civil rights framing of irregular migrants. The United Farm Workers, and the labor movement more generally, continued to view "back door" migrants as a threat to organizing efforts (Zolberg 2006, 341–2). Democrats with strong labor constituencies favored only a limited legalization program and sought to impose sanctions on employers of irregular migrants. The increase in refugee flows in the 1970s only heightened the tensions on Capitol Hill, because this influx of low-skilled migrants was seen as a further threat to the structures of the welfare state, which labor and African American constituencies were fighting to preserve (Gimpel and Edwards 1999, 133). In 1977, the Carter administration's attempt to broker a compromise through its comprehensive immigration reform proposal failed to gain traction in Congress. The decision in the fall of 1978 to create a Select Commission on Immigration and Refugee Policy ("The Hesburgh Commission") was in large part an attempt by Democratic legislators to postpone dealing with their own divided constituencies (Tichenor 2002, 233).

It was at this moment, when legislative responses to the country's dramatically increasing population of irregular migrants remained elusive, that high-profile litigation campaigns intervened in the national debate. As courts began hearing the multiple lawsuits on behalf of undocumented Texas schoolchildren, judicial proceedings offered opportunities for advocates to mobilize the liberal Washington policy community around the civil rights framing of irregular migrants. As Michael Olivas has shown, liberal supporters were particularly engaged by litigation challenging Texas's exclusion of undocumented children from public schools. Between 1977 and 1981, MALDEF Legal Director Peter Roos repeatedly solicited statements of support from Carter administration officials and encouraged the liberal legal community to write editorials, host fundraisers, and file amicus briefs on behalf of the plaintiff children (Olivas 2005, 204). Leveraging contacts with Assistant Attorney General for Civil Rights, Drew Days, and with Secretary of Health, Education, and Welfare Joseph Califano, Roos succeeded in convincing the Justice Department and the Solicitor General to enter the litigation on the side of the children (Olivas 2005, 207). The March 1980 trial in the consolidated *In re Alien Children* class action further cemented high-profile liberal support. Once Peter Schey's legal team had juridically cemented a civil rights reading of the issues, Judge Woodrow Seals's racially insensitive remarks and subsequent public apology during the trial could then become a media story that would galvanize public attention (Olivas 2005, 217). In the assessment of legal aid attorney Larry Daves, who assisted MALDEF on the Texas schools litigation, the involvement of "experts from the civil rights establishment [was] ultimately what carried the day," both in the initial District Court victories and in the Fifth Circuit's affirmance of these decisions.[38] Seen from another angle, it was the particular jurisprudential regime deployed by both legal teams – one that convincingly associated undocumented migrants with symbolically redolent legal categories of Warren Court civil rights jurisprudence – that generated both recognition and engagement on the part of the broader liberal legal community.

Unfolding at approximately the same moment, litigation challenging the government's Haitian refugee policies offered a parallel track for converting established civil rights groups to the cause of immigrant rights. The temporary restraining order against the INS issued by a Nixon-appointed federal judge in May 1979 was a breakthrough moment in legitimating the immigrant rights narrative. The exhaustive trial between the fall of 1979 and the spring of 1980, in which the plaintiffs rhetorically emphasized the racial identity of Haitian asylum seekers, opened political space that migrant advocates consciously exploited. In the spring of 1980, attorneys for the Haitians succeeded in convincing members of the Hesburgh Commission to travel to Miami, where they heard firsthand testimony from five hundred refugees.[39] Later that year, again as part of a political strategy to garner support for the litigation, members of the Haitian defense team organized meetings on Capitol Hill for refugees to personally describe their experiences, energizing the Congressional Black Caucus Haitian Taskforce. This framing of refugees as a racially disadvantaged minority was influential in convincing leading black legislators who had previously opposed refugee legislation to vote for the 1980 Refugee Act (Gimpel and Edwards 1999, 131), suggesting the catalytic potential of a civil rights legal framing for constructing a new political narrative around vulnerable migrants.

The auspiciousness of the political moment was not lost on some of those directly involved in litigating the cases, whose professional prestige had been palpably enhanced when immigrant rights arguments were vindicated in federal court.[40] In the spring of 1981, in the aftermath of the *Haitian Refugee v. Civiletti* trial, attorney Rick Swartz left his position at the Washington Lawyers Committee for Civil Rights and sought funding from the Ford Foundation for a new lobbying organization – the National Immigration Forum – that would bring the civil rights approach to immigration directly into the political sphere. Armed with the momentum generated by developments in court, Swartz turned his attention to the congressional politics of immigration. The release of the Hesburgh Commission's Report in March 1981 had propelled immigration policy to the top of the national agenda, and Swartz and MALDEF President Vilma Martinez emerged as the two most vocal advocates for a civil rights approach (Laham 2000, 55). Drawing on professional prestige palpably enhanced by successes in court, they actively lobbied the White House and Congress to reject the commission's recommendation for the imposition of an employer-sanctions regime, arguing that it would endanger important civil liberties values and create discrimination against members of minority groups.

As Congress began debating the Simpson-Mazzoli immigration bill in early 1982, developments in court generated additional materials with which to construct a new immigration lobby. The Haitian refugee litigation produced a particularly dramatic development in the form of a June 1982 decree from Judge Spellman ordering the INS to release each of the 1,700 Haitian plaintiffs from detention once individual counsel was secured for filing an asylum claim.[41] Technically speaking, the court order shied away from a constitutionally based ruling on the merits. However, the decision to grant parole to such a large number of unauthorized migrants generated substantial attention within the legal profession. Leaders of both the American Bar Association and the American Immigration Lawyers Association endorsed an ambitious initiative to secure individualized legal representation for Haitians dispersed across the country (Helton 1984/1985). The very fact that the case generated the largest pro bono effort ever organized was decisive in energizing the legal profession's participation in the legislative politics of immigration (see Chapter 4). Not surprisingly, the legal profession's engagement further tipped the Democratic Party's position away from a materialist approach to immigration enforcement. During the summer and fall of 1982, a nascent network of civil rights organizations, civil liberties groups, and professional bar associations that had supported the Haitian litigation worked together to mobilize against proposed amendments to the Simpson-Mazzoli bill that aimed to streamline exclusion and deportation hearings (Gimpel and Edwards 1999, 140).

As momentum gathered in Washington for incorporating civil rights concerns into immigration reform, the Supreme Court's *Plyler* decision in June 1982 symbolically raised the stakes. The 1975 Texas Statute at issue in the case had not attempted to control immigration directly, yet Justice Brennan's decision nevertheless drew a direct connection to ongoing federal inaction on immigration reform. As recounted by scholar Aristide Zolberg, who testified before congressional hearings at this time, the Supreme Court's decision in *Plyler* contributed to the sense among legislators that immigration was "out of control" and that swift action needed to be taken (Zolberg 2006, 361). Yet, by framing the integration of undocumented residents as an issue of social justice, Justice Brennan's decision also offered symbolic support to efforts to frame debate in terms of immigrant rights. The decision made clear that the justices were not willing to wholly subsume immigration under the protections of strict scrutiny, but neither were they willing to dismiss immigrant rights claims entirely. Organizers such as Swartz and Martinez could now emphasize that judicial authorities supported their position that immigration was not just about material interests but was a "difficult and philosophical issue" in which "fundamental protections of liberty and civil rights were at stake."[42]

Proceeding in rapid succession, legal interventions for immigrant rights in the late 1970s and early 1980s had the cumulative effect of legitimizing and strengthening the appeal of a noneconomic framing of immigration reform. Action in court was a key contributor to the nascent National Immigration Forum "getting a seat at the table" in congressional immigration debates.[43] Having merged in 1982 with a much older organization – the American Immigration, Citizenship, and Refugee Conference – composed of predominantly white ethnic groups, the National Immigration Forum set up taskforces and meetings to bring together a new nonpartisan immigration lobby that included a broad consortium of more than ninety ethnic and religious groups and legal organizations. Drawing upon the organizing model of the Leadership Conference on Civil Rights, the forum described itself as an "immigration rights advocacy group" (Graham 2003, 120). It endorsed an amnesty program that would allow Hispanic families to remain together and waged an all-out war against employer sanctions in the name of civil rights protection. Swartz was particularly energetic in positioning the National Immigration Forum as an alternative to the Federation for American Immigration Reform (FAIR), an organization formed in 1979 to lobby in favor of limitations on total admissions and against any legalization. Speaking on behalf of the forum, Swartz labeled FAIR's positions as "nativist chic" and suggested that this narrative might open the door to the kind of racially tinged right-wing groups seen in Western Europe.[44] Although Swartz, Martinez, and their allies were not ultimately able to block employer sanctions provisions from being included in the Immigration Reform and Control Act that was passed in October 1986, they succeeded in ensuring that procedures would be set up to periodically evaluate the impact of sanctions on job discrimination and that the Justice Department would pursue discrimination claims (Gimpel and Edwards 1999, 168).

The civil rights approach to immigration changed the way that key players understood the issues. The formalization of immigrant rights through litigation contributed to catalyzing a civil rights immigration coalition that made possible the civil rights components of the Immigration Reform and Control Act, the comprehensive legislative reform of U.S. immigration policy enacted in 1986. In the decades to come, this lobby, known as "the groups," would continue to exert a strong influence over U.S. immigration policy debates, an aspect of the U.S. legislative politics of immigration that has been extensively studied by scholars of immigration politics (Gimpel and Edwards 1999, Haus 2002, Newton 2008). So, for now, we leave the U.S. story and turn to the initial efforts of French legal activists to develop formal rights for noncitizens. At the same time that immigration in the United States was being transformed into a civil rights issue through legal interventions, legal actors in France were also beginning to engage with the legal issues raised by immigration restrictionism.

THE FRENCH CONSEIL D'ETAT'S POST-1968 JURISPRUDENCE

Unlike their U.S. counterparts, aspiring legal activists in France did not have an extensive body of constitutional jurisprudence on which to build their claims. Indeed, the practice of rights-based judicial review had been introduced only recently into the politics of the Fifth Republic. Having confined itself for the first thirteen years of its existence to the limited political mandate set by its Gaullist designers, France's Constitutional Council roused itself in 1971 and declared itself competent to apply the ensemble of rights-based provisions of France's constitutional texts in all of its future decisions. Yet it was not obvious at the time how widely this *"bloc de constitutionnalité"* would be applied because the Constitutional Council's institutional mandate was confined to reviewing the text of statutes before they were enacted into law and did not extend to judicial review either of the laws already in application or of administrative action.[45] This narrow constitutional jurisdiction was particularly limiting for those seeking to influence the politics of immigration, because France's immigration policies were at this time almost entirely elaborated through administrative action rather than legislation.

While French constitutional jurisprudence remained shielded from influence through litigation, this was not the case for the parallel system of administrative law and administrative review. In the Fifth Republic, as the power of the presidency expanded, France's highest administrative jurisdiction, the Conseil d'Etat, increasingly gave its review of administrative acts a constitutional tinge by declaring that the general principles of law that it is charged with enforcing result from the Preamble of the 1946 Constitution, even as their authority is also confirmed by legislative texts (Brown and Bell 1998, 219). This jurisprudential development by the Conseil d'Etat followed the lead of the Constitutional Council,[46] but it also built upon a tradition in French administrative law forged progressively by a combination of jurisprudence and doctrine over the course of the nineteenth and early twentieth centuries. The two main conceptual pillars of this tradition consist of the ideas that administrative authority must adhere to formalized procedures and that it must be exercised in the service of the public (Chevallier 1989, 313, Koopmans 2003, 139). The tradition recognized that standards for public authority should be different from those applied to private actors, which is why administrators were to be judged not by the judicial branch but by a special jurisdiction – the

Conseil d'Etat – operating at the pinnacle of state administration. Its corps of elite civil servants were to be the "conscience" of the state, steering administrators away from actions taken for reasons of expediency and thus ensuring the maintenance of *Etat de droit*, a state in which public action is entirely encapsulated and ruled by the law so that "its various organs cannot act except by virtue of a juridical habilitation and may only use the avenues authorized by law" (Chevallier 1999, 14). The Conseil d'Etat's legal grammar thus centers not on protecting against the danger that the coercive tools of the state will be co-opted for narrow factional purposes, but on the risk that the state – whose independent existence is unquestioned – might become unbound from legality and slip into rule by exception.

Of particular importance to those seeking to impact administrative policies concerning immigration was the fact that, in the 1970s, the Conseil d'Etat was moving toward a more probing administrative control that emphasized the need for greater equality between the state and those it administered. In its 1971 *Ville Nouvelle-Est* decision, the Conseil d'Etat stepped onto the terrain of administrative fact finding by requiring state planners to demonstrate that their decision to proceed with a contentious local economic development initiative had been taken only after conducting a full study of the plan's environmental impact.[47] In the same month, the Conseil d'Etat extended its review of administrative rule making, holding in its *Damasio* decision that discretionary "interpretive circulars" could be distinguished from "regulatory circulars" and "orienting circulars" and that the latter two categories – insofar as they created new norms – justified judicial scrutiny of whether their content was contrary to principles of legality or the relevant empowering provisions in legislative texts.[48] These decisions might be read, as some commentators suggest, as signs of the Conseil d'Etat's willingness to respond to post-1968 public criticism of the unilateralism and secrecy of the Gaullist state (Brown and Bell 1998, 229–30). In any event, the Conseil d'Etat's experimentation with judicial policy making and balancing approaches called into question the status quo of postwar administrative managerialism by establishing a jurisprudential regime of heightened concern for autocratic tendencies within the executive branch.

But would immigration policy be included in the domain over which the Conseil d'Etat asserted this framework of legality in administration? The control of immigration was an area in which administrative discretion was long established. In a series of decisions during the 1950s, the Conseil d'Etat had determined that administrative tribunals held no legal authority to review the basis of individual expulsion orders issued by the Minister of Interior in the name of public order.[49] And because the postwar regime governing immigration allowed the administration wide discretion to determine what types of activities constituted a "menace to the public order," this effectively gave bureaucrats carte blanche over immigration matters.

Despite these obstacles, aspiring legal activists in France were encouraged by what they perceived as a general embrace of legality in other areas of legal and political life in the 1970s. At the Cour de Cassation, France's highest court of appeals for private and criminal matters, proactive litigation by the legal department of the *Confédération Française Démocratique du Travail* (CFDT) was producing a significant expansion of labor rights (Willemez 2003). In partisan electoral debates, heavy-handed policing techniques and "bureaucratic totalitarianism" were being publicly criticized, and public liberties emerged as a prominent rhetorical theme in French politics (Agrikoliansky 2005). Finally, the public campaign, led by respected jurist René Cassin, for France to ratify the European Convention on Human Rights reinforced the discursive salience of fundamental rights and liberties (Madsen 2005, 60–2). Aspiring legal activists saw their role as bringing immigration policy making within this expanding legal regime.

PROTECTING IMMIGRANT WORKERS FROM THE POLICE STATE, PART I – THE MARCELLIN-FONTANET CIRCULARS

France's shift toward immigration restrictionism supplied ample material for immigrant rights test cases. In December 1972, administrative circulars issued jointly by Minister of Interior Raymond Marcellin and Minister of Labor Joseph Fontanet instructed prefects to deny requests for regularization if an immigrant worker's employer could not show that the National Employment Agency was unable to find a French worker to fill the position. Prefects were also instructed to deny requests for regularization if the immigrant's employer failed to provide adequate housing for the worker. The circulars also changed the rules for issuing residency and work cards for all immigrants, not just for irregular migrants making the initial attempt to regularize their status: prefects were to replace the temporary work authorization card, previously issued during the first year of employment, with a one-year visa pasted onto the immigrant's employment contract, and residence cards would now last no longer than the duration of a work permit. The consequences of this tightened criteria for regularization were harsh, because a denied request would result in an expulsion order. For this reason, the circulars elicited widespread mobilizations on the part of immigrant workers, who saw these administrative acts as part of a policy to reduce the population of foreign workers by restricting access to residency and work permits.

In one of its earliest efforts to use appellate litigation, members of the nascent legal network associated with the *Groupe d'Information et de Soutien des Travailleurs Immigrés* (GISTI) coordinated with attorneys affiliated with the CFDT labor federation to petition the Conseil d'Etat to overturn the controversial circulars. Because GISTI was not yet registered as an official association, the case was brought in the name of a Portuguese immigrant and CFDT unionist, Antonio Da Silva, who held work and residency permits, but for whom it was argued the circulars would impose multiple obstacles when it came time to renew these permits. The CFDT filed a separate petition based on its organizational interest in policy making that impacted its members, and the two cases were consolidated when they were finally heard by the Conseil d'Etat in January 1975.

The arguments in both petitions were anchored on the constitutional principle of the right to work, a right contained in the Preamble to the 1946 Constitution. Associating an official work permit, once granted, with an individual's "consecrated" freedom to work, the CFDT petition asserted that the administration could not subsequently place limitations on guarantees that it had already established.[50] The circulars' various provisions – delaying the issuance of a permanent work permit by one year, harmonizing the duration of work and residence permits, and conditioning the issuance of a work permit on the employer having advertised the job with the national employment agency – were argued to effectively bind immigrant workers to their employers insofar as the new rules prevented workers who changed employers from renewing their residence authorization. Similarly, the provision conditioning residence and work authorizations on the employer's commitment to supply adequate housing were criticized as a means by which employers and the state would jointly exercise greater social control over foreign workers.

GISTI's petition challenging the Marcellin-Fontanet circulars likewise cast the regulations as an autocratic administrative attempt to exploit the labor of immigrant workers. The argument was that immigrants were being treated by the police state as a commodity that could be used and then discarded. Through administrative fiat, the circulars had illegally changed a well-defined existing regime in which labor contracts, once signed by the employer and employee, were not assumed to have any fixed expiration. GISTI's challenge to the circulars urged the Conseil d'Etat to consider immigrant workers who had been given an employment contract as part of the national community. As such, they should be protected from the precarity associated with a regime of short-term permits. Drawing parallels between the circulars' reinforcement of policing and administrative control that threatened the liberties of foreign workers and the "regime of exception" associated with a police state, it called on the Conseil d'Etat to apply its recently developed jurisprudence asserting review over the administrative practice of regulating by informal circular.[51]

The Conseil d'Etat did eventually overturn several of the provisions of the Marcellin-Fontanet circulars, although it avoided discussing the constitutional right to work and justified its decision solely on the basis of statutory interpretation. According to the decision, the administration had inappropriately added conditions to existing laws when it instructed prefects to refuse immigrant residence permits based on the quality of available acceptable housing and to delay the issuance of a work permit by one year.[52] And by ordering that *all* regularizations of foreigners who had entered as tourists be prohibited, the administration had inappropriately added to the relevant legislative and regulatory dispositions governing its action. The decision in *Da Silva* articulated no explicit evolution in jurisprudential principles and was only a partial victory, because the Conseil d'Etat upheld the provisions of the circulars harmonizing the duration of work and residence permits as well as the requirement that jobs be posted with the National Employment Agency.

Nevertheless, GISTI's jurists celebrated the decision as a vindication of their arguments, taking it as a sign that the Conseil d'Etat was now willing to scrutinize government policy making in the area of immigration. For GISTI, *Da Silva* was the first Conseil d'Etat decision for which it could claim credit as an organization. The group's press conference announcing the victory was so celebratory that lawyer Philippe Waquet, who had authored GISTI's *Da Silva* petitions, was summoned by the president of the *barreau* and reminded of the "prudence" and "discretion" appropriate to a member of the legal profession.[53]

PROTECTING IMMIGRANT WORKERS FROM THE POLICE STATE,
PART II – VALÉRY GISCARD D'ESTAING'S MIGRANT
RETURN PROGRAM

Between 1974 and 1977, the government issued a stream of restrictive immigration policies, giving GISTI's aspiring legal activists additional opportunities to go to court. Litigation was brought against a set of four 1974 circulars that suspended all new labor immigration, as well as a fifth circular that prevented foreigners arriving without a labor contract from being issued a short-term residence permit. Cases were also organized against two 1974 circulars restricting migration from France's former colonies in Sub-Saharan Africa, against the government's "return assistance program" promulgated by memorandum in June 1977, and against a 1977 decree placing conditions on family reunification.

In November 1978, the Conseil d'Etat declared all of these restrictionist circulars, as well as the return assistance program, either fully or partially illegal.[54] It was not a complete victory for the plaintiffs; the Conseil d'Etat found no legal obstacle to the circular provision instructing prefects to deny residence permits to foreigners entering France clandestinely, and it gave a careful reading to France's treaty obligations with its former colonies, allowing the government to restrict labor migration from some of these countries. Nevertheless, these holdings demonstrated a willingness on the part of the Conseil d'Etat to review, and in some cases overturn, immigration circulars that arguably departed from the existing legislative and treaty regime.

The following month, the Conseil d'Etat went a step further when it overturned the 1977 family immigration decree, thereby annulling a cornerstone of the government's restrictionist immigration policy. Because the Conseil d'Etat's reversal of the family immigration decree exceeded its other decisions in terms of both legal and political significance, this decision merits extended discussion. The decree in question had been promulgated by Lionel Stoléru, the Giscard government's secretary of state for immigration, and followed two earlier revisions of procedures governing immigrant family reunification.[55] As a tactic to forestall criticism, the 1977 decree explicitly guaranteed the right of immigrants who had resided in France for at least three years to bring their immediate family members to join them. However, this was simply sugar coating, because the decree's aim was essentially restrictionist. It achieved this goal by making family migration conditional, for a period of three years, upon the agreement of immigrant spouses seeking residence permits not to take up any employment. The decree's legality was attacked by both GISTI and the CFDT, who collaborated in drafting their petitions to the Conseil d'Etat. A separate petition was filed by lawyers affiliated with France's other national labor confederation, the Confédération Générale du Travail (CGT).

In attacking the legality of the 1977 decree restricting family reunification, GISTI and the CFDT returned to the right to work arguments that they had used in challenging the Marcellin-Fontanet circulars. They claimed that, according to Article 34 of the Constitution, only the legislature could set conditions on the exercise of a fundamental principle of law, such as the right to work. Interestingly, however, GISTI's petition also invoked a second line of argument, challenging the decree as a violation of the hitherto unenunciated "right to family life," for which the language of the Preamble to France's 1946 Constitution provided a possible textual basis ("the nation will assure to each individual and to families the conditions necessary for their development"). The authors of GISTI's petition were undoubtedly aware, through their links to the Conseil d'Etat, that the Conseil's own advisory section had already, in

October 1977, issued a nonbinding advisory opinion criticizing the government's proposed policy on the basis of this very principle of the right to family life, finding it unreasonable that both migrant spouses would not be able to work when this had become the norm for French families (Fournier 2014).[56] Sensing a receptive attitude among the members of the Conseil d'Etat, GISTI developed a discursive association between the right to family life and a narrative about executive overreach in immigration matters more generally. Its petition to the Conseil d'Etat placed the decree within the extremely harsh context of government proposals to revoke residence cards, to end all immigrant family reunification, and to carry out mass removals.[57] According to this narrative, the decree was yet another example of the administration regulating the situation of immigrants through a process of "infra-droit," or nonlaw.

The Conseil d'Etat's December 1978 decision in the *GISTI, CFDT et CGT* litigation overturned the government's 1977 family immigration decree and, in doing so, established the right to family life as a newly justiciable fundamental principle of law.[58] It declined to hold that the decree had violated the right to work of immigrant family members. However, the Conseil d'Etat declared that foreigners authorized to reside in France had the right to lead a normal family life and that this right included the ability to be reunited in France with their immediate family members. The government could refuse family reunification in individual cases on the basis of concerns for public order, subject to review by an administrative tribunal. However, the decree forbidding all immigrant family members from working went beyond defining the conditions under which the right could be exercised and illegally curtailed a fundamental constitutional right.

The accompanying legal conclusions authored by the Conseil d'Etat's judicial advisor, the *commissaire du gouvernement*,[59] explained the reasoning by which this new right to family life should be applied to foreigners. Working from the proposition that the requirement of individual examination is central to standards of legality in administration, the judicial advisor concluded that immigrants authorized to reside in France were just as deserving of these legal protections as French citizens, declaring that, "Our tradition is one of rights of man and not just of citizen and it proclaims principles that surpass our frontiers."[60] Moreover, while it presented its decision as an extension of general principles of legality, the Conseil d'Etat seems to have been aware of the political context because its judicial advisor explains in his conclusions that, "One of the main interests of these appeals is that they allow us to focus [*faire le point*] on the question – subject to much controversy – of the rights of foreigners to residence and work."[61] At the end of his conclusions, in what could best be described as a version of dicta, the judicial advisor elaborates some of the broad principles that, in his view, should guide immigration policy making, listing a number of guarantees that the administration must uphold. These include the rights of foreigners who have been authorized to reside and work in France to "a minimum of stability in their situation ... and a progressive consolidation of these situations," and "the right – unless legislation exists to the contrary – to not be expelled from our territory except for reasons of public order, and public order must be interpreted restrictively."[62] France's legal and policy-making circles were thus alerted to the applicability, despite the restrictive turn in immigration policy making, of certain general principles of legality in this domain formerly left to administrative discretion.

IMMIGRANT RIGHTS LEGAL NARRATIVES OUTSIDE OF FRENCH COURTS

The extension of a rights-oriented jurisprudential regime into the domain of immigration policy making had a particularly dramatic impact in France, where the prevailing political discourse around immigration up to this point had been resolutely materialist. French administrative elites in the decades after World War II abandoned their initial plans to promote the social insertion of immigrant workers and it was understood that those who arrived to replenish the country's depleted labor force would return to their countries of origin when their labor was no longer needed (Lochak 1985, 158). This was the dominant view among politicians on the political right, who saw immigrant workers as dispensable sources of labor (Viet 1998, 385). Moreover, many in France's political class were loath to admit that colonial groups, against whom they had recently suffered humiliating defeats, were owed any kind of right to residency (Weil 2004, 111).

While it was generally more sympathetic to immigrants and their working conditions, the Left's position on immigration was in flux during this period. François Mitterrand was busily constructing a coalition to anchor the newly revived Socialist Party, but he initially took no strong position on immigration policy. His 1972 "Common Program" made only vague references to immigrant workers as one of many groups exploited by the capitalist class (Viet 1998, 397). The low visibility of the issue was compounded by the fact that immigrant activists initially had few organizational links to France's national labor confederations, which constituted a major institutional force within the Left. The primary strategy of France's communist-affiliated labor federation, the CGT, was to preserve support among its basic constituents, the skilled French workers in the traditional large-scale industries, while France's other national labor federation, the CFDT, for most of the 1970s remained paralyzed by a split between constituents favoring border closure and those seeking to unionize immigrant workers (Grillo 1985, 234–9). The small circle of jurists who represented the CFDT and the CGT in legal challenges against restrictionist policies were significantly ahead of their national union leaders in embracing the cause of immigrant workers.

In this context, litigation against the Marcellin-Fontanet circulars was politically significant insofar as it constructed a narrative for collective mobilization on the part of France's various immigrant communities and their small circle of supporters. The direct policy impact of the official case disposition was relatively minimal.[63] The importance of the litigation derived instead from the informal narrative assembled by legal proceedings that associated rights with the domain of immigration. For local movement leaders, contesting the circulars in court was seen as a way of mobilizing a nationally diverse coalition that brought together Portuguese, North African, and African migrants alongside members of the French working class (Bouziri 2005). "We have formulated an appeal to the Conseil d'Etat," declared leaders of the new *Mouvement des Travailleurs Immigrés*, "so as to make it clear that under these labor contracts we are made into salaried slaves."[64] At a moment when the wave of migrant worker factory strikes that had begun in 1970 was losing momentum due to internal divisions, the act of publically claiming rights under French law provided a platform for rallying rank-and-file participants in immigrant movements. The catalytic effects of legal contestation were likewise apparent to members of GISTI's immigrant defense network. GISTI's press conference in January 1975 celebrated the group's role in overturning parts of the Marcellin-Fontanet circulars while linking action in court to the ongoing protest activity of immigrant workers (Ginesy-Galand 1984, 182). For both immigrant activists and their supporters, the Conseil d'Etat's willingness to scrutinize government immigration circulars validated a rights-based narrative that was already in the process of development.

These efforts gained further momentum in response to the more draconian policies adopted, starting in 1977, by the Giscard government. As immigrants mobilized to protest these policies and to claim their place within French society, their cause attracted growing support from prominent leftist political figures. By early 1978, French politics began to see what historian Vincent Viet terms an "osmosis" between, on one side, partisan and syndical organizations and, on the other side, a network of civil society groups with very diverse sensibilities but united by their opposition to immigration policies that seemed "not to respect human rights by designating foreigners as scapegoats for unemployment" (Viet 1998, 404).

At this formative moment in the politics of immigration, the Conseil d'Etat's intervention in November and December 1978, first striking down numerous provisions of restrictionist immigration circulars and then overturning an entire administrative decree, was appreciated by immigrant defenders as offering valuable resources for sharpening their ongoing criticism of the Giscard government. The potential jurisprudential significance of the Conseil d'Etat's intervention, particularly the decision overturning the family immigration decree, was immediately apparent to commentators at the time.[65] Yet, as the holding rested on principles of legality in administration, this new jurisprudence would not formally prevent the government from enacting similarly restrictive immigration policies legislatively. In other words, the ruling did not deter the Giscard government from moving forward to finalize a new legislative program whose ultimate aim was to reduce France's foreign population through a repatriation program in which it was hoped the Algerian government would cooperate (Weil 2004, 144–87).

Faced with a government determined to act, the task for immigrant defenders was to use the court decision as leverage for winning over a wider audience. In other words, they would need to translate a technical development in administrative law into a narrative with broader political implications. Aware that the political stakes were high, GISTI carefully crafted a note interpreting the Conseil d'Etat's intervention and announcing its importance to immigrant political activists and their supporters. With a touch of bravado, this note was also circulated to local prefectures charged with implementing immigration policy, purposefully formatted in the style of an official circular and claiming to provide "instruction" for how street-level officials must apply the decisions.[66] Presenting the Giscard government as wedded to a policy paradigm of "nonlaw" and "systematic recourse to clandestinity," GISTI's note went on to set these policies in opposition to an alternative policy paradigm based on immigrant inclusion. It was this alternative paradigm, according to GISTI's note, to which the Conseil d'Etat had given its imprimatur in what was clearly "a serious blow to the government." And GISTI was in a position to know, the note asserted, because the Conseil d'Etat's holding was made "in conformity with the arguments developed by GISTI in its appeals." These so-called instructions thus went far beyond technical explanation insofar as they reassembled the case holding into a narrative pitting respect for the principle of immigrant rights – which had received legally authoritative legitimation – against the deceptive and excessive tendencies of the Giscard government. Not surprisingly, the minister of interior responded with irritation, asserting that this "excessively liberal interpretation" misrepresented the decision and that GISTI was in no position to instruct administrators.[67]

Yet by the time the Giscard government could respond, opposition to its legislative agenda had begun to congeal around this new narrative of legality and immigrant rights, constructed jointly by the Conseil d'Etat's interventions and by the interpretation given to them by immigrant defenders. Public figures on the political left now calculated that taking up the cause of immigrant rights had become an effective political strategy, and associative leaders such as the CFDT's Hubert Lésire-Ogrel distanced themselves from the government's proposals, asserting that, "fundamental liberties are in jeopardy, the right of immigrants to live and to have a family life and a future ... the forced departure of immigrants touches too many essential things for us not to struggle against it" (Weil 2004, 177). By June 1979, when the legislature debated the text of the government's proposals for a forced return program, resistance had solidified even among centrists. In the intervening two months, the Conseil d'Etat's advisory section issued an uncharacteristically blunt opinion that reflected many of the arguments developed by groups publicly opposed to the project, and prominent Gaullist legislators in turn drew on these arguments to criticize the government during legislative debates (Weil 2004, 172–9). In December 1979, the government was forced to withdraw its legislative program for reducing the stock of France's foreign workers, having underestimated the extent to which opposition would crystallize around a legalized framing of immigration policy. Although immigrant rights, as a discursive construct, were never in any technical sense binding on legislators, a narrative – forged through juridical activity – that associated immigration restrictionism with rule by exception acquired substantial political authority.

These developments turned out to have far-reaching political ramifications, insofar as the tarnishing of President Valéry Giscard d'Estaing's immigration policy program proved to be an unanticipated boon for his political adversary, François Mitterrand. In the process of joining other critics of the government who positioned themselves as vocal defenders of immigrant rights, Mitterrand discovered a valuable weapon to use not only against the government but also against his communist competitors within the Left, who had been slower to embrace a rights-based political discourse (Viet 1998). Issued in the context of debates leading up to the 1981 election, his 110 *Propositions* proposed giving noncitizens voting rights in local elections as well as full associational rights.[68] These rights were necessary, according to Mitterrand, so that immigrants might have the opportunity to fully participate in society.

This *prise de position* was cemented following the Left's 1981 presidential victory, not least because during the campaign Mitterrand had presented himself as offering voters a clear electoral program, a contract to break with the past and usher in a new political regime. During the new government's first year in office, fidelity to its electoral program guided its actions "to the point of fetish-ism" (Weil 2004, 196). The creation of a "Secretary of State for Immigrants" within the new Ministry of National Solidarity, which took over the immigra-tion portfolio from the Ministry of Labor, aimed to demonstrate symbolically that the nation's solidarity extended to all. No longer would immigrants be seen simply as workers; rather, they were integral members of society and education and social insertion programs were required to address their needs. Minister Nicole Questiaux declared that her ministry's actions would be guided by "sol-idarity with all, French and immigrants alike, without discrimination," and she urged legislators to quickly reverse the previous policies enunciated in "often illegal circulars, often hastily prepared, sometimes brutal declarations, and unpublished instructions," and replace them with a politics founded on respect for immigrant human rights (Weil 2004, 199). The immigration law of 1981, granting foreigners associative rights as well as social security and unem-ployment benefits was a dramatic instantiation of this approach.

We can see the durable effect of the rights-based framework for immigration when the political winds in France shifted due to the rising electoral popular-ity of far-right politicians promoting a discourse that equated immigration and insecurity. The Socialist Party's unfavorable electoral showing in the spring 1982 cantonal elections, and the sense that the 1981 regularization had pro-duced negative political effects, prompted some ministers in the Mitterrand government to advocate a change in its immigration position. Nevertheless, during cabinet debates, ministers such as Laurent Fabius vocally insisted that a distinction be made between unlawful immigrants, on the one hand, and, on the other hand, lawful immigrants "who can and must stay" (Favier and Martin-Roland 1997, 173). The impact of the immigrant rights political nar-rative was also felt among political and administrative elites who identified themselves as representatives of France's republican tradition (Viet 1998, 414). President Mitterrand eventually pursued a compromise: regular migrants would be included and definitively given residence rights while irregular migrants would face a politics of exclusion.

Thus, although French judges in the early 1980s lacked retrospective pow-ers of judicial review to use as a stick against restrictionist statutes, juridical framings made prominent contributions to constructing an enduring politi-cal narrative about the place of France's postwar cohort of migrant workers, and their families, within French society. A public report assessing expert opinion on France's politics of immigration identifies the 1982–4 period as "completing the definition" and confirming the "new rules of the game" for immigration politics (Gaxie 1995, 35). The immigration law passed by the Mitterrand government in July 1984 brought about a "stabilization" in the terms of partisan debates (Viet 1998, 415). Although the 1984 law contained a number of provisions to finance voluntary repatriation of immigrants, a signal of the influence of the far-right on both political parties, it nevertheless introduced the ten-year residence card. This replaced a system in which mandatory annual or tri-annual application for renewal of residence authorization had kept immigrants in France in a state of permanent instability. The statute concretized in law "the recognition of a durable installation in France of immigrant populations" and the dissociation of the right to residence from economic activity (Lochak 1985, 168). In this respect, the 1984 law represented a realization, on the part of the government and the legislature, of the impossibility of sending postwar immigrants back to their countries of origin. This outline for the politics of immigration "traced a line for all governments to come" (Blanc-Chaléard 2010, 492). French governments in subsequent years would reinforce the rigor of border controls while expressing their commitment to integrating those already present. The process of contesting immigration policy in court contributed to changing the discourse on immigration, with the effect that the guest workers who had reconstructed postwar France would be seen no longer as a temporary presence but rather as a group who should be incorporated into French society.

CONCLUSION

The period of the late 1970s and early 1980s has been identified by one prominent commentator as coinciding with a "transformation of immigration law" that moved immigration jurisprudence toward greater adaptation with the contemporary politico-legal environment (Schuck 1984). My analysis adopts a different approach. Rather than conceptualizing changes in immigration law in functionalist terms, this chapter has emphasized the substantial experimentation and engineering involved in the assemblage of new juridical frameworks for immigration. Existing jurisprudential regimes needed to be connected to the immigration domain through creative legal argumentation that qualified events and relationships in new ways. At the same time, immigrants needed to be disassociated from the national security framework that had previously permeated this area of case law. Immigrant defenders played a central part in this process that filtered and translated both the complex lived experience of immigrants and the diversity of activities implicated in immigration control. To the extent that immigration policy was incorporated into jurisprudential regimes for protecting minority rights, on the one hand, and curbing administrative rule by exception, on the other, it was the result of this process of creative engineering.

However, this is not the end of the story. The process of contesting immigration policy in court did not just overturn particular policies subjected to litigation. Rather, courtroom proceedings and judicial texts assembled rights-based discursive framings that were appropriated and reassembled into broader political narratives. Strikingly, the judicial decisions that activists had to work with were often only narrow or partial victories, and their holdings placed no formal limits on national legislative action. Legally assembled framings became forceful and widely meaningful because activists glossed their content and actively disseminated their interpretations, and because social movement organizations, administrative elites, and other political actors chose to accept these readings as statements of "law."

In other words, if legal engagement had lasting impact, it was not because it coerced immigration policy makers but rather because the "passage of law" (Latour 2002, 139–206) offered receptive audiences something around which to mobilize. In the United States, law's passage contributed key building blocks, conceptually and organizationally, for an immigration–civil rights lobby that continues to make itself felt. Legally generated assemblages were likewise potent in France. Advocacy before the Conseil d'Etat generated a narrative of legality that irreversibly associated both the Giscard government and its plans for a forced return program with the taint of autocracy. At the same time, judicial vindications of "immigrant rights" provided a platform for movement leaders to build and strengthen coalitions among diverse immigrant associations and with other political groups. In other words, law did not simply block policies from being enacted; rather, at a formative period for immigration reform lawmaking, legal contestation of immigration matters had radiating effects, defining political identities and crystallizing political agendas. As we will see in Chapter 4, victories in court exerted a long-term propulsive force not only on their audiences but also on their progenitors, drawing jurists who had contributed to the engineering of immigrant rights further within the ambit of the legal field.

4

Institutionalizing Legal Innovation

Having had some notable victories in court in the late 1970s and early 1980s, immigrant defenders in the United States and France sought to sustain their activities and build upon this momentum. For attorneys with ambitions to influence policy on a national scale, this was the moment to translate recent high-profile litigation on behalf of vulnerable migrants into broader professional recognition for their project. In the U.S., legal services attorneys working with the National Center for Immigrants' Rights (NCIR) were particularly busy: in the summer of 1981 they were in the midst of preparing their first brief to the Supreme Court in the *Plyler* litigation, and the organization was also sponsoring a National Immigration and Refugee Consultation in Washington, D.C.[1] Meanwhile, across the Atlantic, the jurist members of the *Groupe d'Information et de Soutien des Immigrés* (GISTI) were exploring how to find a balance between their ongoing involvement with immigrant social movements, their enhanced prestige among jurists, and the prospect of increased policy influence within the newly elected Socialist government.

Yet even as it showed signs of coalescing, immigration-centered legal activism needed to acquire greater solidity and weight if it was to withstand the tensions created by its various commitments to legal expertise, emancipatory social change, and elite policy engagement. These tensions soon became apparent when early litigation victories offered opportunities for career advancement in the policy-making sphere, threatening to rob legal activism of its core talent. Instability was also created by the dissolution of several key immigrant movement organizations whose struggles had formed the basis for court-centered contestation. Most notably, both CASA and the Foyer Coordinating Committee (discussed in Chapter 2) ceased their operations after struggles with leadership turnover. If legal activism wanted to avoid the same fate, it would need to develop relatively more institutionalized structures.

Aspiring legal activists in the United States had a relatively well-defined idea of what this process of institutionalization would involve. As discussed in the following text, foundation-sponsored public interest law offered an existing organizational repertoire into which immigrant rights legal activism could readily be integrated. This process of institutionalization had an appreciable impact on the four national legal organizations with which U.S. immigrant rights legal activism would come to be most closely associated: the National Immigration Law Center (previously the National Center for Immigrants' Rights), the American Civil Liberties Union (ACLU) Immigrants' Rights Project, the Center for Human Rights and Constitutional Law (previously the National Center for Immigrants' Rights, Inc.), and the National Lawyers Guild's National Immigration Project. My analysis explores how this engagement with elite supporters of public interest law progressively solidified the project of immigrant rights legal activism at the same time that it subtly shifted its content.

Unlike their U.S. counterparts, French legal activists had no ready organizational model to follow. My discussion therefore emphasizes the ongoing experimentation that has accompanied institutionalization of immigrant rights legal activism in France, focusing on the operations of a single organization, GISTI, and its network of affiliated jurists. Although in recent years other associations have begun to regularly collaborate with GISTI in petitioning courts to review immigration policies, it is GISTI that has most explicitly identified its work with the project of legal activism and that has used this term to describe its activities. As I show, GISTI's jurists have drawn on a variety of existing French traditions of protest and advocacy, continually combining them in new ways so as to recruit sufficient support to sustain their project amidst a shifting political environment.

Though they had access to different potential sources of support, aspiring immigrant rights legal activists in both the United States and France similarly sought to safeguard their project and ensure its long-term realization. Their innovative project had reached what we might call the *prototype phase* by the summer of 1981; judicial recognition meant that it was no longer simply an idea on paper. At the same time, the project's future was far from assured. Over the next two decades, additional supporters of the immigrant rights legal activist project would be recruited, seduced, developed, and brought on board. This process of association and mediation would give the project greater heft and solidity, placing legal activism into association with each state's broader "legal complex" (Halliday, Karpik, and Feeley 2007, Karpik and Halliday 2011). However, institutionalization would also inevitably attenuate the project's connection to locally based mobilizations, moving it away from direct action and toward strategies that engaged with official state institutions.

U.S. LEGAL LIBERALISM AND PUBLIC INTEREST LAW

In the United States, an organizational repertoire for institutionalized legal activism preceded both the turn toward restrictionism in immigration policies and the rise of immigrant defense networks in the 1970s. The breakthrough in the entrenchment of a "liberal legal network" had come a decade earlier, when key members of the legal establishment came to understand a liberalized legal system "as an instrument of modernization and as the responsible, establishment alternative to anarchy" and committed themselves to the construction of vigorous legal aid programs (Teles 2008, 33). However, if the initial goal was to provide low-cost legal assistance, then the federal government's new legal services system soon moved beyond this mandate and became an important site for proactive efforts to use courts for broad policy change. Early directors of the Office of Economic Opportunity (OEO) Legal Services Program encouraged the development of a cadre of young lawyers operating through "legal services backup centers" and dedicated to litigation strategies that would result in social change at the systemic level. Due to its strong support from liberal elites, this proactive approach would continue to feature strongly in federal legal services activity even after the OEO component was replaced in 1974 by the Legal Services Corporation (LSC), a public corporation with a presidentially appointed board of directors.

In addition to encouraging the federal legal services program, leaders of the liberal legal network worked to strengthen legal activist initiatives in the private sector. The Ford Foundation, in particular, systematically directed resources to groups aiming to propel liberal policy reform through litigation. The result was a flowering of legal activist projects, which extended across policy areas as diverse as civil rights, juvenile rights, women's rights, prisoners' rights, environmental protection, welfare rights, and consumer rights. These efforts, like the federal legal services backup centers, drew on a popularized model for how courts might be effectively leveraged for social change that was grounded on the landmark litigation campaigns of the National Association for the Advancement of Colored People (NAACP) Legal Defense Fund (Rabin 1975, 218). In retrospect, it is evident that this reading of legal history involved a good deal of mythologizing and exaggerated the extent to which NAACP attorneys had in fact exerted control over the sequence and pace of test-case litigation (Tushnet 2004, Mack 2005). Regardless of its historical basis, however, the myth of attorney-led law reform was a powerful motivator for legal activist efforts.

The rise of the public interest movement in the late 1960s and early 1970s provided these efforts with a label – "public interest law" – flexible enough to subsume the diversity of initiatives in which the liberal legal network had become engaged. By the 1970s, one could speak of a prototypical "public interest law firm" that operated as a nonprofit law office, either inside a parent organization or as a self-contained organizational unit, and devoted most of its activity to "impact" litigation (Handler, Ginsberg, and Snow 1978). Supported by a secretarial staff and paraprofessionals, the staff attorneys in these organizations spent the majority of their time on litigation-related work and did not think of themselves as having permanently left the private practice of law (Nielsen and Albiston 2006, 1606–10, Rhode 2008, 2050–4). Although they operated primarily as tax-exempt institutions, public interest law firms strongly resembled their corporate-commercial counterparts. Extending beyond the public interest movement's original environmentalist and consumer initiatives, the label of public interest law was applied to a wide range of liberal initiatives and this "public interest law sector" came to be understood as an integral part of the U.S. legal profession (Weisbrod 1978).[2]

The Ford Foundation's decision in 1970 to become a principal support for public interest law organizations was crucial, as it encouraged other private foundations in the 1970s to do the same (Harrison and Jaffe 1973, Trubek 2011, 418–20). Operating in coordination with leaders of the American Bar Association (ABA), private foundations offered political capital that allowed public interest law firms to maintain the benefits of tax-exempt status (Hilbink 2006, 411–17). In addition to protecting public interest law from its critics, leaders of the U.S. liberal legal network also engaged in congressional lobbying to revise legislative guidelines for attorney's fees awards to the benefit of public interest litigators.[3] Most prominently, the Civil Rights Attorney's Fees Award Act of 1976 created a presumption in favor of awards to prevailing plaintiff attorneys in civil rights lawsuits, and the Equal Access to Justice Act of 1980 made the federal government liable for attorney's fees in civil rights cases where the government's action causing the litigation or its legal position in the litigation was not "substantially justified."

As Michael McCann has argued, legal elites were responsive to U.S. public interest law initiatives because the young attorneys who proposed these initiatives shared, or at least claimed to share, a preference for professionalized reform rather than for radical social change (McCann 1986). Within these broad parameters, however, the multiplicity of legal activist initiatives supported by liberal elites during this period suggests that members of the

U.S. liberal legal network were not wedded to any rigid concept of what public interest law entailed. Rather, they were willing to consider supporting any
project that could claim a plausible link, either organizationally or conceptually, to existing efforts to promote a liberalized legal system (Cummings and
Trubek 2008).

These underlying dynamics exerted a strong influence over the emerging area of immigration-centered legal activism. Leaders of the liberal legal
network encouraged efforts to bring immigrant rights litigation into the
inner-circle of public interest law. The Ford Foundation, in particular, took
an energetic interest in immigration-centered activity starting in the early
1980s. Immigration at this time was seen by Ford Foundation leaders as an
increasingly politically salient issue on which a major funding program could
potentially structure national debate. The "problems" of large-scale refugee
flows from Haiti and undocumented migration from Mexico fell within the
foundation's existing concerns, and the foundation saw itself as "uniquely
qualified" to marshal the substantial resources required to address these policy issues.[4] These considerations resulted in the creation in 1982 of a separate program to fund immigration-related projects. During the 1980s alone,
the foundation dispensed approximately $25 million in funds as part of its
newly created "immigration and refugees program" (McClymont and Golub
2000).[5] Moreover, this sustained Ford Foundation investment was especially
influential in the institutionalization of immigrant rights legal activism during this period when public sources of support were contracting. As the LSC
and its backup centers were targeted by conservative critics, private foundations stepped in to provide sustaining support for this component of their law
reform program.[6] Aspiring immigrant rights legal activists would leverage
this injection of targeted private-sector funding from liberal elites in order to
expand and institutionalize their organizations.

AN INSTITUTIONALIZED IDENTITY FOR IMMIGRANT RIGHTS LEGAL ACTIVISM IN THE UNITED STATES

As they sought to ensure the long-term sustainability of their efforts following
important litigation victories, aspiring legal activists were enthusiastic about
the prospect of associating their project with public interest law. Developing
relationships with elite supporters of public interest law would allow legal
activists to "consolidate and then expand" their organizational infrastructure
and was viewed as a necessary step to sustaining their position "in the vanguard
of the most important immigration litigation today."[7] From their perspective,
institutionalization would allow immigrant rights organizations to litigate on

equal terms with the most highly accomplished private law firms. It seemed obvious that immigration policy could be matched with the well-established public interest law firm model and that organizations with staff attorneys and sustained material support from private foundations would be best positioned to succeed in contesting immigration policy in court.

This mutual attraction between practitioners of immigration-centered legal activism and elite sponsors of public interest law is particularly apparent in the organizational transformations undertaken by the NCIR. As discussed in previous chapters, NCIR had come into existence in 1979 when Los Angeles–based legal aid attorney Peter Schey secured LSC funding to create an immigration-focused legal services backup center. Coordinating with the National Lawyers Guild's network of immigrant defenders, the organization had played an important role in the Sbicca factory immigration raid case, in early Haitian refugee litigation, and in legal challenges brought on behalf of undocumented children in Texas. As things turned out, however, NCIR's exclusive reliance on public funds was short-lived; legislative restrictions on LSC activities, which came into effect in January 1983 while the new backup center was getting off the ground, substantially limited its ability to engage in proactive litigation. NCIR was also destabilized by the departure of its founding director, attorney Peter Schey, who made the decision to operate independently rather than be hampered by the new legal services funding restrictions.

At a moment when NCIR's continued existence was uncertain, the Ford Foundation's budding interest in supporting immigrant rights initiatives offered a crucial source of stability. NCIR received its first grant from the Ford Foundation in 1983 in the form of $150,000 in funds to create an Immigrant Children's Rights Project that would provide legal assistance to clients ineligible under new legal services restrictions. Ford Foundation program officers were reassured that the first step of NCIR's newly hired director, Gilbert Carrasco, as he sought to place the organization on more solid footing, consisted of recruiting an advisory board comprised of prominent immigration attorneys, including the Executive Director of the American Immigration Lawyers Association (AILA).[8] The organization soon became a regular beneficiary of Ford Foundation support, relying on increasingly sizable grants to fund its litigation activities. As federal support for legal services continued to shrink throughout the 1980s, NCIR responded by diversifying its funding sources and seeking out additional foundation grants. By the end of the 1980s, only one-third of its funding came from federal legal services financing.[9]

The link between external financial support and the institutionalization of immigrant defense efforts is also apparent in the immigration-centered activities of the ACLU. The involvement of the ACLU's national office in immigration policy reform had been minimal throughout the 1970s. Even though ACLU Executive Director Ira Glasser in 1980 recognized the potential in this area for "a major legal movement with systematic efforts to rationalize the law," he remained reluctant to devote resources to immigration-centered legal activism.[10] News that the Ford Foundation would be dedicating substantial funds to immigration-related projects tipped the balance in favor of involvement. In 1983, the ACLU Foundation, the organization's tax-exempt arm, submitted a proposal to the Ford Foundation for an Immigration and Aliens' Rights Task Force and received $300,000 in funds to distribute to local affiliates who submitted proposals for litigation activities.[11] Two years later, the program was reorganized and centralized as it became clear that local affiliates did not have adequate resources to undertake activities without additional assistance from the national office. Lucas Guttentag, a young attorney who had started his career at the Center for Law in the Public Interest, was hired to serve as full-time national director of the Aliens' Rights Task Force. The task force subsequently moved toward further centralization, hiring an additional staff attorney and a paralegal to better enable litigation from a national perspective. Coordination with affiliates was facilitated by organizing national conferences of attorneys, publishing a newsletter and legal research memoranda, and maintaining a national immigration docket that listed, summarized, and indexed the organization's ongoing litigation concerning immigrant rights. These developments aimed to "significantly increase the ACLU's activity and effectiveness in the field."[12] A new name, the Immigrants' Rights Project, reflected this transformation from a task force of affiliates toward the public interest law firm model, which foundation support had both facilitated and encouraged.

At the same time that private foundations were propelling an institutionalization of immigrant rights legal activism, attorneys' fee awards offered another potential avenue for movement in this direction. Starting in October 1981, attorneys' fee awards under the Equal Access to Justice Act, which the Ford Foundation had lobbied to enact, supplied a complimentary source of funds so long as litigators could show either that the government's action causing the litigation or that its legal position in the litigation was not substantially justified. The Haitian refugee litigation of the early 1980s resulted in awards of several hundred thousand dollars in attorneys' fees for NCIR.[13] The ACLU Immigrants' Rights Project likewise obtained substantial income from attorneys' fees for successful litigation of immigration enforcement practices.[14] Attorneys' fees were a prerequisite for the sustained operations of Schey's organization, the National Center for Immigrants' Rights, Inc. (which operated entirely separately of the original NCIR), as it moved toward a self-funded model.[15] Indeed, by the early 1990s, the considerable attorneys' fees awarded in several long-lasting class action cases covered the majority of the organizational budget for Schey's operations.[16]

This newly available institutional support for immigration-centered legal efforts likewise had an impact on the activities of the National Lawyers Guild's immigrant defender network. By the early 1980s, the National Lawyers Guild's National Immigration Project had opened a permanent office in Boston and its members were becoming increasingly involved with the emerging nationwide Sanctuary Movement on behalf of Central American refugees.[17] The Central American Refugee Defense Fund (CARDF) was founded in 1982 by National Lawyers Guild affiliated attorneys Marc Van Der Hout and Carolyn Patty Blum, with the aim of mobilizing a legal wing for the Sanctuary Movement's grassroots solidarity efforts.[18] In 1983, CARDF created its own newsletter, *Network News*, and received a fifteen thousand dollar grant from the Ford Foundation to sponsor a conference on Central American refugee defense.[19] While its founders had originally envisioned raising sufficient funds to operate as an independent national backup center, they ultimately determined that taking this route was unwise in a field already occupied by Ford Foundation grantees. To eliminate duplication of efforts, CARDF moved its operations to Boston in September 1984 to share facilities with the National Lawyers Guild's National Immigration Project.[20] Rather than creating a new backup center, its founders would come to rely on close collaborations with NCIR and the ACLU Immigrants' Rights Project, organizations that were in a position to supply the necessary resources to litigate national class action cases on immigration issues. In a grant application to the Ford Foundation in 1989 to fund an immigration detention project, the National Immigration Project insisted that it had been "vigilant about complementing rather than duplicating" the work of other national experts – and Ford Foundation grantees – in this area.[21]

This pattern of interorganizational division of labor was explicitly encouraged by Ford Foundation leaders. Perhaps most importantly, the Ford Foundation's close relationship with the Mexican American Legal Defense and Education Fund (MALDEF), which was "expected to carry primary responsibility for addressing immigrant civil rights issues," ensured that litigation challenging discrimination on the part of domestic law enforcement officials would become increasingly separated from legal activism challenging immigration enforcement.[22] Although NCIR had played an important role in litigating the Texas schools case during the late 1970s, the Ford Foundation's new crop of immigrant rights grantees were encouraged to concentrate on lawsuits against immigration agencies and their officials. Moreover, recognizing that immigration-centered legal activism was a "polycentric" field in which no organization was preeminent, the program staff of the foundation undertook the project of "rationalizing" the immigration law area so that grantees would not duplicate each others' work.[23] The ACLU Immigrants' Rights Project developed a specialization in constitutional due process issues after grant administrators at the Ford Foundation made it clear that other grantees were handling refugee and asylum law issues and duplication of efforts should be avoided.[24] Meanwhile, NCIR was cultivated by its funders as the expert on "public benefits issues" as they affect immigrants.[25] For its part, the National Immigration Project chose to focus on the nexus of immigration law with criminal law issues, in keeping with the National Lawyers Guild's historical tradition of activist defense work. In practice, many cases involved a combination of these sets of issues, and specialists in different areas regularly shared expertise. The organizational files of both the ACLU's Immigrants' Rights Project and the National Lawyers Guild's National Immigration Project preserve extensive litigation-related correspondence exchanged between the two groups, testifying to the close working relationships that developed between organizations that historically had espoused divergent ideological commitments. Nor were prior antagonisms an obstacle to collaboration, as demonstrated by the fact that NCIR ultimately forged a pragmatic partnership with Schey's operation in order to support the latter's class action lawsuit against detention practices involving noncitizen minors.[26]

By the early 1990s, immigration-centered national legal organizations in the United States felt confident that their role was to focus on impact litigation and to provide technical assistance for other groups who worked at the grassroots. Following the enactment of the 1986 Immigration Reform and Control Act (IRCA) legalization program, and the Ford Foundation "deliberately channeled funds" to "national legal organizations undertaking litigation activities that benefitted from a national perspective," who were expected to provide nationwide support services on immigration law issues to both legal services and other nonprofit agencies.[27] When NCIR changed its name in 1990 to the National Immigration Law Center (NILC), this in part reflected the fact that the organization now relied on a national advisory board of leading attorneys and advocates in the field of immigration and civil rights "to shape priorities and legal strategies" and "to help identify important trends in immigrants' rights, set program priorities, and coordinate the delivery of services."[28] The ACLU Immigrants' Rights Project likewise moved toward a more legalized approach, in which staff attorneys aimed to "conceptualize suits to ensure consistency with issues in other suits and affirmatively identify which issues raised by administrative practices are more susceptible to formal legal challenge, focusing on addressing complex constitutional questions through litigation."[29] National legal organizations embraced the institutionalization of their organizations and the spread of formalized internal operations. Far from something to be resisted, institutionalization became an achievement to be celebrated. In its forty-page report to the Ford Foundation in 1991, NILC systematically detailed the "project goals," "achievements," and "work remaining to be accomplished" for each of its initiatives, suggesting the degree to which it had professionalized its operations.[30] Similarly, by the early 1990s, the ACLU Immigrants' Rights Project celebrated the fact that it employed five full-time staff and had more than doubled its initial budget through support from seven separate foundations.[31]

At the same time that they inscribed their activities in a recognizably professionalized form, U.S. immigrant rights legal activists were drawn toward the legal field in ways that went beyond requests for financial support. In particular, they sought to capitalize on the bar's budding interest in immigration issues as "a major problem of our time" in which lawyers had an important role to play.[32] A watershed moment came in 1982 when the private bar was mobilized to meet the legal needs of Haitian asylum seekers whose systematic detention by the INS had been the subject of an early legal activist campaign. Having come down to Miami in June 1982 to assist the Haitian defense team in securing an injunction to release the Haitians, Michael Posner from the Lawyers Committee for International Human Rights committed his organization to ensuring that the 1,700 Haitian class members in *Louis v. Nelson* would be provided with individual legal counsel as a condition of their release. The Lawyers Committee's Refugee Rights Project director Arthur Helton spent the following two years marshaling "one of the most ambitious pro bono enterprises ever attempted," which included training sessions that were attended by more than 1,200 lawyers (Helton 1984/1985, 48). With funding from the Ford Foundation, and the endorsement of former ABA president Chesterfield Smith, who led the court-appointed committee to oversee the program, a broad network of legal groups evolved around the Haitian representation effort. As members of groups such as the Association of the Bar of the City of New York and the Chicago Bar Association started handling these cases, immigration-related pro bono work gained a reputation among the corporate bar as "a sexy area" (Rosenau 1989, 60). These early collaborations with leaders of the private bar were key to the creation of a "cadre" of lawyers willing to volunteer their time and political influence on behalf of immigration and refugee issues.

For their part, several key members of the Haitian defense team – whose litigation efforts sparked these collaborations with the bar on immigration and refugee issues – were able to parlay positive attention from the legal establishment into positions of leadership in bar associations. In 1982, Ira Kurzban and Rick Swartz both joined the board of AILA. The following year, Swartz was active in pushing the ABA House of Delegates to establish a coordinating committee on immigration, which would subsequently organize more than a dozen large-scale immigration pro bono projects through state bar associations (Wharton 1983, 59). Meanwhile, Kurzban focused his attention on AILA, aiming to make the organization more accessible to a new generation of immigration lawyers. Elected as AILA's president in 1987, he turned his main focus away from impact litigation to focus on institution building.[33] His leadership tenure coincided with the creation of a Legal Action Center within the organization's new tax-exempt wing, the American Immigration Law Foundation. By the early 1990s, those who had pioneered immigrant rights legal activism a decade earlier comprised a majority of members of AILA's newly formed Asylum Committee and had assumed the leadership of immigration committees in sections of the ABA.[34] While many of these individuals no longer devoted the majority of their professional energies to activist litigation by this time, their high-profile involvement with bar associations had made it easier for legal activist efforts to leverage the corporate bar's resources in class action lawsuits seeking to bring systemic reform to the U.S. asylum system and to expand immigrant access to the 1986 IRCA legalization program.[35]

As immigration policy turned to increasing restrictionism during the 1990s, the ongoing interest in immigration matters on the part of leaders of the bar and private foundations, in combination with sweeping changes to immigration law, fueled a further expansion and rationalization of the immigrant legal services field. After 1996, federally funded legal services programs faced further restrictions on providing services to noncitizen clients.[36] In response, a new cohort of immigrant-specialized nonprofit organizations, funded by private foundations and local bar associations, came to take the place of legal services lawyers (Hing 2000, Cummings 2007, 914). With the capacity of the immigrant legal services field thus expanded, staff attorneys at NILC, the ACLU, and the National Lawyers Guild's Immigration Project identified an increased need for their organizations to provide training sessions, technical assistance, and policy-oriented litigation to this expanded network of community-based service providers. These developments in turn solidified the stratification between staff-led immigrant rights backup centers and organizations dedicated to local capacity building. At the same time, the funding streams available to institutionalized legal activism became increasingly distinct from those targeted to community-based immigrant advocacy.[37] By the mid-1990s, immigrant rights legal activist organizations had cultivated a highly specialized and legally centered niche within the immigrant legal services field.

The evolving format of the National Immigration Project's *Immigration Newsletter* provides a particularly concrete record of this move toward legalization. During its initial decade, the *Immigration Newsletter* consisted of a mimeograph containing a diverse mix of cartoons, political manifestos, and personalized accounts of developments in the working lives of individual immigrant defenders. Articles were generally less than two pages in length and contained no footnotes. However, the transition to a subscriber-oriented publication in the fall of 1980 increased the need for professionalization. As a result, the April 1981 edition began the practice of providing footnotes for all legal articles. By 1985, lengthy articles such as "Recent Trends in Asylum Denials on Mandatory and Discretionary Grounds" and "Committee of Central American Refugees v. INS: A Challenge to Transfer of Refugees to Remote Detention Facilities" were followed by several pages of footnoted legal references. Over the next ten years, the newsletter gradually adopted many of the features of a traditional bar association journal, applying rigorous standards for facts, citations, and accuracy, while abandoning the more relational and political content of earlier years. In practice, soliciting professionalized law review–style articles was not always easy because, as the field of immigration law expanded, other professional organizations and law schools began producing immigration-centered law journals.[38] In 1998, as electronic communication became on option, the effort to sustain a publication that had become a cross between a law review and a membership journal was finally abandoned and the newsletter was discontinued.

Even before this point, however, the newsletter's rule-oriented compilation of judicial and legislative developments stood alongside other efforts in an increasingly institutionalized immigrant rights legal community. In retrospect, this process occurred quite rapidly, as legal activists adapted the template of the public interest law firm and applied it to immigration work. This model structured interorganizational relationships as well as organizational strategies. Both the desire to show concrete results to external supporters and the pressing need of professionalized organizations to remain solvent were an integral part of the law firm model of public interest law. As we will see in Chapter 5, the litigation strategies that emerged from this association with the model of public interest law firms – in particular, the desirability of showing litigation's concrete outcomes – gave rise to a very particular type of regular interaction with the government officials responsible for immigration-related policy making. However, before considering how routinized immigrant rights litigation strategies have structured immigration politics, it is necessary to step back from the American picture and examine an alternative model of combining law with political engagement.

FRENCH TRADITIONS OF SPEAKING FOR THE PUBLIC THROUGH LAW

While the leaders of the ABA embraced participation in government action and liberal political mobilization in the 1960s and 1970s, the French legal profession did not play a similarly influential role. On the one hand, the Fifth Republic's power structures relied upon and privileged specially trained cadres of administrative elites, relegating lawyers to operating within a judicial system that was in crisis. On the other hand, this exclusion from state power was partly self-enforced. Despite the major changes taking place in French society, the *barreau* remained attached to a classical model of legal practice that was generalist in orientation and uninvested in the market for corporate legal services (Karpik 1999, 315). Faced with competition from a new generation of young lawyers, leaders of the bar were primarily concerned with securing their own professional position and prestige. For their part, the post-1968 generation of law graduates held little hope that a profession that they saw as failing to keep up with the times would provide support for social change and resigned themselves to creating alternative professional networks and collaborating with grassroots social movements.

Yet as they sought to contribute to movements for change, young jurists in the 1970s faced serious conceptual hurdles in identifying an appropriate role for legal strategies in this social movement milieu because at this time influential leftist public intellectuals were insisting that expert knowledge was at the core of existing relations of hierarchy. The new model of political activism, exemplified by Michel Foucault's engagement with prison issues, was grounded on the notion that power could best be resisted by generating a *contre-expertise* through the synthesis of subaltern voices; it explicitly eschewed engagement with state structures. This notion of *contre-expertise* posed particular challenges for jurists, especially given the fact that French legal theory remained resolutely attached to legal formalism (Chevallier 1993). It was not obvious how juridical knowledge, whose *raison d'être* was enabling the functioning of the republican state, could play a part in fundamentally rethinking state structures.

This is not to say that the Foucauldian approach, in practice, eschewed all expressions of commitment to abstract principles. The visible presence at public political protests of both Jean-Paul Sartre and Foucault signaled their willingness to pay homage to a venerable French tradition of defending abstract ideals through principled acts of protest, including acts of protest undertaken in the courtroom (Noiriel 2010, 102–25). Indeed, over the course of the twentieth century, prominent figures in French political life had regularly taken to the streets to defend the abstract notions of liberty and legality. During the period of the Dreyfus Affair, at the turn of the twentieth century, public denunciation in the courtroom and in the press was a key strategy adopted by the *Ligue des Droits de l'Homme* as it sought to promote its vision of a liberal and secular republic against the conservative alternative (Naquet 2009). More recently, in the early years of the Fifth Republic, attorney Robert Badinter channelled the Dreyfusard model of denouncing injustice as part of his crusade against capital punishment, using the courtroom as a stage on which to plead for its abolition (Cassia 2009). These diverse acts of political engagement demonstrate that left-leaning political activism – in practice – could be successfully reconciled with legally based activity, so long as the latter operated in the spirit of denunciation rather than in cooperation with the state.

GISTI's pioneering conceptual innovation was to identify a programmatic justification for this ongoing practical hybridization of the Dreyfusard model, embodied in the lawyer-orator denouncing injustice in the name of abstract liberal principles, with newer post-1968 notions of political activism through locally generated *contre-expertise*. The vision developed by the group, expressed in its early publications, was that the extension of general principles of legality was *itself* a contribution to the immigrant cause, because it removed immigration from the space of "nonlaw" that had previously defined this domain of governance.[39] This innovation solved the problem of how juridical expertise might be reconciled with post-1968 political struggle by linking the activity of formalizing and rationalizing the law with the emancipatory effect of deconstructing immigration governance's logic of exclusion. It was a vision of legal activism in which GISTI's diverse membership of juridically-inclined civil servants, lawyers, and social workers all found inspiration.

However, identifying a conceptual justification for legal activism in France would not by itself ensure its viability. To be sustainable, GISTI would need to put this programmatic vision into practice and deepen its degree of realization. As described in the section that follows, the process by which GISTI's innovative vision came to life has been relatively more organic than top-down. In contrast to the U.S. experience of extending existing legal activist organizational models into the realm of immigration law, GISTI's institutionalization has operated through experimentation and remains grounded on informal networks extending inside as well as outside the state.

AN INSTITUTIONALIZED IDENTITY FOR IMMIGRANT RIGHTS
LEGAL ACTIVISM IN FRANCE

The first half of the 1980s found French immigrant rights legal activism at a crossroads. Like many comrades among France's political left, GISTI's members greeted the May 1981 election of Socialist Party presidential candidate François Mitterrand with euphoria.[40] Strengthened by its record of victories before the Conseil d'Etat, which it did not fail to point out to the new government, GISTI introduced itself as an association, founded in 1972 by jurists and social workers, that "has strived to promote and defend the rights of immigrant workers and their families, and that has not ceased (in its publications, its interventions, and its judicially-oriented activity) to challenge the segregationist politics endorsed by the previous government."[41] Its letter to the incoming president called for detailed legislative modifications, which it felt were "necessary to install a new politics of immigration that dignifies France." The immediate aftermath of the Socialist victory was a moment in which GISTI felt that its project had received a double vindication, judicial and electoral. At least initially, this celebration seemed warranted, as the Mitterrand government expressed its intention to facilitate foreigners' access to permanent residence and enacted a legalization program that regularized the status of 132,000 foreigners (Weil 2004, 220).

However, it soon became clear that the Socialist victory in fact posed serious challenges for GISTI's project. Having been promoted to cabinet positions within the new government, the elite civil servants among GISTI's founders effectively left the organization. The legal activism of GISTI's collaborators within the Confédération Française Démocratique du Travail was becoming even more thoroughly incapacitated at this time, as the union's leadership in 1978 had adopted a strategy of "resyndicalisation" and increasingly viewed the judicial strategies of its legal department as a distraction (Noblecourt 1990, 135). Generally speaking, among leftist groups with close ties to the newly elected government, there was an unspoken expectation on the part of the Mitterrand government that they would refrain from criticizing its policies.

The period of 1981 to 1985, when the Socialists took the reins of power for the first time during the Fifth Republic, was thus a time for vigorous discussions on how GISTI's project should proceed in the new political environment, and debate centered on what type of activity to pursue. At a meeting of GISTI's members shortly after the close of the government's regularization program, one faction criticized the group for being insufficiently involved in assisting migrants hoping to benefit from the regularization.[42] Others responded that local immigrant-run associations were better placed for this work, and that the particular form of action for legal activists should be supplying juridical support for collective actions rather than for individuals. Moreover, given the changed political context following the Socialist victory, they suggested that their network should orient itself toward a new type of activism, namely direct and informal interventions with the relevant authorities. A decision was made that members of the group who wished to engage in grassroots work with local associations would continue to do so. However, debate continued over the appropriateness of such work for the association as a whole, and there was a manifest concern that GISTI had not yet developed a coherent organizational strategy for the new political context.

If the extent to which GISTI could or should be involved in grassroots work remained unresolved, the question of what concrete role it would play in the messy business of brokering political compromise was an even more complicated matter. After some debate, the group arrived at the position that GISTI need not refrain from making informal responses to policy proposals when contacted by members of the government, although there was a consensus that this advisory role "should not go so far as providing counter-proposals."[43] Yet in October 1981 when the government stood behind legislation formalizing sanctions for irregular entry and unauthorized employment, GISTI accused the Socialists of hypocrisy for copying the restrictionist policies of their predecessors and, under the leadership of attorney Arlette Grunstein, it petitioned the Conseil d'Etat to overturn both the decree and the two circulars implementing the law.[44] GISTI's lawyers also began an extensive test-case campaign challenging the ability of the police to conduct controls of immigration status alongside immigrant housing inspections.[45] While both campaigns achieved moderate success in court, these actions came at the price of political isolation, as GISTI was accused by its former leftist partners of disloyalty to the new government.

The electoral *alternance* in May 1986, which demonstrated the growing influence of the *Front National* and its anti-immigrant rhetoric, confirmed GISTI's rupture with the government but also opened a door to collaboration with a newly reconstituted civil society movement. GISTI found itself qualified to play a particularly prominent role in this new movement: its new president, Danièle Lochak, had achieved the rank of professor of public law and had gained a reputation as one of the leading scholars of French administrative law, and several of the association's affiliated jurists, including Philippe Waquet and François Julien-Laferrière, had established themselves as leading litigators in private practice. Bolstered by the professional recognition of its leadership, GISTI joined the Ligue des Droits de l'Homme in leading a coalition of civil society associations and labor unions in a weeklong protest against the government's proposed immigration and nationality laws, which were denounced in the strongest terms. According to the Ligue des Droits de l'Homme, the treatment of foreigners was, "a question around which the French political and intellectual field is structured: between Dreyfusards and anti-Dreyfusards, indigenophiles and partisans of colonization, Vichystes and Résistants."[46] Similarly, GISTI's president characterized the immigration law of 1986, which reestablished the pre-1981 regime for expulsions and gave more power to prefects in issuing removal orders, as a "contamination" of far-right xenophobic ideas into mainstream political discourse (Lochak 1987, 56). GISTI's efforts to petition the Conseil d'Etat to overturn the administrative circulars and decrees implementing these restrictive immigration laws served as a complement to its more visible public protests against the new policy.[47]

This denunciatory stance was in some sense a return to an activist modality familiar from the mobilizations of the 1970s, but the nature of the immigrant "cause" to which GISTI now attached itself, and to which it offered its specifically juridical expertise, was becoming hard to pin down. Expanding beyond the issue of immigrant workers' stability of residence, the defense of immigrants was increasingly associated with activism related to the treatment of asylum seekers. GISTI member François Julien-Laferrière's involvement in asylum issues through the organization *France Terre d'Asile* enhanced the group's litigation competencies in this area, and starting in the 1980s the two groups began to collaborate in litigating asylum issues.[48] This move toward specialization and informal division of competencies would continue. In 1989, a new association, *L'Association Nationale d'Assistance aux Frontières pour les Etrangers* (ANAFE), was created with GISTI's support to provide assistance to immigrants and asylum seekers detained when attempting to enter France. Nevertheless, it was GISTI that continued to handle complex legal questions in this area. For instance, when the government detained asylum seekers in a hotel near Roissy Airport without statutory authorization, this covert practice was publicized and condemned by ANAFE, but it was GISTI that formally contested the legality of this "zone of nonlaw" in a lawsuit reported in the media as giving the government "a lesson in administrative law."[49] Amidst this diversification of its activities, GISTI made the decision to drop the word *travailleurs* from its name. As this name change indicates, legal activism to defend the immigrant cause was no longer seen as tied to the immigrant worker debates of the 1970. Moreover, GISTI's project was proving sufficiently malleable to encompass an increasingly diverse array of immigration-related causes with which the group's juridical expertise had become associated.

This organizational adaptation to the changing politics of immigration was accompanied by an appreciable degree of rationalization and systematization in GISTI's organizational practices. In the latter half of the 1980s, GISTI substantially developed its record-keeping techniques, progressively acquiring systems for tracking membership and member dues that made for a strong contrast with the group's initial roster of seventeen members and thirty-four handwritten correspondent addresses.[50] Staff members were hired to "systematize" GISTI's training programs for local immigrant associations, and the association began receiving public funding in the form of a contract to organize regular legal training sessions for government-employed social workers.[51] At the same time, the group consciously sought to improve the organization and presentation of its written publications. Handwritten pamphlets were replaced by a paid-subscription journal, *Plein Droit*, launched in 1988. In addition, GISTI began to market a series of handbooks on immigration law to practicing lawyers. By the mid-1990s, GISTI was regularly contracting training sessions in immigration law with local bar associations, offering a standard program with a fixed price per day.[52]

In part, these steps toward greater institutionalization responded to the perceived need to secure GISTI's financial stability. Starting in the mid-1980s, the organization's main funder, the *Comité Catholique contre la Faim et pour le Développement*, which had provided funds for GISTI to open its own offices, made it clear that it preferred to support defined programs rather than all of the organization's operating expenses.[53] As GISTI began to develop specialized budget lines for its operations, it looked to its informal contacts within the public sector for financial support. Funding for the campaign to publicize asylum rights was obtained through informal inquiries with personal contacts within the government.[54] Securing access to funding from the Ministry of Social Affairs' Direction of Population and Migrations became more "ritualized" beginning in the late 1980s.[55] Moreover, when the Socialists returned to power, it was the prime minister's office that contacted GISTI in order to share the news that a budget line had become available for associations whose activities centered on human rights issues. The close personal nature of these contacts is evident in letters using first names rather than more formal means of address.[56]

At the same time that GISTI moved toward more systematized and institutionalized activities, it increasingly concentrated its efforts on challenging administrative regulations rather than entering into political struggles at the local level. Although the association maintained its weekly drop-in consultation sessions out of a ritualistic commitment to this tradition, the internal debate over how to prioritize legal expertise and locally based activities was tacitly settled in favor of the former. By the mid-1980s, GISTI staff had decided to "channel and restrain" requests for legal assistance from locally based social workers.[57] From this point, grassroots organizing would be handled by separate organizations, such as the *Collectif des Accidentés du Travail, Handicapés et Retraités pour l'Egalité des Droits* established by GISTI staff member Patrick Mony in 1985. In contrast to the close contacts that characterized its involvement with the SONACOTRA residents movement of the 1970s, GISTI remained largely uninvolved in the grassroots movement of second-generation immigrant youth that developed in the 1990s against the *double-peine* (the penalty of expulsion associated with a criminal conviction).[58] Similarly, it was activists affiliated with the emergent antiglobalization movement, rather than GISTI, that took the lead in supporting the series of spontaneous sit-ins and squats organized by the various "collectives of *sans-papiers*" once this movement had burst onto the scene in the early 1990s (Péchu 2006, 296). While several of GISTI's jurists represented participants in the *sans-papiers* movement, the organization by the 1990s had clearly moved away from its early aspiration to provide ongoing support at the local level.[59]

As the politics of immigration continued to be the subject of intense political debate throughout the 1990s, role of lawyer-orator on behalf of France's community of human rights and humanitarian associations became an institutionalized aspect of GISTI's organizational identity. In debates over the enactment of restrictionist immigration laws in 1993, GISTI publically accused the conservative government of "harboring a profound scorn for the family life of foreigners" and "enacting a veritable coup d'état" against rule of law.[60] GISTI adopted a public position in favor of open borders, prompting a debate within the Left over whether this response to the government's increasingly restrictionist policies was too radical.[61] Despite calls from some within the leftist political establishment for a more pragmatic stance on immigration matters, GISTI maintained its strongly critical position even after a subsequent electoral *alternance* returned a government of the left to power in 1997; its public statements emphasized the inadequacies of a 1998 immigration law that reversed some but not all of the restrictionist measures enacted by the previous government.[62] When a government of the right returned to power in 2002, GISTI coordinated a civil society campaign against what it saw as an entrenched policy regime that allowed France's immigrants to be treated as "disposable."[63] The organization has led a collective of French left-leaning associations in calling for freedom of movement for all people across national borders since the mid-1990s, a campaign that included collaboration with filmmakers and even a rock concert to publicize the idea of open borders.

Activism in court, which has tended to operate in an abstract and formal register, provides an additional tool for this principled denunciation of immigration policies. Rather than wading into the details of street-level implementation, GISTI has preferred to focus on abstract formal legality and over the past four decades its jurists have gained confidence and become adept at bringing abstract challenges before the Conseil d'Etat. GISTI organized more than twice as many abstract challenges before the Conseil d'État in the 1990s as it did in the previous two decades, and this number doubled again after 2000 (Lochak 2009, 44). The contrast between this litigation approach and American-style public interest law was made clear to me when I initially asked GISTI members about their law reform efforts, and the term *law reform* elicited puzzled looks. As they saw it, the task of pushing courts to apply existing principles of legality is ontologically distinct from the pragmatic trade-offs of policy reform. This is not to say that GISTI's legal activists are advancing the law in a way that is purely speculative or academic; rather, they see themselves as advancing the rights of foreigners by virtue of the principled consistency of their program. The attachment to a principled agenda can be seen in every issue of GISTI's journal *Plein Droit*, which opens with an unsigned editorial laying out the principles to which the association is attached and describing how enacted policies have fallen short of these principles. Among the most prominent of these principles are the guaranteed provision of social assistance, the right to asylum, and the right of migrants settled in France to work and to enjoy a family life. These themes form continuous threads of coordinated activity before the courts and are the basis for contesting immigration policy.

The sustainability of this model of legal activism relies upon a loyal and tight-knit circle of affiliated lawyers who are willing to file judicial petitions in GISTI's name for little or no fee.[64] There is no equivalent to the position of the staff attorney within U.S. public interest law firms. GISTI's paid staff have relatively little involvement in formulating or drafting legal arguments. After a decision has been taken to challenge a particular administrative action in the association's name by the group's inner-circle of members, the role of GISTI's paid staff is generally limited to keeping records of the petition's progress. Organized litigation is instead conducted by GISTI's unpaid members. A common link for many of GISTI's early lawyer supporters was that they had participated in the Mouvement d'Action Judiciaire legal network at the beginning of their careers. By the 1990s, the circle had come to include a number of Danièle Lochak's former students who completed an internship with GISTI as part of their legal training. Lochak's respected legal scholarship and close relationship with the Ligue des Droits de l'Homme further strengthened the group's reputation and attracted a new generation of legal academics and litigators as prospective GISTI members.

GISTI's legal activism has also made good use of its network of social contacts among the upper echelons of the judicial world. Its landmark 1978 victory was achieved in part because the case served as a "catalyst" of initial signs of change in the Conseil d'Etat's position on immigrant rights, signals that were already perceptible to GISTI jurists working within that institution though they were not made public (Genevois 2009, 71). Knowledge of discussions taking place within the Conseil d'Etat likewise proved helpful in making legal activists aware that certain provisions of the 1996 Debré immigration law, concerning proofs of adequate housing for immigrant residency permits, had received criticism from the Conseil d'Etat at the drafting stage and were thus susceptible to legal challenge (Guiraudon 2000, 210). In both instances, the source of GISTI's privileged access to this source of legal authority was the fact that its jurists operated in the same Parisian microcosm occupied by French administrative elites. Particularly as their careers advanced, GISTI's legal activists encountered members of France's governing class by virtue of where they lived and who they knew. At the same time, this relationship with the Conseil d'Etat has been actively maintained through the organization's careful cultivation of a reputation for eloquence and abstract reasoning, qualities that, as Michèle Lamont has shown, are essential resources among French elites (Lamont 1992). Although her presence is not required, Danièle Lochak has been known to attend the public audiences for GISTI's cases before the Conseil d'Etat, where she is addressed as *"Madame le professeur,"* signaling both the respect that this title conveys as well as GISTI's willingness to incorporate a subtle reputational leveraging into its organizational strategy.

Indeed, operating in an organizational context in which reputation and informal networks are indispensable, GISTI has devoted substantial effort to maintaining its "brand name." One way of doing so has been limiting access to GISTI membership by making it conditional on sponsorship by two existing members. The organization has never made any strong attempt at recruitment. Over the years, jurists who demonstrated an expertise in immigration law were invited to join GISTI's selective membership and were generally eager to become associated with such a prestigious group. Rather than seeking to expand its membership as other associations have done, GISTI has consciously maintained a niche identity.[65] The organization has devoted substantial time and effort to organizing colloquia and publications celebrating its litigation successes and has invited famous jurists to comment on their significance. For instance, the 1992 edition of GISTI's immigrant rights legal guidebook has a preface contributed by the Vice President of the Conseil d'Etat at the time, Marceau Long (GISTI 1992). The success of GISTI's legal activism has rested in part on its ability to leverage a circle of supporters and to build a network of contacts that remains largely personalized and informal in nature.

This proximity to the state, while it has been effective in providing access to the upper echelons of French administrative law,[66] has nevertheless supplied a source of angst for GISTI's legal activists. The generation that began their careers in the 1970s maintained a strong attachment to an ethos of urgency and spontaneity, accompanied by a fear of being co-opted by the state. Even as this image of spontaneous mobilizations grew more distant from reality, the group has struggled to maintain its critical autonomy. In 1992, the association used the twentieth anniversary of its creation to recall its foundational principles and to explore the tensions involved in juridical engagement with a state whose policies continued to promote restrictionism.[67] The following year, fearing that these principles were being compromised through association with a government of the right keen to appease far-right voters, GISTI announced its resignation from participation on the National Consultative Committee on Human Rights. Although GISTI continued to receive its regular funding from the Ministry of Social Affairs, GISTI's president expressed concerns that her association might become accustomed to money and would find itself distracted by having to support the enhanced operations that more funding would allow.[68]

While they are fearful of being co-opted by the state, GISTI's legal activists in recent years have expressed a parallel fear of being seduced into the sphere of the market. This antimarket discourse is an outgrowth of the evolving politics of the French legal field, which since the late 1980s has pitted business lawyers against those defending the traditional model of courtroom defense (Karpik 1999, 285–312). To maintain its separation from market forces, GISTI has made a point of routinely linking immigration issues to larger political debates and its journal, *Plein Droit*, has regularly published short essays by historians, sociologists, anthropologists, and philosophers that address legal issues only at the most abstract level. Similarly, when referring to the informal procedures used to make a decision of whether and how to litigate, legal activists voiced pride in what they referred to as their "artisanal" approach, insisting that public representation should be distinguished from the strategic lobbying work of interest groups.[69] GISTI made the decision to avoid hiring professional public relations staff for fear that the group's political positions would become oversimplified when targeted to the media.[70]

Looking beyond these calls to prevent mission-creep, however, the preceding discussion has highlighted the extent to which GISTI's project has sustained itself over time through a combination of tinkering and flexibility. Indeed, over the past ten years, as new sets of actors have become involved in providing immigration-related legal services in France, GISTI's organizational identity has continued to evolve. As jurists affiliated with other organizations, such as the Cimade and Amnesty International France, have gained confidence in formulating petitions for judicial review, GISTI can now no longer claim to stand alone as the legal wing for all of France's immigrant defense mobilizations.[71] With no externally imposed division of labor in immigration-related legal expertise, the dynamics of these collaborations remain informal although there is a general tendency for GISTI to take charge of litigation in complex cases.[72] Perhaps most telling of the changes in recent years, at a colloquium dedicated to the emerging area of French legal activism on behalf of prisoners' rights, GISTI's legal activists embraced their identity not as a *sui generis* innovation but rather as role model for "collective action à la française" (Slama and Ferran 2014, 9). GISTI's broad vision of "eradicating the zone of non-law" has not only proved sufficiently flexible to accommodate substantial organizational translation over time, but also has encouraged emulators among legal activists in other policy domains.

CONCLUSION

In the United States and France, attorneys who began their careers as immigrant defenders have been drawn over time toward more institutionalized modalities. In the United States, it was the process of seeking external support that especially propelled the institutionalization of immigrant rights legal activism. Organizations strove to demonstrate, both to their professional peers and to supporters within the liberal legal network, that their litigation activities were having a concrete impact. Staff-led immigrant rights legal organizations with largely paper memberships replicated the organizational model of public interest law. In the process of doing so, they implemented more professionalized human resources practices and developed formalized structures for communicating with local affiliates. They also rationalized their collaborations with each other, allowing for effective division of labor. Perhaps the most striking aspect of institutionalization, however, is the degree to which immigrant rights legal activism has gravitated toward the legal profession. Immigration-centered legal activism emerged as a form of practice characterized by regular interactions with the institutional structures of the U.S. legal profession as well as frequent partnership with the private bar's pro bono initiatives.

By contrast, in France, there has been little direct involvement in, or support for, legal activism on the part of leaders of the legal profession. Planned litigation has remained a voluntary activity carried out by a small circle of committed jurists whose reputation attracted the best and the brightest to join their ranks. Unlike the situation in the United States, an organizational template for institutionalized practice was not ready for adaptation. Instead, aspiring French legal activists have taken inspiration from the historical precedent of lawyers and intellectuals speaking on behalf of abstract notions of liberty and legality. Despite a professed aversion to institutionalization, French legal activists' organizational practices have nonetheless experienced an appreciable systematization and formalization. They have also been gradually incorporated into what legal sociologists Terrence Halliday and Lucien Karpik have identified as a liberal-leaning "legal complex" operating inside and outside of the state (Halliday and Karpik 1997, Halliday, Karpik, and Feeley 2007). We see this move toward institutionalization in the efforts of GISTI's jurists to secure their organization's reputation with sources of legal and political authority.

It is important to distinguish the analysis of institutionalization offered here from anti-immigrant polemics asserting that immigration-centered legal activism was the brainchild of liberal elites.[73] Lawyers and legal organizations are reduced in these polemics to mere instruments for advancing an existing liberal agenda through the courts. Against these top-down conspiracy theories, the history of immigrant rights legal activism demonstrates the extent to which national legal organizations in each country emerged through a process that was more horizontal than vertical. As detailed in Chapter 2, immigrant rights legal activism developed into a distinct professional community because idealistic jurists joined in local struggles that renegotiated migrants' normative claims on the law. Moreover, as the discussion in this chapter demonstrates, the process of institutionalizing legal activism also involved substantial translation and adaptation. Rather than operating as a cut-and-paste process, it unfolded through a series of mutually reciprocated associations between ambitious immigrant defenders, their various supporters inside and outside of the state, and an evolving immigrant social movement environment. It was through this combination of entrepreneurialism and experimentation that the project of institutionalized immigration-centered legal activism ultimately coalesced.

It is clear, however, that the process of institutionalization that began in the 1980s moved immigrant rights legal activism progressively further away from local social movements and increased its proximity to the space of official policy making. While legal activists in both countries continued to identify their work as political, they took pride in having established reputations with sources of legal authority. For example, American and French jurists alike celebrated the fact that high courts had subscribed to their publications. This in turn inspired greater attention to rigorous legal argumentation and analysis. In the United States, successes in court encouraged immigrant defense lawyers to pursue litigation strategies that adopted a "national perspective" and to create organizations that operated with only loose connections to the struggles of local movements. Similarly, in France, legal activism, which was initially grounded in local immigrant social movements, became part of a largely Paris-based network of human rights and humanitarian associations with a strong programmatic agenda. Not only was it challenging for legal activists to maintain contact with political struggles at the local level, but litigation efforts conceptualized from a national perspective were also more obviously relevant to programmatic debates over immigration policy. In both settings, liberal elites became a supportive audience for immigration-centered litigation. The flip side of this development was that the new organizational forms facilitated through the support of elite benefactors – a network of specialized public interest law firms in the United States and a circle of principled lawyer-orators in France – allowed for a relatively reduced competence for coordination with grassroots immigrant social movements engaged in direct action strategies.

Regardless of the organizational models that American and French legal activists cultivated in concert with their supporters, one important effect of institutionalization was that it expanded the quantity and scope of immigration policies that would be subjected to litigation. As immigrant rights legal activism acquired a solid base of support and adopted sustaining organizational form, challenging immigration policies in court became a routine dimension of immigration politics. In other words, at the same time that immigrant rights legal organizations were building and maintaining relationships with their supporters in the legal profession, their litigation efforts brought them into increasingly regular contact with the government administrators whose policies they opposed. The next two chapters look more deeply at the courtroom work of institutionalized immigrant rights legal activism to elucidate the patterns and practices produced in the process of seeking judicial review of immigration-related administrative policy making.

5

Enacting Adversarial Legalism through Class Action Lawsuits

After two decades of increasingly institutionalized litigation efforts, U.S. immigrant rights legal activists in the mid-1990s found themselves the subject of unwanted legislative attention. The Illegal Immigration Reform and Immigrant Responsibility Act (IIRIRA), signed into law in September 1996, contained language that severely limited class action lawsuits challenging Immigration and Naturalization Service (INS) policies and practices.[1] Placed alongside IIRIRA's other restrictionist provisions, such as those establishing an "expedited" removal process and curbing judicial review of final deportation orders, the provision restricting class action litigation can be seen as part of a broad legislative effort to alter the role of federal courts in immigration matters.[2] At the same time, IIRIRA's class actions provision is worthy of particular attention as it offers a revealing commentary on how immigrant rights legal activism had come to be perceived by actors within the government.

The legislative architects of this jurisdiction-stripping provision were explicit about how they understood the "problem" that it was designed to address. Describing the purpose behind IIRIRA's class action restriction, Senator Alan Simpson explained, "We got rid of layers of people who love to bring class actions and disrupt the normal course of INS work."[3] The chief counsel to the Senate's Immigration Subcommittee was even more direct in his explanation of legislative motivation: "We're tired of these suits every time you don't give out benefits to as many people as some lawyers think you should."[4] Representative Lamar Smith, the Chairman of the House Subcommittee on Immigration, expressed his critique in a similar manner: "Any individual immigrant may still sue the agency and obtain specific relief, but broad class action suits … will be curtailed. Immigration lawyers have used such suits to accomplish what they cannot accomplish through legislation or regulations."[5] Legislators expressed a determination to strip away a legal mechanism that had been used with notable efficacy for court-propelled policy change. Their public statements give some indication of the degree of antagonism that had developed between immigrant rights legal activists and the agency that was the target of these lawsuits.

In an influential series of essays almost thirty years ago, Martin Shapiro speculated that assertive judicial review of administrative practices would inspire hostility on the part of agency officials and focus them on the appearance of fairness rather than on substance (Shapiro 1988, 110–11). Along similar lines, Robert Kagan's seminal study of "adversarial legalism" marshaled a broad array of empirical evidence to support the view that lawsuits by rights advocates have often stimulated legal and political counterattack by administrative agencies that treat judicial decisions that reject their policies "as just one more political obstacle to be overcome by tactical means" (Kagan 2001, 171). A recent study of organizational responses to legal mobilization in the area of disability rights confirms this tendency on the part of public administrators to adopt negative attitudes toward lawyers who organize lawsuits challenging administrative practices (Burke and Barnes 2012).

Yet, as other empirical studies have shown, organized litigation does not always "succeed" in constructing a culture of adversarial legalism and administrative recalcitrance. In some instances, legal activism directed against local public administration has strengthened the hand of internal reformers favoring "systemic legalized accountability" (Epp 2009). At the federal level, court decisions prompted by organized litigation, rather than inspiring hostility, at times have instead "established a new policy status quo" by altering public expectations about the responsibilities of government (Melnick 1994). Although assertive judicial interventions can set in motion cycles of interaction that amplify conflict and lead administrative policy makers to focus on second-order policy questions about the scope of standing and judicial reviewability (rather than considerations of substantive policy), the emergence of this "deconstructive" pattern of juridification is context-dependent (Silverstein 2009). For instance, organized litigation is more likely to be construed as an intrusive activity that impedes an agency's mission when judges assertively interpret legislation in ways that are contrary to the expectations under which the law was initially enacted (Silverstein 2009, 274–9).

Without contesting these findings, I want to suggest that the practical achievement of "adversarial legalism" in a given policy domain depends not only on the initiative of judges but also on dynamics that are cultivated among other routinized participants in the litigation process. As this chapter explains, legal proceedings against U.S. immigration policy administrators have been characterized by a highly pragmatic organizing logic that places legal activists in close contact with the day-to-day institutional and operational terrain of immigration policy. Through repeated interactions, litigators and agency administrators have been regularly brought into contact. The result of these legal performances has been the construction of a collectively held narrative among immigration officials in which judges and formal law fall into the background while those responsible for organizing lawsuits against immigration policy practices assume, in the eyes of their administrative interlocutors, the dual roles of protagonist and target for counterattack.

The set of class action litigation campaigns organized against the INS during the 1980s and 1990s provides the material for developing an understanding of how this antagonistic dynamic emerged. It was during this period that immigrant rights legal activists were first brought into regularized contact with national immigration officials, who previously had not been the subject of organized litigation. My close study of these interactions concentrates on the modality of the performances that they constructed. I argue that understanding how immigration class action lawsuits were experienced by their participants is important if we want to fully understand the responses that organized litigation elicited beyond the courtroom.

The analysis in this chapter starts by elaborating the unique set of features that came to be associated with immigration class action lawsuits – across a range of issues – starting in the 1980s. It then lays out the culture of interaction engendered by repeated recourse to this distinct legal instrument by legal activists seeking to influence national immigration policy making. The final section explores the shifting dynamics operating in more recent years, as legislative jurisdiction-stripping introduced new actors and sites of interaction between legal activists and immigration policy makers.

CLASS ACTION LAWSUITS AGAINST THE INS

For U.S. immigrant rights legal organizations, class action lawsuits have offered a powerful instrument for influencing national immigration policy making. While the class action lawsuit has long been a feature of federal litigation, the potency of this instrument was substantially enhanced during the 1960s and 1970s. In the mid-1960s, Congress revised the class action rule so as to allow plaintiffs to seek injunctive relief on behalf of groups of individuals with no prior legal relationship so long as they could show that their legal opponent had acted in a manner generally applicable to the class as a whole (Redish 2009, 10–11). Case law generated by civil rights litigation and public interest litigation likewise contributed to extending the power of the class action mechanism. Federal courts routinely assumed that plaintiffs in civil rights class actions adequately represented their proposed class and that the class actions posed no danger of conflict between lawyer and client (Bell 1976, 493). Judicial willingness to apply these standards to public interest litigation organized against federal agencies further extended the reach of the class action mechanism (Schuck 1983, 151). During the 1970s, courts hearing class actions were willing to issue consensual remedial decrees and permanent injunctions when administrative agencies had been judged to be in violation only of statutory provisions rather than of constitutional rights.

For aspiring immigrant rights legal activists, starting in the early 1980s, the class action mechanism offered a clear path for bringing public officials under substantive judicial oversight. Immigration and refugee statutes were providing opportunities for legal activism by simultaneously creating new entitlements for migrants and limiting existing rights, and immigration-centered public interest organizations were gaining the institutional and juridical capacity to litigate these cases.[6] In 1984, the director of the National Center for Immigrants' Rights summed up a generalized sentiment when he told his advisory board, "We cannot effect change through law if we are unable to proceed through class actions."[7]

Beyond the basic characteristic of generalizing judicial holdings to a large number of class members, however, immigrant rights class actions starting in the early 1980s also became associated with a specific and regularized organizing logic. First of all, the immigration class action came to be deployed most regularly in cases challenging the practices of a particular administrative agency. Legal activists learned through experience that it was not particularly difficult to use class action lawsuits to convince courts that the INS was acting abusively. For much of its history, the INS was a "beleaguered bureaucracy" that had few political allies (Morris 1984), and the underdeveloped asylum system offered multiple opportunities for legal challenges. The lesson taken from initial cases challenging the INS's handling of Haitian asylum claims in the late 1970s and early 1980s was that an effective strategy for systemic reform consisted of focusing on the traditionally poor reputation of the agency charged with immigration policy implementation and identifying "structural defects" in its patterns of behavior (Kurzban 1981). In addition, litigating against an agency that chose to defend actions that were demonstrably abusive proved to be fertile ground for attorneys' fee awards.[8] Legal activists learned from these early experiences with class actions that they had good chances of winning attorneys' fees when litigating against the indefensible practices of a politically isolated agency. Conversely, they came to understand that the odds that a court would find the government's conduct "substantially unreasonable" and award attorneys' fees were much less favorable when litigation targeted congressional statutes and thereby raised abstract issues of policy.

In addition to targeting INS policies and practices, immigration class actions came to concentrate on using federal district court orders as leverage for policy change. Rather than seeking to obtain doctrinal innovations, legal activists were content to secure orders from district courts that placed them in a position to redesign INS operations. The specificities of U.S. immigration jurisprudence weighed into this tactical choice. As political scientist Anna Law has demonstrated, the fact-intensive and procedurally focused review of lower federal courts has typically been more conducive to immigrants winning their cases than the abstract consideration of national sovereignty concerns that has come to characterize the U.S. Supreme Court's institutional mandate (Law 2010). This insight about where they had the best chances of winning their cases was something that legal activists understood intuitively, and their litigation strategies steered courts to focus not on rarefied principles that might activate plenary power considerations but rather on the case-specific "record of systematic abuse" on the part of the agency.[9] From their perspective, class action lawsuits against INS practices – even when they resulted in nonconstitutional holdings – offered an attractive means to compel changes in immigration policy making.

Before taking a closer look at how this instrument for immigration-centered law reform operated in practice, it is important to sketch briefly the basic background for the major immigrant rights litigation campaigns that deployed the class action instrument. Litigation during the 1980s and 1990s is the focus because this was the period in which the immigration class action operated in its most unadulterated form. Within this period, I focus on class actions in which national legal organizations played a leading role and where the petitioners withstood government motions for dismissal. Although the cases I discuss in this chapter are only a subset of all immigrant rights cases litigated during this period, the selective sampling makes possible a close examination of the routinized interactions between repeat players for which class action lawsuits set the stage.

One important group of immigration-related class actions in which these routinized interactions developed were lawsuits organized with the participation of national legal organizations that challenged the treatment of migrants fleeing conflict in Central America. The Refugee Act of 1980, which brought U.S. law into alignment with international refugee law, provided a legal hook for these cases, which followed on the heels of successful efforts on behalf of Haitian asylum seekers. The political associations of these litigation campaigns were inseparable from the Reagan administration's treatment of the Central American conflict as a Cold War issue and from the contestation of these policies by a nationwide Sanctuary Movement that reached its peak activity during the 1980s (Coutin 2006).[10] Among the earliest class action lawsuits in this area, the *Perez-Funez* case alleged that the INS routinely coerced unaccompanied minors in its custody into accepting immediate repatriation through the "voluntary departure" procedure. Similar issues concerning advising individuals of the right to apply for asylum as well as of due process rights were subsequently raised in a nationwide class action lawsuit, the *Orantes-Hernandez* case, brought on behalf of all Salvadorans in INS detention. The *Flores* class action lawsuit, filed on behalf of a fifteen-year-old from El Salvador who was detained for five months in a detention facility designed for adults, also targeted INS detention policies. Finally, the government's handling of asylum and removal hearings became a focus for legal activists' efforts on behalf of Central Americans. The *American Baptist Churches* (ABC) class action accused the government of nationwide systematic bias in the adjudication of Salvadoran and Guatemalan asylum claims. Two additional class action cases, *Mendez v. Thornburgh* and *El Rescate Legal Services v. Executive Office for Immigration Review*, challenged aspects of asylum processing and adjudication in the Los Angeles and San Diego INS districts. All four of the national immigrant rights legal organizations discussed in Chapter 4 contributed to this body of cases.

The Immigration Reform and Control Act of 1986 (IRCA) provided the impetus for legal activists to challenge INS practices on a second front. The law included a general legalization program for noncitizen residents as well as programs that regularized the status of eligible members of population-specific groups: (1) seasonal agricultural workers and (2) Cuban and Haitian nationals. The INS's handling of the legalization became the subject of a substantial corpus of class action lawsuits organized by immigrant rights legal activists.[11]

A third important body of cases consisted of class action lawsuits challenging the U.S. government policy of intercepting Haitian vessels on the high seas to prevent their occupants from reaching U.S. territory. Immigrant rights lawsuits targeted various aspects of the Haitian interdiction program, ranging from questioning the statutory authorization for the interdiction program to challenging the adequacy of detention conditions for HIV-positive Haitians held at the U.S. military facility in Guantanamo Bay.[12] These class actions on behalf of interdicted Haitians were organized by seasoned immigrant rights legal activists in collaboration with other nonprofit organizations and corporate pro bono counsel.

Although many other class action cases were organized, this subset provides a representative snapshot of the most significant areas of immigration-centered class action litigation during this period. They are particularly vivid exemplars of a broader pattern of interaction that developed around the class action mechanism as it was wielded against federal immigration officials.[13] Having laid out the historical context for the cases, the rest of my analysis concentrates on how the emergence of the immigration class action lawsuit contributed to constructing an enduring association between judicial intervention and administrative antagonism.

THE AMPLIFICATION OF ADVERSARIAL CONFLICT

The first thing that becomes apparent when looking at the records of immigrant rights class action campaigns during the 1980s and 1990s is the extent to which these lawsuits were fact-intensive undertakings. A highly partisan process of evidence accumulation began even before the cases were filed in court. Legal activists made liberal use of Freedom of Information Act (FOIA) procedures, seeking any and all government documents potentially pertinent to the subject of the lawsuit and thus avoiding any possibility that their cases would not meet the threshold for certification as a national class.[14] For example, in the *Orantes* litigation campaign, FOIA procedures were used to conscript agency officials into compiling the immigration records of all individuals required to return to El Salvador as well as all documents and records relating to policy and practice regarding Salvadorans.[15]

Once a federal district court had certified a class and rejected motions to dismiss the case, the gates were opened to the next phase of documentary stockpiling through the process of discovery. In the *ABC* case, the INS was required to produce thousands of pages of documents held in its central and regional offices, and attorneys conducted depositions of dozens of government officials (Blum 1991, 352). The class action challenging the legalization program compelled the agency to provide litigators with the worksheets used by individual INS officers across the country.[16] Class action lawsuits concerning various aspects of the Haitian interdiction program used the discovery process to force the government to turn over surveillance videos, Coast Guard reports, flight manifests, Joint Task Force directives, and interagency memoranda – six thousand pages in all (Goldstein 2005, 244). Through these ambitious discovery requests, the process of evidence gathering in immigration class action lawsuits became like a war dance preceding courtroom combat: it was long and strenuous, as the two sides assessed the strength of their adversary's evidentiary arsenal and calculated the cost of defeat.

It was a process that was burdensome and labor intensive for both plaintiffs and defendants. In the words of one legal activist who participated in several class actions targeting INS practices, "We had a good chance of winning so long as we could garner the necessary resources to bring the lawsuit."[17] The resources of corporate law firms were particularly helpful in this respect, supplying "deep pockets and endless resources" (Goldstein 2005, 53) to assist in the voluminous and wide-ranging discovery process. Moreover, the party-driven nature of the process meant that INS officials were required to sit for questioning in the plush corporate law firm offices of pro bono collaborators in immigration reform litigation.[18] Thus, in addition to having their internal memoranda subjected to public scrutiny and criticism, agency officials were forced to make themselves available for depositions conducted on their adversaries' turf.

While this use of the discovery process allowed legal activists to take the initiative, it relegated judges to the supervisory role of umpires shaping the balance of power between opponents. For instance, in the ABC class action, a key turning point was the judge's decision to allow litigators to substantially revise the focus of their claims. Such decisions, while clearly unfavorable to the agency, produced no precedent-setting rule. Sympathetic judges exercised influence over the outcome of these cases but did so largely in the background and thus without attracting condemnation from agency officials.

By contrast, interactions between litigators and agency officials were frequent and came to be highly adversarial. Class action lawsuits challenging immigration policy administration required the specification of a concrete administrative adversary. The target of unflattering attention could not be generalized to "the state" in its entirety, because U.S. civil procedure directs plaintiffs contesting executive policies to focus on the allegedly abusive actions of one or more discrete units of the public administration. Starting in the early 1980s, the role of administrative target was filled by the INS. Legal activists focused attention not on the content of regulations (and what they say about government policy), but rather on the inequities created by the agency's street-level practices. Even in instances in which there was good reason to suspect that street-level practices were the manifestation of deliberate policy choices made at the highest levels of government, legal activists centered their legal attacks on the agency charged with implementing these policies. This meant assembling an arsenal of documentation regarding agency practices rather than debating the legality of these policies in the abstract. The fact-intensive nature of the process was particularly evident in cases that involved efforts to demonstrate that a pattern of agency behavior existed even though the pattern was nowhere embodied as policy in a formal regulation. Not only did this process isolate the agency from broader political structures, but it also left the agency thoroughly exposed to the massive scope of national class action lawsuits.

Courtroom exchanges amplified the tendency of immigration class actions to target the "agency" as an isolated institution characterized by distinct and recurring pathologies. With the judge and media as audience, trials were an opportunity for legal activists to conduct a public shaming of the agency. The records of the *Orantes* trial, which began in 1985 and lasted for more than a year, give a sense of this potential of immigration class actions to generate drama. The testimony of 175 witnesses set the stage for a highly dramatic exchange that reached a fever pitch just before the court heard the testimony of Aryeh Neier, the co-chairman of Americas Watch, when priests at a church two blocks away from the court declared their church a sanctuary in a ceremony filmed by television cameras.[19]

Sympathetic district court judges occasionally echoed and amplified the dramatic rhetoric developed by plaintiffs' attorneys. For instance, when defending interdicted Haitians detained at Guantanamo Bay, legal activists argued that INS officials were aware that medical care was lacking in detention facilities but had repeatedly failed to act and had deliberately ignored the medical advice of military doctors. The district court's opinion subsequently took up this framing of events, labeling the agency's practices "callous and reprehensible" and concluding that "Defendant INS has repeatedly failed to act on recommendations and deliberately ignored the medical advice of U.S. military doctors."[20] The fact-centered nature of class action lawsuits against agency practices, by emphasizing the impact of policies and their human consequences, held ample potential for high courtroom drama that symbolically reinforced the targeting of the agency.

In this combative environment, the opportunity for a truce – through party initiated settlement – was always an option. Often the parties chose to settle before the case went to trial, but even in those cases that did reach the trial stage, there were numerous opportunities for negotiations between the parties to achieve a settlement. The opportunity for settlement meant that the decision to litigate became a matter for pragmatic calculus that weighed a variety of considerations: the likelihood of success, the importance of the rights at stake, the number of people impacted, the availability of alternatives to litigation, the estimated cost of litigation and whether sufficient funds are available.[21] From the time an immigration class action lawsuit was filed, legal activists were engaged in negotiations with the government at multiple levels. As litigation proceeded toward setting a trial date, the interest for both sides in discussing a settlement increased. This did not prevent settlement negotiations between the parties from being conducted in a tough and highly adversarial tone. When advocates were aware that the agency wanted to settle, they often used this knowledge to ask for greater concessions. Negotiations in some cases went on for years, while the fact-intensive discovery process played itself out. As one government attorney put it, "All class actions take on a life of their own after a while. They run their course. Either the plaintiffs will get something out the case and will want to settle or the agency will get tired and want to settle. After a while they collapse under their own weight."[22]

In short, the process of litigating an immigration class action lawsuit gave legal intervention an aura of subjectivity. Legal activists approached the settlement process understanding that they had a good chance of prevailing in the courts, while recognizing that the agency's lawyers likewise felt they would prevail and that the truth probably lay somewhere in the middle. Particularly in constitutional due process or equal protection cases, where debate centered on differing assessments of the rationality of the administration's actions, there was substantial room for legal subjectivity. In these cases, tenacious bargaining and savvy strategizing sometimes carried the day even in the absence of any explicitly articulated legal theory.[23]

Indeed, U.S. immigrant rights legal activists had particularly little time for abstract questions of legal coherence as they became increasingly immersed in the world of administrative implementation. Class action litigation produced settlement agreements and injunctive orders that were lengthy and detailed and thus subject to interpretation. Unsurprisingly, litigators tended to give broad readings to their provisions, thereby extending a case's life for as long a period as the agency was required to make a showing of compliance. Moreover, in some instances (most notably the *ABC* settlement), the agency agreed to give attorneys a lead role in the process of implementing a judicially supervised remedy. When this was the case, the line between implementing an agreement and appropriating policy-making functions was a thin one; district court judges were a presence in the background for administrative officials, but it was the attorneys who drove the process of implementation and who set the bar for agency compliance. The *Orantes* class action is another good example of this open-ended monitoring. Litigation had resulted in an injunction, still in effect, requiring the INS to provide an oral notice of rights, including the right to counsel and the right to asylum, to all arrested Salvadoran migrants. Besides the notice of rights, the *Orantes* injunction specified a number of additional administrative procedures to ensure access to counsel: the agency was required to provide an updated list of free legal services providers in all detention centers, and was prohibited from transferring unrepresented detainees out of the district where they were arrested for a period of seven days, and the injunction also prescribed regular access to legal materials and telephones, and mandated lengthier visiting hours for attorney consultation.[24] Legal activists read the injunction as a judicial confirmation of the principle that arrest and detention should be subjected to greater legal supervision, and therefore returned to court multiple times seeking additional orders and remedies to ensure "real compliance."[25] By providing an opportunity to monitor the agency's actions, immigration class action lawsuits opened the door to a cycle of subsequent lawsuits.

Of particular significance for the development of a culture of administrative antagonism, the process of implementing court orders in immigration class action lawsuits brought legal activists into roles considered by some officials to be ministerial functions of the agency. As part of the monitoring provisions set in place by litigation, private attorneys acquired legal authorization to review the operating and training instructions issued by agency leaders. For example, in the *Flores* settlement, the agency was required to allow attorneys to review statistics on juvenile detainees as well as all written agreements between the INS and the various public or private entities contracted to provide the housing of detained minors. Similarly, in the ABC settlement, advocates were given a role in revising and augmenting the training modules and handbooks issued to asylum officers. Unsurprisingly, their contributions aimed to broaden asylum officers' instructions regarding the range of circumstances in which asylum could be granted. The additional materials developed by advocates included examples of situations in which discrimination constituted persecution or where recruitment by the military or by guerrillas did so, as well as training modules on the need for extra sensitivity when eliciting testimony from individuals who have experienced trauma.[26]

The ABC settlement went further in this direction than most others, demonstrating the fine line between supervising implementation and acquiring administrative functions. Immigrant rights litigators borrowed mechanisms of judicially supervised administrative oversight developed in civil rights Title VII employment discrimination lawsuits and applied them to the immigration policy context.[27] The goal was structural change of the U.S. asylum system to bring it into conformity with rights-expanding international standards for refugee status determination. To this end, legal activists crafted a settlement that would provide them with administrative data, monitoring systems, and mechanisms for enforcing compliance. As part of the settlement, attorneys were provided by the agency with funds to hire a full-time coordinator to oversee INS compliance. The coordinator devised plans, which the government funded, to conduct a public information campaign, including television, radio, and print advertisements, as well as leaflets and posters, to inform Salvadoran and Guatemalan migrants of the benefits potentially available under the agreement. The agency was required to provide the settlement coordinator with numerical evidence demonstrating that it was making progress in providing benefits accorded to class members, which attorneys then needed to assess.[28] Also, as part of the settlement, the parties agreed to ask the General Accounting Office to conduct two reviews of the asylum process, and allowed the plaintiffs to enumerate specific matters on which the agency would be assessed (Blum 1991, 355). This case shows most clearly how U.S. immigrant rights litigation involved legal actors in the operational details (allocation of resources, setting of standards, design of operations, etc.) of the administrative world. Lawyers organizing lawsuits against the agency acquired substantial control over agency operations.

INSTILLING ADVERSARIALISM: JURIDIFYING U.S. ADMINISTRATIVE POLICY MAKING ON IMMIGRATION

What were the administrative responses that developed around legal activity and legal actors in this immigration policy context? The first thing that becomes clear is that, starting in the early 1980s, U.S. administrative officials acquired a keen awareness of immigration class action litigation and those responsible for organizing it. From the perspective of the INS, class action lawsuits aimed "to not only establish rights for individual aliens, but also to stop limit, or fundamentally change the manner in which the Service operates."[29] As they threatened to impede the agency's mission, these legal attacks organized by "activists and public interest groups" called for an aggressive response that would "preserve the authority" of the INS. Starting in 1981, important immigration litigation began to be handled by a task force that marshaled the combined forces of the INS General Counsel's Office, an INS field attorney, a Department of Justice Civil Division attorney, and an Assistant U.S. Attorney.[30] As INS operations continued to inspire regular class action challenges, the task force approach was institutionalized in the newly created Office of Immigration Litigation within the Department of Justice, which in 1983 assumed primary responsibility for coordinating nationwide litigation.

Beyond the organizational reforms inspired by class action settlements and structural injunctions, these interactions indirectly contributed to reinforcing a disposition toward defensiveness and recalcitrance within the INS. Because officials did not want to be seen as pushed around by private lawyers, the INS acquired a reputation for "blood-and-guts litigation" and for refusing settlement offers (DeBenedictis 1992). INS leadership took the approach that negotiating with litigators would be tantamount to letting "the [Leonard] Weinglasses of the world" run the agency.[31] Commissioner Alan Nelson initially resisted issuing any legal instructions for implementing the 1986 IRCA legalization program because he was irritated that class actions had already been filed within days of the legislation's passage. He relented only when the agency's attorneys explained that refusing to instruct employees on legally defensible procedures would make the INS more rather than less vulnerable in the inevitable litigation onslaught.[32] Similarly, faced with repeated challenges to its asylum procedures, the agency's response was to retreat into its bunker and resist proposing final asylum regulations to implement the 1980 Refugee Act (Beyer 1992, 463).

For their part, the agency's attorneys adopted the position that the INS needed to strengthen its legal defenses and implement a military discipline within its legal team if it wanted to fend off litigation attacks. One General Counsel described his effort to "provide a definite chain of command" and designate an area of legal responsibility and accountability among the agency's lawyers, declaring that "[the] goal is to develop this office into a first-rate professional law firm that gives our client, the people of this nation, the highest quality representation."[33] Other agency officials took similar efforts when legal activism exposed the agency to negative publicity, sending a memorandum to government attorneys with the instructions that "[i]f the Commissioner and the General Counsel are likely to read about the case in the newspapers … then they should be informed as early in the process as possible."[34] Government attorneys pushed the INS policy-making process toward a greater concern with litigation defense, and in several instances policy was hastily changed as part of the agency's strategy to have courts dismiss ongoing litigation.[35] As legal scholar Margaret Taylor points out, the agency's impulse to hastily formulate a litigation strategy had the effect of locking officials into policy positions before they had time to think them through, thereby heightening the adversary nature of a policy dispute and giving policy deliberations a court-centered focus (Taylor 2002, 311). Dialogue in these situations shifted to what was defensible in court.

As part of this enactment of adversarial legalism, defenders of immigrants were depicted as conspirators aiming to undermine rational governance. In May 1987, the agency sent covert observers to attend the discussion of litigation strategies sponsored by immigrant rights advocates at the National Lawyers Guild's annual conference.[36] The aim of doing so was to prepare for, and possibly preempt, challenges to the implementation of the legalization program, so that the agency would not be as vulnerable as it had been a few years earlier when faced with class actions on behalf of Haitian asylum seekers. In the eyes of the agency, groups such as the New York Civil Liberties Union, the National Lawyers Guild, the Washington Lawyers Committee, and the

American Civil Liberties Union (ACLU) were conspiring in assembling yet another "coordinated and consolidated attack" designed to undermine administrative functioning. Agency leaders attributed conspiratorial qualities to relatively routine lawyering techniques, writing that, "A network of expert witnesses is being assembled and ... [advocates will] build a paper trail of complexity and ingenuity."[37]

On occasion, the INS did opt for a more accommodationist response. For instance, in response to class action litigation targeting the IRCA legalization program, the agency liberalized its interpretation of the statute's "continuously physically present" requirement for legalization.[38] The agency had already been considering liberalizing its interpretation for several months, but the class action filing forced its hand. However, accommodationist moves like this were more the exception than the rule. The agency's typical response to class action lawsuits challenging the implementation of the IRCA legalization program was a stubborn insistence that district courts did not have jurisdiction to hear these claims. Class action litigation had set up a two-player game in which the habitual response of the agency to litigation consisted of defensiveness and a resort to jurisdictionally based legal arguments.

In 1989, a new INS commissioner who arrived with a more conciliatory approach agreed to settle a number of unresolved class action lawsuits. The agency had been particularly embarrassed by an injunction issued in the *Mendez* class action lawsuit, in which the judge inveighed against the incompetence of asylum officers and required that their training sessions be video recorded and submitted to the court (Beyer 1992). Moreover, a massive discovery effort in the *ABC* class action had turned up a "smoking gun." A video-recorded training session showed an INS supervisor making racially tinged disparaging remarks about Salvadoran asylum seekers. The agency entered into settlement discussions in the *ABC* lawsuit with a desire to bring to a close a fraught decade for the U.S. asylum system and allow its newly revamped Asylum Office to make a fresh start. In January 1991, only a few months after new regulations for the Asylum Office were issued, a settlement agreement in the *ABC* case committed the government to rehearing the asylum claims of all Salvadoran and Guatemalan applicants (see Figure 2). To the agency's chagrin, legal activists celebrated the settlement as a "stunning victory" (Blum 1991, 355).[39]

In the immediate aftermath of the *ABC* settlement, the INS agreed to settle a number of other immigration-related class action lawsuits. The *Flores* settlement in 1991 committed the agency to revising its juvenile detention practices. Later that same year, the INS agreed to a modification of the *Orantes* injunction after legal activists had returned to court seeking additional orders and

FIGURE 2. The *ABC v. Thornburgh* litigation team celebrates their settlement agreement outside the U.S. District Court for the Northern District of California in January 1991. From left: Marc Van der Hout, Lucas Guttentag, Ellen Yaroshefsky, Carolyn Patty Blum, Debbie Smith, Jim Garrett, and Lori Schechter. In the background are two Salvadoran men holding a banner for CRECE-CARECEN, the organizations of Central American refugees and Central American refugee centers. Photo courtesy of Carolyn Patty Blum.

remedies that would ensure access to counsel in the context of a massive new INS detention program in South Texas. The following year, after the Supreme Court rejected its argument that class action challenges to the 1986 IRCA legalization lacked jurisdiction, the INS agreed to settle the suit brought against its administration of the agricultural worker legalization program. Also in 1992, the government formalized its standards for the certification of interpreters in immigration courts, thereby bringing closure to the *El Rescate* lawsuit. The agency's willingness to settle even extended to a long-standing class action lawsuit that traced its origins to the 1978 Sbicca factory raid, producing a settlement in which the INS committed – for a period of thirty months – to provide a "Miranda-like warning" to all noncitizens taken into custody by immigration enforcement officers.[40]

However, the mood soon soured as it became clear that settlements were perceived by legal activists as victories and that they provided a wedge for advocates to involve themselves heavily in agency policy determinations. The INS felt it had made settlements that were "even-handed and fair to everyone," and the General Counsel at the time expressed irritation with immigrant rights advocates who, "believe it is part of their job to [announce] they 'won' in the settlement" (DeBenedictis 1992). Another General Counsel during this period argued that gestures at cooperativeness simply left internal procedures exposed to direction by outsiders with little concern for bureaucracy's organizational maintenance imperatives, writing that, "Ambitious interlocutory orders entered in the course of class action proceedings . . . have brought a halt to large chunks of INS enforcement, even though, in the end, perhaps only a minority of the class would wind up proving that they had actually been harmed by the challenged practice or were among those entitled to the ultimate relief in the case" (Martin 2002, 321). In particular, class action litigation concerning the timeliness of work permits for asylum seekers, while crucial in propelling reforms within the asylum system, placed the newly established Asylum Office in a "hole that got deeper and deeper" and from which it could not extricate itself (Beyer 2000). The implementation of the *ABC* settlement was overwhelming for the agency, but it paled in comparison to the obligations with which they were saddled as a result of class actions challenging INS policies in the legalization program enacted in 1986. These lawsuits, which the agency saw as encouraging spurious filings, created temporary immigration benefits for "an indeterminate population" and forced the agency to direct resources to receiving and processing applications (Martin 2002, 321).

In other words, although there have been important differences in how administrative authorities in Republican and Democratic administrations interact with practitioners of immigration reform litigation, a number of common themes emerge. One key element in administrative litigation narratives is the dislocating effects of immigration centered legal activism. The *ABC* settlement produced a "tidal wave" that brought asylum adjudication to "the verge of complete collapse" (Beyer 1992, 483). As more than one government official stated in an interview, class actions may lead to important changes, but they are also responsible for "gumming up the whole works." Another central theme is the agentive powers, and hubris, associated with some class action litigators. When asked about the ways that class actions had propelled regulatory developments during the 1980s and 1990s, administrators acknowledged that some of those cases had propelled change but expressed sarcasm about the sizable egos of certain litigators.[41] In the words of one longtime government attorney, these veteran immigrant rights litigators are "people who have made a living out of litigating against the government; when an agency acts, you can always find someone who said a dumb thing with 10,000 employees and sometimes it's easier than finding class members."[42] According to this view, the legal system gives individual practitioners of immigrant rights legal activism the tools to take advantage of the government.

In the mid-1990s, this administrative narrative of an agency beleaguered by an onslaught of lawyer-driven litigation made its way into the legislative politics of immigration. INS officials, acting directly or through the Department of Justice, actively encouraged legislators to address "the problem with judicial review as it had come to be exercised" (Martin 2002, 322). This was not the first time that the agency had sought to foreclose class action lawsuits. In 1981, the Reagan Justice Department had been instrumental in drafting the "Fair and Expeditious Appeal, Asylum, and Exclusion Act," which would have precluded class actions by tying judicial review to final orders of removal and thus prevented lawyers from "subverting immigration processing."[43] Examples of litigation brought on behalf of Haitian asylum seekers were repeatedly cited in the analysis accompanying the legislation.[44] To the agency's disappointment, Congress failed to act on the bill. However, in 1996 the political context in Congress was different. Legislators were primed to comprehend litigation against the INS through the now well-established and politically popular critique of liberal judicial activism (Tushnet 1997). Moreover, this was a period in which immigration debates were politically linked to legislative discussions of crime, terrorism, and "welfare fraud" (Gimpel and Edwards 1999, 212–16). Legislators were thus more receptive to INS complaints that class action lawsuits threatened to paralyze immigration enforcement efforts.

The multiple laws passed in 1996 demonstrate the extent to which legality in immigration had moved from an ancillary theme to a major debate in the politics of immigration. The Anti-Terrorism and Effective Death Penalty Act (AEDPA) and the IIRIRA are best known for expanding the category of crimes that carry severe consequences for noncitizens seeking asylum, legal permanent resident status, citizenship, or relief from removal. In barring judicial review altogether for most aliens with criminal convictions and blocking judicial review of decisions on most forms of discretionary relief, Congress went far beyond the limitations on certain types of lawsuits with which the agency was most concerned (Martin 2002, 322). However, in addition to punishing migrants with criminal records, IIRIRA also sought to punish their lawyers by severely limiting courts from granting classwide injunctive relief in legal challenges to removal-related operations.

INS officials saw the new statutory restrictions on courts' immigration jurisdiction as a congressional acknowledgment and affirmation of the agency's previously subordinated position. Having been made the target of class action lawsuits for many years, they now compensated for what they saw as legislative liberation from a position of subservience to lawyers. Less than three weeks after the passage of IIRIRA, government attorneys sought the dismissal of four of the five unresolved class actions challenging the implementation of the legalization program.[45] In their enthusiasm, lawyers for the INS also asked a court hearing a class action lawsuit challenging the agency's document fraud policy to reconsider its decision that the immigration service has misled people into giving up their right to hearings, a case not directly related to the deportation process and thus not evidently subject to the new statute's restrictions on class actions. As David Martin, the INS General Counsel put it, the new laws meant that court injunctions would no longer be "breathing down our necks" and the agency could put its past problems behind it.[46] In the weeks following the passage of IIRIRA, attorneys in the Office of Immigration Litigation joked that they would be out of work because the statute had placed so many restrictions on federal court review of immigration matters.[47]

IMMIGRANT RIGHTS LEGAL ACTIVISM AFTER (ATTEMPTED) JURISDICTION STRIPPING

An unexpected effect of this move to restrict judicial involvement in immigration matters, however, was that it galvanized U.S. liberals and energized their support for rights-based activism on behalf of noncitizens. One prominent commentator compared IIRIRA's "attack on access to the courts" to Franklin Roosevelt's court-packing plan.[48] Liberals described the statute's jurisdiction-stripping provisions as "mean and petty" and criticized the Clinton administration for failing to address the issue and the danger it posed as a precedent.[49] Restrictions on judicial review over immigration matters, and the stripping of jurisdiction over class actions in particular, were located by legal commentators within a familiar conservative strategy of diverting attention from substantive policy debate by attacking the courts (Volpp 2000, 466n. 16). In becoming the victim of attack, immigrant rights legal activism reinforced its link to the cherished liberal causes of school busing, abortion, prayer in schools, and death penalty defense. Legal activists could point to the injustice of restrictions on review, arguing that, after losing a series of class action challenges, "the government didn't just move the goal posts: it wanted to tear them down."[50]

As things turned out, all was not in fact lost. Indeed, if the goal of those who wrote the jurisdiction-stripping provisions had been to close off judicial review of immigration matters and put immigrant rights legal activists out of work, then subsequent developments have demonstrated the difficulty of doing so. First of all, the 1996 legislation did not prevent legal activists from monitoring the enforcement of cases that had already generated permanent injunctions or settlement agreements. National legal organizations, in the years since 1996, have continued to work with local groups across the country to monitor enforcement of the permanent injunctions or settlement agreements obtained in the *ABC, Perez-Funez, Orantes-Hernandez, Flores, El Rescate,* and *Mendez* cases. One aspect of this monitoring includes the initiation of remedial lawsuits to address problems related to class members' rights. Although the judge who originally heard the *ABC* case is no longer available to adjudicate them, actions in federal district court to enforce the settlement continue to be brought using a standard complaint form that has been developed for this purpose.[51] Compliance with the *Orantes* injunction, which courts have thus far refused to remove, likewise continues to weigh on the minds of administrative officials. Indeed, the perceived burden of continued judicial supervision under the *Orantes* injunction was part of the motivation for the Department of Homeland Security's unsuccessful efforts in 2006 and 2007 to have Congress further tighten the rules governing immigration-related class certifications (Family 2008, 117). Consideration of these existing class action remedies featured prominently in legal activists' recent formulations of strategies to defend migrants fleeing new forms of violence in Central America.[52]

Although the 1996 legislation did not put them out of work, there was a sense among legal activists in the immediate aftermath of its enactment that a concerted campaign was needed to defend the jurisdiction of courts as a matter of principle. According to the government's interpretation of AEDPA and IIRIRA at the time they were enacted, these statutes stripped the courts of jurisdiction to review agency determinations concerning both removability and eligibility for discretionary relief in individual cases. The fear among legal activists was that this would effectively preclude any judicial review of decisions made by the Board of Immigration Appeals (BIA) and thus leave the executive branch's interpretation of the Immigration and Nationality Act without external oversight. Although this had not been the main focus of prior legal activist campaigns, it seemed important to defend judicial review on principle, lest the 1996 statutes undermine the entire mechanism for bringing immigration matters to the courts. Moreover, the 1996 statutes had restricted the types of immigration-related agency practices outside of a final order of removal that could become the subject of independent action in district courts. This jurisdiction-stripping provision cut even closer to policy-related litigation efforts, threatening to undermine challenges to a range of agency policies and practices that had previously been the focus of legal activist campaigns.

Rather than attempting to address these jurisdiction-stripping provisions through class action lawsuits, which they feared might get bogged down in a procedural morass, legal activists experimented with a new model of systemic challenge. Led by the ACLU Immigrants' Rights Project, they developed a campaign to bring the issue of judicial review in immigration matters before the Supreme Court through the strategic litigation of individual cases. The campaign involved communicating with the immigration bar so that suitable test cases could be identified across the federal judicial circuits. It also entailed collaboration among activists and legal academics to develop arguments that would resonate with the Supreme Court at the level of constitutional principles. In addition, a publicity campaign was organized to generate momentum to encourage the Supreme Court to hear the issue. This test-case strategy was new terrain for immigrant rights legal activism, taking it out of the familiar realm of fact-intensive class action suits. Moreover, it raised the risk that the Supreme Court would deepen the scope of its plenary power jurisprudence by upholding the government's interpretation of the statutes.

After five years of coordinated efforts, however, legal activists could claim victory in their struggle to preserve the principle of judicial review. By a margin of five to four, the Supreme Court in its 2001 decision in *INS v. St. Cyr* preserved judicial recourse for individual noncitizens facing adverse decisions from the BIA. Without overturning the relevant statutory provisions, the decision interpreted them as not depriving federal district courts of jurisdiction to review habeas corpus petitions challenging decisions of the BIA.[53] The government's maximalist interpretation of the 1996 laws and its rush to dismiss all pending cases contributed to undermining its credibility, as it provided a number of sympathetic test cases and created the impression that the BIA's decisions were politically influenced (Taylor 2002). In a second decision issued the same year, *Zadvydas v. Davis*, the Supreme Court affirmed that the 1996 immigration reform statute did not preclude federal courts from reviewing substantial constitutional challenges to agency decisions and actions not related to a final order of removal.[54] Using a test case strategy, these litigation campaigns had isolated the 1996 judicial review provisions as extremist, and the Supreme Court in the summer of 2001 was sufficiently moved by this framing of the facts and issues to assert its willingness to intervene in immigration matters. Immigrant defenders and government attorneys alike were put on notice that the Court might be willing to move away from its traditional deference to administrative determinations in this area. As one government attorney put it, "Courts got it into their head that something was broken with immigration and adjudication. It used to be that we never lost a Supreme Court case, but now they are less deferential."[55] From the perspective of the agency, the decisions in *St. Cyr* and *Zadvydas* were an additional source of vulnerability at a moment when a Justice Department policy aiming to "streamline" procedures for immigration status determination had the unanticipated consequence of pushing unprecedented numbers of individual immigration appeals into the federal court system.[56] Although the 2002–3 streamlining program was relatively short-lived, its long-term and indirect effects continue to be felt. For instance, as the influx of individual appeals into the courts has made splits between the federal circuits more common, litigators with no link to existing advocacy networks have seized on immigration cases as a vehicle for securing a reputationally enhancing audience before the U.S. Supreme Court, a development not entirely welcomed by immigrant rights advocates (Morawetz 2011). In sum, legal activists' strategy of using test cases to challenge jurisdiction stripping has been one of several factors contributing to a broader acceleration of interactions between courts, administrators, and litigants around immigration matters.

However one assesses the results of this juridification of immigration policy administration, the apparent potency of a test case strategy in the immigration context does not mean that legal activists have abandoned familiar litigation models. The 1996 jurisdiction-stripping provisions made it more difficult to litigate class actions but not impossible. Moreover, by 2005, when Congress through the REAL ID Act modified some of IIRIRA's provisions and returned oversight of BIA decisions to the circuit courts, the struggle over jurisdiction stripping appeared to have subsided.[57] Legal activists could therefore return to focusing on the substance of agency practices, and they wasted no time in doing so. For instance, in the fall of 2005, Peter Schey's recently renamed organization, the Center for Human Rights and Constitutional Law, filed a class action lawsuit against the newly created Department of Homeland Security, challenging its failure to implement the U visa provisions of the Victims of Trafficking and Violence Protection Act of 2000, thereby effectively denying immigrant crime victims a path to legal status.[58] In recent years, the ACLU Immigrants' Rights Project likewise has initiated a series of class action lawsuits challenging various aspects of the agency's implementation of legislative provisions mandating increased immigrant detention.[59] As a result of these lawsuits, district court judges have issued injunctive relief requiring the agency to provide a bond hearing to detainees confined for six months or longer and to provide legal representation to mentally disabled individuals in all aspects of their removal and detention proceedings.

While no immigrant rights class action lawsuit has yet been organized to challenge the Obama administration's use of prosecutorial discretion to defer deportation, sympathetic federal district court judges have in the past showed a willingness to allow lawsuits to go forward against the prosecutorial discretion programs of previous administrations.[60] As prosecutorial discretion becomes a growing feature of immigration policy making, advocates welcome executive actions to defer deportation but contest assertions that agency implementation of these actions is entirely immunized from federal court review (Wadhia 2013). From the perspective of the government attorneys who would be on the other side of a class action lawsuit challenging the implementation of these executive actions, the possibility that legal activists "will find a way to get prosecutorial discretion into federal court" does not seem far-fetched even as judicial review in this area remains especially deferential.[61]

As for legislative jurisdiction stripping, certainly the 1996 statutory changes have prevented class actions from challenging issues related to review of individual removal proceedings. Yet current case law continues to allow independent district court action through class action lawsuits so long as litigators can couch the alleged harm as raising a separate type of issue. In the view of government attorneys, the class action mechanism continues to give immigrant rights legal activists the tools to take advantage of the government. As one veteran government attorney put it, "You just go to court and file a complaint and say these regulations suck and I'll tell you why once I get discovery time, and the system permits that."[62] Class action challenges to immigration agency policies and practices thus remain a major feature of U.S. legal landscape.

At the same time, immigration-related class action litigation has recently been increasingly utilized in challenges to immigration policies enacted by the states. In the context of federal gridlock on immigration reform and proactive efforts by groups favoring immigration restrictionism, state initiatives related to immigration control multiplied in the first decade of the twenty-first century. Many of these cases challenging state and local provisions are brought as class actions in federal court. For example, the ACLU and the National Immigration Law Center collaborated with civil rights organizations to file a class action lawsuit challenging a provision of Arizona's State Bill 1070 requiring police to demand immigration papers from those suspected of unauthorized entry.[63] Similarly, class action lawsuits have targeted state-level policies that refuse public benefits to beneficiaries of the executive branch's "deferred deportation" programs.[64] While the move to focus on state lawmaking is an important development that has shifted the dynamics of litigation, it can also be seen as the extension of a familiar model of fact-intensive class action litigation.

In sum, it seems clear that the statutory changes enacted in 1996 have not caused any wholesale abandonment of the immigration class action lawsuit. Attorney Lucas Guttentag, who served as longtime national director of the ACLU Immigrants' Rights Project, points out that class action cases were never the only available strategy for legal activism and that, in at least one area, organized litigation challenging the constitutionality of an immigration statute had been attempted even prior to the 1996 reforms.[65] However, he agrees that class action cases continue to be a staple of immigrant rights litigation, even as the *St. Cyr* case demonstrates the viability of alternative models. In the assessment of veteran litigator Peter Schey, class action work continues to be the most substantial way to impact nationwide policies, and legislative restrictions on jurisdiction have not prevented his litigation model from remaining "pretty much the same since 1980."[66] Legal activists have been able to circumvent many, but not all, of the 1996 jurisdiction-stripping provisions that targeted their activities, according to Dan Kesselbrenner, who has directed the National Lawyers Guild's National Immigration Project for more than two decades.[67] It is now harder to challenge some types of agency policies but there are still plenty of harms to litigate.

CONCLUSION

In January 2004, the U.S. District Court for the Eastern District of California approved a final settlement agreement in the class action lawsuit of *Catholic Social Services v. Ridge*. Judge Lawrence K. Karlton's order approving the settlement includes the following language:

> The Court begins by noting that this matter has been vigorously litigated for over 17 years. There is no suggestion of collusion between the negotiating parties to the detriment of absent class members. The parties have notified the class of their settlement in accordance with the Court's order. Though the precise size of the certified class is unknown, it undoubtedly comprises thousands of class members.[68]

After almost two decades of litigation, the U.S. Department of Justice had settled a nationwide class action challenging INS policies implementing a criteria of eligibility – the "continuously residence" requirement – of the 1986 IRCA legalization program. The total attorneys' fees generated by this agreement, which allowed individuals who were excluded from the IRCA legalization to apply for "late amnesty," were in excess of five million dollars.[69] As part of the settlement, U.S. Citizenship and Immigration Services, an administrative successor to the INS, agreed to adjudicate applications for permanent resident status filed by individuals who could show they had been prevented from benefitting from the legalization program due to the INS's restrictive interpretation of the "continuous residence" provision of the statute. Monitoring of the government's enforcement of the settlement by plaintiffs' attorneys resulted in a subsequent court order, in May 2010, instructing the government to reopen certain applications denied for abandonment. Through cases such as this one, the immigration class action lawsuit has provided an instrument for bringing administrative officials and immigrant rights legal activists into regular contact.

As the discussion in this chapter has shown, the organizing logic of these contacts is heavily fact centered. Immigration class action lawsuits continue to involve massive evidentiary efforts by the parties, who are thus submerged in details of the street-level operations of immigration policy administration. Injunctive orders and settlement agreements maintain this practical orientation by spelling out specific procedures and forms that the government is required to develop and by giving plaintiffs' attorneys a role in monitoring and implementation. At the same time that the legal process concentrates attention on empirical detail, the role of abstract legal principles is relatively diluted in this form of immigration-centered legal intervention. As one government attorney observed, with a touch of cynicism, "The only judge of fairness is that everyone thinks it is fair: if you have a system that looks and seems fair, then all is well."[70] Particularly in the context of settlement agreements, assessment of fairness and rationality is highly subjective and case outcomes often depend on the level of resources devoted to evidence gathering and the extent of the parties' litigation fatigue. Judicial jurisdiction, rather than any principled program of substantive law, has emerged as the primary subject of partisanship.

In the decades since 1996, coordinated litigation that previously centered almost exclusively on class action cases brought before federal district courts has become more diversified. Test-case litigation has become more salient for national legal organizations, as the Supreme Court has signaled an increased willingness to examine agency interpretations of immigration statutes. In addition, as state legislatures have become involved in immigration policy making, this has presented a new terrain for legal activism on behalf of immigrants. At the same time, because of the jurisdiction-stripping provisions of the 1996 legislation, it has become more difficult to challenge some aspects of federal immigration policy making through class action litigation.

Nevertheless, the familiar and well-honed class action lawsuit continues to be fundamental to the enactment of U.S. immigrant rights legal activism. It is this modality of challenging immigration policy making that elicits expressions of resignation from U.S. government officials who face ongoing class action efforts. At the same time, with the prospect of another legislated legalization program around the corner, guaranteeing the power of courts to review actual practices of immigration officials implementing this program has become a rallying cause for immigrant rights legal activists and their supporters.[71] Particularly when contrasted with the avenues developed in the civil law system for contesting immigration policy in court, the continued availability and centrality of class action litigation becomes apparent and is perhaps the most striking difference between the two systems.

6

Performing Legal Activism before the Conseil d'Etat

The massive challenges to informal administrative policies, so central to immigrant rights legal activism in the United States, never became a feature of litigation in France. In fact, American legal activists would feel quite disoriented in the French legal system. Not only is the class action mechanism absent from French public law, but France's legal system also offers few tools for effectively enjoining administrative practices.[1] An additional limitation is that French judges can only review administrative "decisions," a term precisely defined in their jurisprudence, and are usually prohibited from reviewing general administrative practices. Moreover, even if an effective class action mechanism were to become formally available in France, it seems unlikely that French legal activists would embrace the pragmatic approach of American class action litigation. While opinions are mixed, there is hesitation about the power that class actions confer upon lawyers; several of my French interviewees expressed the concern that bringing class actions to France would have negative repercussions because lawyers might take advantage of their clients in their efforts to win cases.[2]

While their American counterparts might wonder how it is possible to use courts to shape immigration policy in such a system, French legal activists do have a particularly direct procedural avenue for policy-oriented litigation. The French system of administrative law allows abstract challenges to provisions of decrees and ministerial circulars that are claimed to constitute an "excess of power" on the grounds that they are taken in violation of higher order rules and basic principles of legality. The Conseil d'Etat, as France's highest administrative jurisdiction, is authorized to hear in first instance these abstract *recours pour excès de pouvoir* (appeal on the grounds of excessive power).

Although immigrant rights legal activism in France is not limited to abstract litigation before the Conseil d'Etat, the *recours pour excès de pouvoir* is undoubtedly the form of activity that has become the most routinized component of legal strategy. It is the repeated skilled utilization of this legal instrument that has established the *Groupe d'Information et de Soutien des Immigrés* (GISTI) as a "habitual appellant" before the Conseil d'Etat (Genevois 2009, 68). For French legal activists and their judicial interlocutors alike, the process of bringing abstract challenges to immigration policies has set the stage for ongoing and quasi-ritualized interactions. I therefore return to the analytical approach applied in Chapter 5, bracketing the substantive rules and outcomes produced in these decisions in order to explore the performative dimension of court-centered interactions that extend across individual cases.

My analysis suggests that regularized recourse to abstract review petitions has fueled a juridification of governance, comparable to the transformations observed by scholars of European politics in the realm of constitutional review. As Alec Stone Sweet and others have demonstrated, the process of engaging in repeated dialogues with assertive constitutional courts makes lawmakers more likely to express party programs and social visions in terms of constitutional norms (Stone 1989, Kenney, Reisinger, and Reitz 1999, Stone Sweet 2000). When they are brought into dialogue with courts, legislative policy makers come to enact politics more juridically, understanding their role in terms of a responsibility to protect rights and to engage in balancing of conflicting rights (Stone 1989, 31). To the extent that their exposure to routinized administrative review has brought immigration agency officials closer to the standards of Weberian legal formalism, we might conceptualize their dialogue with the Conseil d'Etat as propelling a parallel form of juridification in the administrative policy sphere.

However, it is important to point out that this juridification of immigration governance through administrative review operates in a different tenor than the process that has been observed in studies of constitutionally based dialogues. As I show, the juridified mode of administrative governance propelled by the Conseil d'Etat's increasingly regularized engagement with immigration issues has not been synonymous with a heightened concern for immigrant rights on the part of either judges or administrators. Rather than rights, the most apparent administrative response to routinized judicial interventions is a heightened attentiveness on the part of immigration officials to the vocabulary and protocols of formal legality.[3]

In what follows, I first map out the formal rules and structures that organize *recours pour excès de pouvoir* and then document the austere and highly stylized modality that has developed around proceedings challenging immigration policies. As I show, it is a modality of litigation in which both legal activists and administrators are positioned as supplicants before the Conseil d'Etat, and in which the relational authority of the Conseil d'Etat, as oracle of the law, is consequently enhanced. Through qualitative analysis of official ministerial archives, media coverage of administrative responses to court rulings, and interviews with administrative officials, I explore the traces left on France's administrative world by this modality of immigration-centered legal activism. The final sections of the chapter explore how, in recent years, the trend toward increased Franco-European interactions has introduced new elements into the performance of bringing immigration issues to the oracle of the law.

THE SETTING OF INTERACTION

For French immigrant rights legal activists, the *recours pour excès de pouvoir* before the Conseil d'Etat has offered a direct means of challenging national immigration policy making. The discussion in Chapter 3 introduced some elements of the Conseil d'Etat's approach to administrative legality, particularly the concept of *Etat de droit*. However, to better understand the particular organizational setting in which routinized immigrant rights legal activism has developed, we need to briefly map out how these proceedings are organized. Distinct institutional and conceptual features of the French system of administrative justice differentiate it from judicial review in the Anglo-American tradition. I focus in particular on how this system operates in the context of abstract review of regulatory texts, because this is the instrument that had been used most extensively by immigrant rights legal activists. Unlike ordinary legal proceedings, which are heard by administrative tribunals of first instance, petitions challenging the abstract legality of ministerial decrees and circulars are adjudicated directly by the Conseil d'Etat.

In France's civil law tradition, the Conseil d'Etat is a mixed administrative-legal authority that technically is located within the executive branch. It is staffed by a corps of elite civil servants, experts in administration as well as in law, who are selected through an elaborate system of examinations and trained as specialists in principles of proper administrative behavior (Stirn 1991). Originally created by Napoleon, the Conseil d'Etat counsels the government on the drafting of laws and regulations through a formal advisory process (Ducamin 1981). Its members are also routinely seconded to advisory positions within the administration. These advisory functions of the Conseil d'Etat are combined with an adjudicatory authority over all government acts. The *Section du Contentieux* serves as France's highest administrative jurisdiction, reviewing questions of law raised on appeal from lower administrative tribunals and courts of appeal and also hearing abstract challenges to administrative regulations in first instance (Massot, Fouquet, and Stahl 2001).

Although it cannot review the legality of legislation, the Conseil d'Etat is authorized to review all applications of the law, from ministerial decrees to decisions of street-level bureaucrats. Proceedings before the Conseil d'Etat are initiated by a *recours*, or petition for review. If the petition passes an initial screening, the *Section du Contentieux* creates a dossier for the case and then undertakes a long process of evidence gathering and legal analysis that occurs largely out of public view (Brown and Bell 1998, 89–125). Specially assigned reporting judges, rather than the parties, play the dominant role in researching the relevant facts and law, and a brief public audience, at which multiple cases are handled in sequence, offers the only glimpse of how this process of investigation has unfolded. The process of legal analysis likewise operates in a black box. Decisions of the Conseil d'Etat are notable for their austere and formulaic aesthetics, typically taking the form of a single-sentence syllogism that instructs the administration on the legality of its actions but that offers no explanation of the interpretative process by which a given conclusion was reached. Decisions generally do not refer to prior judgments, nor do they explicitly lay out binding rules of general application. Jurisprudential frameworks are instead developed in the conclusions drafted by the court's internal judicial advisor, the *commissaire du gouvernement*,[4] and in the postdecision commentary of legal scholars.

For those seeking to bring immigration issues to the attention of courts in France, petitioning the Conseil d'Etat holds great symbolic importance, but it is also a somewhat daunting task. One of my interviewees, Gérard Sadik, who works in a position of leadership within the Cimade, told me that he had for years been too intimidated to try to litigate before the Conseil d'Etat, seeing its adjudication as an inscrutable process in which "you cannot tell when you will win and when you won't."[5] Nevertheless, it is this unique jurisdiction, without any parallel in the American legal system, that has provided the primary action-setting for immigrant rights legal activism in France. Through the jurisdictional avenue of the *recours pour excès de pouvoir*, the Conseil d'Etat issued its celebrated 1978 *GISTI* decision that, as we saw in Chapter 3, annulled a restrictionist family reunification decree at a critical juncture in French immigration politics. This lesson in the power of the *recours pour excès de pouvoir* was not lost on French legal activists, who came to view action from the Conseil d'Etat as "one of the few means of breaking into the impermeable fortress of administrative governance."[6] Immigrant rights legal activists in France have become adept at organizing abstract challenges before the Conseil d'Etat to contest administrative policies. At a conference organized to mark the thirtieth anniversary of the 1978 *GISTI* decision, GISTI's members counted almost one hundred petitions in first instance that had been brought to the Conseil d'Etat over this period (Lochak 2009, 44). A few of these cases concerned government decisions in which the organization's interests were narrowly at stake, such as refusals to communicate administrative documents or to grant access to airport detention centers. However, the vast majority of the cases concerned abstract challenges, either to government decrees or to ministerial circulars and ordinances.

As discussed in Chapter 4, French immigrant defenders are most comfortable disputing policies at the level of fundamental principles, an aim to which the *recours pour excès de pouvoir* is well suited. Among the basic principles regularly invoked by legal activists are the right to social protection, the right to asylum, and the right for migrants settled in France to work and to enjoy a family life. Because the Conseil d'Etat has no power to review legislation for constitutionality, legal activists in France have had no way of asking it to strike down any of the more than one dozen immigration statutes enacted by France's legislature since 1980.[7] Yet they can use the *recours pour excès de pouvoir* to challenge the legality of the numerous decrees, circulars, and ordinances through which this controversial regime of immigration policy making has been administratively implemented. The landmark 1978 *GISTI* decision serves as a symbolic touchstone and exemplar of what this style of adjudication might achieve.

With these considerations in mind, we can examine in closer detail the concrete practices involved in bringing a *recours pour excès de pouvoir* before the Conseil d'Etat to challenge administrative immigration policies. In the sections that follow, I flesh out the performative and discursive roles assembled during three different stages of proceedings before the Conseil d'Etat: (1) commencement of proceedings, (2) *instruction*, and (3) judgment. As I explain, these proceedings establish a dynamic in which the legal activists are cast in a supporting role and the administrators whose policies are contested appear hardly at all. The role of the parties is thus relatively minimal and it is the Conseil d'Etat that plays the dominant part.

SOLICITING A RESPONSE FROM THE ORACLE

In the United States, one of the most striking features of immigration-centered legal activism over the past forty years has been its capacity to amplify conflict between immigrant rights litigators and immigration administrators. In France, by contrast, the adjudication of legal challenges to immigration policies has had the opposite effect. The formalistic, formulaic, and inquisitorial practices characterizing the Conseil d'Etat's system of administrative review have effectively prevented adversarial legalism and its associated features from making an entrance onto the French political stage. Rather than performing the parts of attacker and defender, advocates and administrators have been cast in more passive roles. In short, the adversarial relationships cultivated by the pattern of organized immigration litigation in the United States have not materialized in France.

This is not to say that French legal activists, like their U.S. counterparts, did not seek to use law to constrain the restrictionist tendencies of immigration policy making. Indeed, immigrant advocates in France continue to view action from the Conseil d'Etat as one of the few means of breaking into the "impermeable fortress" of administrative governance.[8] In their statements to the media and to the general public, legal activists are openly critical of official immigration policies and repeatedly express their solidarity with extreme-left political mobilizations.

Yet, while advocates may talk of storming the citadel of administration, this adversarial tone has been almost entirely absent from the aesthetics of petitioning the Conseil d'Etat. Legal activists are keenly aware that their petitions to the Conseil d'Etat must conform to the formal language and condensed style of argumentation characteristic of French administrative law. As one seasoned practitioner of immigration policy litigation put it, "If you want the Conseil d'Etat to exercise control, the key is to go slowly. Above all, one should not be disagreeable."[9] Another advocate recalled that younger members of the immigrant rights practice community are sometimes frustrated when those with more litigation experience insist on dropping audacious arguments from their petitions on the grounds that they would not be received well by the Conseil d'Etat.[10] As a rule, legal activists' petitions have avoided combative language and have maintained a moderate tone.

We can see this approach in GISTI's petitions to the Conseil d'Etat. To take a concrete example, in February 1985, GISTI submitted a series of petitions asking the Conseil d'Etat to annul the decrees and circulars implementing the immigration law of July 17, 1984. As discussed in Chapter 3, this law had significantly altered the regime for immigrant admissions and residence in France and was initially considered by immigrant supporters as a major victory. However, by the fall of 1984, the Mitterrand government was giving worrying indications of its wavering commitment to the spirit of the law: a circular from the Ministry of Social Affairs had made "proof of proper insertion" a condition for immigrant family reunification. In a letter to the government sent for publication in *Le Monde* newspaper, GISTI denounced the "Le Pen effect," which was producing this governmental "volte-face" to the detriment of immigrants.[11] When the government did eventually enact a series of regulations implementing the new legislation, these regulations made access to permanent residence conditional on family members having entered through the official reunification process. For GISTI, these actions called into question the government's commitment to the "fundamental and inalienable right to immigrant family reunification." Using the *recours pour excès de pouvoir* mechanism, GISTI's petitions to the Conseil d'Etat challenged the legality of these administrative policies.

The first thing to notice is that, while GISTI's public responses to the government's immigration policy making were expressed in a strident and denunciatory tone, this combativeness is nowhere to be seen in the petitions that presented their arguments to the Conseil d'Etat. The text of each of the petitions begins with precisely the same deferential and solicitous formulation:

> The association here before you defers to the censure of the Conseil d'Etat [the pertinent decree or circular] in all the headings which cause it harm. It asks to be notified of the public hearing at which the Conseil d'Etat will examine this complaint.[12]

The remaining text of each of the two- through five-page petitions includes a brief discussion of formal and substantive legal avenues by which the pertinent regulation might be found illegal. The substantive arguments are gestural, encompassed in a few paragraphs. They explain why, according to GISTI, the regulations violate the spirit of the new immigration legislation.

The brevity and deferential tone illustrated by this example are regular features of legal activist petitions and are not coincidental. Jurists have learned to keep their submissions short. As one advocate explained, "ten pages with ten different points is too long since the Conseil d'Etat just needs one good *moyen* [legal avenue] and they will consider the case."[13] Overall, I did not come across any written submissions by the parties to immigrant rights litigation that exceeded a dozen pages, and most were five to six pages in length.

This form of bringing immigration to the law is notable not only for its deferential tone but also for the way in which it has focused debate at the level of abstract principles as opposed to concrete administrative behavior. In a *recours pour excès de pouvoir* challenging the legality of a regulatory text immediately after its enactment and before it has been applied, evidentiary submissions on the part of advocates are minimal if not absent altogether. The document "stockpiling" characteristic of the class action litigation favored by U.S. immigrant rights advocates and wielded as a weapon against administrators has not been a feature of French legal activism. Instead of discovering patterns and practices of street-level administrative illegality, French advocates in their submissions to the Conseil d'Etat have invoked a substantive vision of Republican social incorporation. In line with the hierarchical ontology of French legal formalism, the aim has been to demonstrate that the regulatory texts at issue were not logically in keeping with these basic principles.

Rather than being passionately accusatory in tone, petitions to the Conseil d'Etat are more likely to display a studied courtesy as they politely suggest ways in which administrative policies "misrecognize" fundamental legal principles, such as security of residence and social inclusion. For example, when challenging regulatory texts in the mid-1980s establishing procedures for family reunification for resident foreign workers, GISTI opened its petition to the Conseil d'Etat with an invocation of what it identified as essential principles for the politics of immigration: "guaranteeing foreigners their fundamental rights against the risks of arbitrary practices, and improving the juridical and material situation of foreigners already installed in France or authorized to reside there."[14] The petition requested the Conseil d'Etat to undertake a careful reading of existing law, arguing that doing so would reveal a principle of social inclusion underlying relevant legislative authority and contained in the spirit of *Etat de droit*. It was this principle that, according to GISTI, prevented the government from placing conditions on family reunification.

These fundamental principles of security of residence and social inclusion have also been read by advocates into the legal regime governing asylum. For example, GISTI's 1992 petition challenging the adequacy of asylum procedures argued that the right to work, social protection (including access to medical care), and free legal aid must be guaranteed to all those seeking asylum in France. Taking away the possibility of employment for those seeking asylum was argued to misrecognize the "signal characteristic" of the refugee regime.[15] French legal activists similarly took issue with the fact that asylum seekers applying through the new territorial asylum procedures, unlike those applying through the regular asylum process, were required to pay the cost of their own interpreters.[16] They argued that fragmenting the asylum regime through a diversity of procedures would result in an overall dilution of rights. Here again, lawsuits focused debate at the level of abstract principle rather than highlighting the shortcomings of particular administrative entities.

Thus, it is not particular administrators or particular administrative agencies who have been exposed to criticism when advocates challenged immigration policies. Instead attention focused on the normative content of the texts, which were argued to "misrecognize the law" by placing conditions on the exercise of rights and creating the potential for precariousness of residence. While U.S. immigrant rights litigation has frequently targeted the specific administrative agencies charged with immigration enforcement, exposing individual public officials to scathing criticism, in France it has been the rules that were singled out rather than those who drafted them.

Not only were administrators not the target of judicial activity challenging France's turn to restrictionism, but advocates and their causes also receded out of focus. The petitions submitted by immigration-focused legal activists simply served to summon the judicial protagonist onto the stage. Once a petition had been filed and a response from the administration had been received, performative agency was wholly assumed by the Conseil d'Etat. The process of ascertaining facts and interpreting the meaning of existing norms took place outside the view of the parties. Experts working within the Conseil d'Etat searched out the law, taking the legal avenues identified by the parties only as a point of departure. It was also their prerogative to request evidentiary materials, such as statistics from the relevant minister about the subject in question. In this judicial process, wedded to the assertion of formalistic neutrality, advocates were relegated to a relatively minor role.

The slowness and lack of transparency of the Conseil d'Etat's procedures has had the effect of sapping the urgency from disputes over immigration policy. In a number of cases, by the time the reporting judges completed their investigations into the relevant facts and legal issues and a date for the audience was finally set, several years had passed since the petition was initially submitted. In 1992, the Vice President of the Conseil d'Etat wrote to GISTI acknowledging that it had come to his attention that, "a certain number of your petitions are in process before the Conseil d'Etat for five years and I have asked the Secretary General to find out where we are with these cases. The first request for judgment deposed in May 1987 was judged in May 1992. For the three others, Monsieur Errera, the reporter, has just turned in his report. They will likely be judged before the end of the year."[17] The interesting part about the letter is that not only had the cases been "in process" for many years, but neither the Vice President of the Conseil d'Etat nor those who had submitted the petitions had any sense in the interval of when the dossiers would eventually be made ready for judgment. The signature of the letter, "very cordially," gives some indication of the banality of this inscrutable process that was driven entirely by the Conseil d'Etat rather than by the parties.

Not only did the lengthy period of instruction significantly dilute any oppositional dynamic between the parties, but there was also no opportunity for adversarial relations to be openly manifested once an immigration-related petition was eventually scheduled for a brief public audience before members of the Conseil d'Etat. In the French system of administrative justice, the audience occurs after the instructional evidence-gathering phase is completed. Although they were the only moments when the parties actually met formally in person, the audiences in immigration cases were more similar in appearance to a business meeting than a trial: adjudicators dressed in suits rather than robes and the room had an overall air of courteous ennui while the reporter and *commissaire du gouvernement* read out their reports.[18] Outside of brief clarifying questions posed by the presiding judge, the parties typically had no opportunity to speak, and they did not address each other directly at any point during the audience. There were no opening or closing statements, and the drama was also dampened by the fact that the audience examined not just one but a series of petitions in a single sitting. When the Conseil d'Etat issued its decisions, usually several weeks after the date of the audience, the parties were rarely present.

Moreover, the texts of these decisions were thoroughly imbued with the trappings of formalism's deductive logic. Take as an example the Conseil d'Etat's decision of April 21, 1997, issued in response to GISTI's challenge to a circular applying provisions of the Second Pasqua Law allowing expulsion of foreigners for specific violations of immigration law, criminal law, or a combination of the two. The minister of interior's circular had sought to familiarize prefects with the various infractions contained in the law and had informed them of their authority to issue a removal order to any foreigner whose presence posed a threat to public order. GISTI had made a number of substantive arguments about why the circular exceeded the bounds of the law. The Conseil d'Etat decision responded to these allegations with a single paragraph as follows:

> Whereas by the terms of [the law as amended in 1993], a removal order may be issued "if a foreigner's residence permit has been retracted or not renewed, if this retraction or refusal has been pronounced, by application of existing legislative and regulatory dispositions, by reason of a threat to public order." Whereas the power thereby conferred to the administration cannot be legally exercised with regard to a foreigner except when his residence permit has been retracted or not renewed by application of a statutory or regulatory provision; whereas in declaring [in the circular] that these measures could be taken "for reason of public order" and that the retraction of a residence permit *should not occur* [emphasis mine] "except when the title has been delivered in error, because the foreigner has a record that must lead to the refusal of the permit demanded," the Minister of Interior has not enunciated dispositions that exceed the field of application of [the legislation] and which [GISTI] would be receivable in requesting the annulment.[19]

As the text of this decision illustrates, the immigration decisions of Conseil d'Etat adhere to the cryptic and formulaic style that is a general feature of judicial decision writing in France. The decision at first seems to reject GISTI's claim, but upon close reading it becomes apparent that the Conseil d'Etat interpreted the circular so as to limit its application, by instructing prefects that they could *only* retract a residence permit if it had been issued in error. The last sentence signals that issuing a removal order by virtue of a discretionary administrative decision to the effect that the individual's removal would benefit public order – as a literal reading of the circular would seem to allow – would indeed render the circular illegal. However, from the text of the decision alone, it is impossible to know the legal reasoning by which the Conseil d'Etat deduced this result. The decision simply instructed the administration in a precise and technical tone, eschewing dramatic flourish and rigidly adhering to the image of dispassionate expertise.

Moreover, the legal solutions favored by the Conseil d'Etat offered scant opportunity for accusing these judges of taking policy making into their own hands. While it is certainly possible to find differing assessments of the Conseil d'Etat's immigration doctrine, no one could plausibly classify its mode of argumentation as politically motivated legal instrumentalism. One favored method used by the Conseil d'Etat to align immigration-related administrative policies with legal principles without criticizing administrators involved "emptying a regulatory text of its venom," whereby the terms of the regulatory text were interpreted in a way that was, from the perspective of immigrant rights advocates, "clearly more favorable than a literal reading of the text."[20] This is an established way by which the Conseil d'Etat saves a text, "patching things together," rather than explicitly ruling against the government, and it has been used with notable frequency in immigration cases.

Yet even when overturning immigration regulations, the language of the Conseil d'Etat's decisions tended to be terse and dispassionate, gesturing at formalistic principles of good administration rather than asserting individual rights. For example, the same circular discussed in the preceding text also instructed prefects on how to implement another provision of the Pasqua Law of 1993, which allowed for a foreigner given an order to depart from the territory to be assigned to his residence if he could demonstrate that it was impossible to immediately travel to his own country or to another country. The Conseil d'Etat interpreted and pronounced upon the legality of this section of the ministerial circular with the following paragraph:

> Whereas in permitting prefects to place under house arrest a foreigner with an order to depart the territory who could not "for an objective reason, be placed in immigration retention (for example, by reason of lack of space)" [the circular] has the effect of extending the field of application of the house arrest provision [of the statute]; whereas the association bringing the appeal is, thus, receivable and founded in demanding its annulment.[21]

The regulatory text was thus overturned, limiting the authority of prefectures to place foreigners under house arrest. Yet the phrasing of the decision did not let it appear as if one of the parties had won and the other lost. The policy had simply been brought into alignment with existing legal principles.

One practitioner of immigrant rights litigation referred to the members of the Conseil d'Etat as "good intellectual mechanics" who see themselves as the "bridges of the Republic,"[22] facilitating a well-run state, and thus the general interest of all, by maintaining standards of good administrative practice.

In the United States, immigration reform litigation inspired hostility on the part of administrative officials. No similar dynamic appears to have been at work in France. Immigrant rights decisions of the Conseil d'Etat, when they did get reported in the media, were very rarely characterized by controversy. Indeed, government responses to Conseil d'Etat pronouncements overturning immigration-related regulatory texts offered nothing more than acknowledgment. "The Minister will conform to the decisions of the Conseil d'Etat," was the only response to the Conseil d'Etat decision overturning multiple provisions of a circular on asylum procedures.[23] Similarly, "Justice has spoken the law, and we must take it into account. But the Prime Minister asks his services to study the margin for maneuver permitted by the decision," was the response to a decision on access to social assistance programs.[24] In some instances, the minister announced the same day the decision was issued that he had ordered a new regulation to be drafted "with modifications precisely as directed."[25] French political life has not been immune to polemics against judges, particularly in the context of the activities of left-leaning investigating magistrates (Roussel 2002). Nor have European courts evaded countermobilizations against unpopular decisions (Alter and Meunier-Aitsahalia 1994). However, this targeting of judges for criticism did not reach the institution of the Conseil d'Etat, even in the aftermath of its most far-reaching immigration decisions.

A similar absence of controversy is notable in the way that administrators responded to questions about how immigration reform litigation has affected their work. The themes invoked were drawn from the ideals of the French legal tradition. "The associations are doing their job by raising problems for the government to fix," was how one former director of juridical affairs described immigration reform litigation.[26] He went on to muse dispassionately about whether the decision of the Conseil d'Etat requiring the translation of asylum hearings would be extended to other administrative procedures, saying that it was "an interesting question." Another longtime public official involved in immigration administration offered a similarly intellectualized analysis of the benefits of litigation, declaring that, "Juridical combat to have the hierarchy of norms respected is always necessary" (Moreau 2009, 245). This register of talking about immigration policy litigation invokes a strongly professed belief in the hierarchy of norms and *Etat de droit*. The recuperation of these themes by administrators who must repeatedly defend their policies against legal challenges demonstrates the power of legal formalism in the French system of administrative justice to transform adjudication from a potential opportunity for amplifying political conflict into a ritualized performance of law's authority.

FROM POLICING TO PROCEDURALISM: JURIDIFYING FRENCH ADMINISTRATIVE POLICY MAKING ON IMMIGRATION

At the same time that it has blocked opportunities for confrontation between advocates and administrators, the Conseil d'Etat's engagement with immigration issues had an indirect but important impact on the modality of French administrative governance. As this section will describe, the recurrent adjudication of immigration regulations reinforced the presence of the Conseil d'Etat, along with its distinct mode of reasoning, in an immigration policy-making process that previously operated as a zone of nonlaw. In other words, these routinized judicial-administrative exchanges effected a "juridification of policy making" reminiscent of the shifting mode of legislative policy making previously observed in studies of the Constitutional Council's routinized interactions with the French legislators (Stone 1989, Stone Sweet 2000).

The scope of this shift toward administrative juridification is highlighted when we place French immigration governance in historical context. As discussed in Chapter 2, immigrant labor from France's colonial territories was welcomed prior to the 1970s but foreign migrants were also heavily policed. They could not register their associations and their residence was tightly controlled using an elaborate system of identity checks and police files (Noiriel 2001). This system of control reached unprecedented proportions during the period of the Algerian struggle for independence, when the administration created an entirely separate governance apparatus for Algerian colonial subjects inside France. Nominal efforts were made to win over the loyalty of Algerian migrant workers through the creation of a separate system of social services. In practice, however, these services maintained close links to the police and stood aside as auxiliary police units, operating outside of the normal judicial or police hierarchies, were given free rein to control the North African immigrant population (Viet 1998, 188–9). Operating as a form of *haut police* (high police), immigration governance as late as the 1970s was a zone of exception within France's *Etat de droit*. It was a domain of the administrative state unconstrained by the well-developed standards of legalized accountability that the Conseil d'Etat supervised in other areas of policy making.

The Conseil d'Etat's repeated engagement with immigration policy making, spurred by legal activist efforts, therefore represents a significant development. Regularized judicial supervision, even if it allows little room for public adversarial contention, has shifted the routine procedures of this area of state administration that previously operated in the shadows of legality. Two dimensions to this juridification of immigration-related administrative policy making merit particular consideration.

First, those responsible for formulating the regulatory texts governing immigration enforcement now pay serious attention to juridical pronouncements. Administrators, while preparing drafts of regulatory texts, routinely compile and analyze immigration-related decisions of the Conseil d'Etat as well as the legal commentary that accompanies these decisions. Particularly when adjudication has signaled a divergence between the position of the government and that of the Conseil d'Etat, administrators have invested extra effort in developing legal rationales for government policies. For example, when legal advisors in the Ministry of Social Affairs began the process of drafting regulations to implement the family reunification provisions of the 1984 Immigration Law, they were keenly aware of the need to align their actions with existing jurisprudence on family reunification, explaining to their superiors, "Taking into account the litigation which marked earlier attempts in this domain ... it is necessary to proceed with an in depth juridical analysis which we will undertake incessantly."[27] That they did so is evidenced by the substantial accumulation of these juridical documents within their archival files. On occasion, the government has even brought in additional "seconded" members of the Conseil d'Etat to lead ad hoc advisory groups to redraft administrative texts with an eye toward identifying novel legal avenues that would make policies less likely to incite criticism on jurisprudential grounds while leaving underlying objectives untouched (Weil 2004, 169–71).

A second dimension of juridification is visible in the government's reliance on private advisory opinions from the Conseil d'Etat, which can preempt an issue from becoming the subject of jurisprudential development. Government officials have moved away from the disdain for legality characterizing prior periods of immigration policy making and have acted to maximize the Conseil d'Etat's involvement at earlier stages of the process by seeking out its advice through the formal advisory procedure. For example, administrators preparing texts implementing immigration legislation in the mid-1980s found it "particularly opportune" to present not only a draft decree but also several circulars affecting the situation of migrant families officially to the Conseil d'Etat.[28] Even though only the decree required an advisory opinion, the "significant jurisprudence" concerning family rights signaled that this was an area of policy making on which the Conseil d'Etat had staked a claim.

The government has an incentive to request and follow advisory opinions closely, although they are nonbinding. As a member of the Conseil d'Etat explained it, "The immigration texts are always contested and the government knows this."[29] From the perspective of administrators, the involvement of the Conseil d'Etat in giving advice on decrees is the primary mechanism by which they experience the "very alert, very precise, and very searching" supervision of the administrative judge.[30] But this process is far preferable to having their regulations annulled as a result of litigation, because the advisory opinions are not made public and the administration is free to adapt the advice as it sees fit. It is still possible that a decree or circular will be annulled because different sections of the Conseil d'Etat handle advice and adjudication and because petitions may call adjudicators' attention to previously unseen legal avenues. Moreover, the government retains the option to enact immigration policy using legislative means, thereby avoiding the coercive power of administrative review altogether. The important point to make, however, is that immigration adjudication has contributed to routinizing consultation of the Conseil d'Etat and its jurisprudence within the administrative process.

Over the past four decades, the territory on which the Conseil d'Etat has asserted its involvement through jurisprudential development has grown to include almost all areas of immigration policy making. It has developed an entirely new jurisprudence on extradition, which previously was considered a political matter. It has also declared itself capable of adjudicating the meaning of international accords governing migration, a prerogative that previously belonged exclusively to the Minister of Foreign Affairs. Indeed, some commentators suggest that immigration issues have provided one of the avenues by which the Conseil d'Etat has maintained its normative relevance when faced with juridical competition from European jurisdictions (Lochak 1993, Abdelgawad and Weber 2008).

Yet, while its immigration jurisprudence has been an asset for the Conseil d'Etat in its struggle to remain influential relative to other jurisdictions, it has not radically shifted the substance of French immigration policies. In principle, a jurisprudence that enunciates fundamental rights for noncitizens may constrain the policy options available to public officials. The Conseil d'Etat's 1978 ruling that noncitizens have a right to a normal family life has certainly exerted a strong and continuing influence over policies concerning family reunification (although it technically does not bind legislative lawmaking). In addition, there is some evidence that the jurisprudence of the Conseil d'Etat has on occasion influenced policy-making debates within the administration, by equipping administrative critics of restrictionism with arguments to counter the positions of their enforcement-minded colleagues (Weil 2004, 176–87,

Bonjour 2014). However, in other instances, the addition of legality has served a primarily cosmetic purpose, enhancing the opportunities for administrative lawyers within the bureaucracy to invent creative ways to justify restrictionist government policies. Internal administrative correspondence has on occasion celebrated "ingenious" juridical rationales allowing policies to survive the Conseil d'Etat's scrutiny.[31] Moreover, even when policies are struck down by the Conseil d'Etat, the judicial pronouncements generally have little to say about the content of immigration policy. As we have seen, the Conseil d'Etat's immigration decisions often invoke general principles of administrative legality without any explicit discussion immigrant rights.

Indeed, the Conseil d'Etat's immigration jurisprudence is a source of disappointment to immigrant rights advocates. After more than thirty years of persistent litigation, French legal activists lament that they have been unable to convince the Conseil d'Etat to adopt their vision of republican inclusion, which holds that long-term resident foreigners should be entitled to the same legal rights as citizens (Alaux 2009, Lochak 2009). Like other defenders of immigrant rights, legal activists are dismayed by the rightward shift in French immigration politics, influenced by the rise of the far-right and its adoption of restrictionist themes since the early 1980s. In the assessment of one veteran litigator, "the cause of legality advances" even if the decisions are not always favorable to the cause of immigrants.[32] In recent years, advocates have organized protests at the doorstep of the Conseil d'Etat to express their frustration with official proceedings that withhold both formal and emotional satisfaction from immigrant defense efforts (see Figure 3).

Thus the initial observation that litigation has not made immigrant rights legal activists more politically visible does not tell the whole story. The inscrutable and austere decisions produced by the *recours pour excès de pouvoir* are part of a broader dynamic in which both legal activists and administrative officials are placed in postures of deference toward the Conseil d'Etat as enunciator of law.

EUROPEAN PRESSURES FOR CHANGE

While its formal and austere register remains the distinguishing feature of France's judge-centered engagement with immigrant rights, it would not be accurate to suggest that administrative legality in France is static or immune to external influence. Indeed, at the same time that the Conseil d'Etat was expanding the scope of its influence and relevance within the administration through its engagement with immigration matters, it faced increasing difficulty in maintaining its normative preeminence in other areas. Particularly in regard to administrative decisions concerning economic competition and access of

FIGURE 3. This rare (and imperfect) photograph shows members of GISTI and the Ligue des Droits de l'Homme at their protest in December 2010 outside the Palais Royal in Paris, following a *référé* decision in which the Conseil d'Etat – to their disappointment – upheld a practice on the part of some French prefects of housing asylum applicants in tents due to the temporary unavailability of other forms of public accommodation (CE réf. 19 novembre 2010, *Panokheel*, n°344286, Recueil Lebon). Photo courtesy of Serge Slama.

foreign firms to French markets, the Conseil d'Etat's traditional manner of oversight has faced a serious challenge from the forces of Europeanization. In recent years, there is evidence that these dynamics of Europeanization are gradually exerting an influence within the traditional French system of public law adjudication, including the proceedings governing the *recours pour excès de pouvoir*. For this reason, it is worthwhile briefly exploring the sources and nature of this change.

It was not until the 1980s that the French system of public law first seriously encountered European pressures for change. Until this point, the Conseil d'Etat had comfortably relied on a doctrinal solution that allowed it to avoid giving direct effect to international treaties or to the interpretation of these treaties by European courts. Its *loi-écran* doctrine asserted that national law completely and exclusively defined the legal conditions in a given policy area and thus made it unnecessary to apply European law. This doctrinal position

was symptomatic of a general French hostility to control by supranational jurisdictions, which extended both to the European Court of Justice (ECJ) and to
the European Court of Human Rights (ECHR). Although France had belat-
edly ratified the European Convention on Human Rights in 1974, the government at the time considered this to be a "superfluous" step, and asserted that
national laws adequately guaranteed the rights of individuals (Abdelgawad and
Weber 2008). As an elite corps concentrated in Paris and operating in close
proximity to the administration, the members of the Conseil d'Etat were institutionally disposed to this Gaullist tradition of defending French sovereignty
(Plötner 1998, 60).

As the political tide turned in favor of European integration, however, the
Conseil d'Etat found itself increasingly isolated by its rigidly nationalist position. As early as 1975, its counterpart at the head of France's ordinary judiciary, the Cour de Cassation, had expressed its willingness to give full direct
effect to international treaties (Lasser 2009, 61–2). By the 1980s, the supreme
courts in two of France's major partners, Germany and Italy, had likewise
adopted more Europeanist positions regarding the direct effects and supremacy of the ECJ's jurisprudence. Moreover, in the mid-1980s the Mitterrand
government abandoned France's long-standing protectionist approach toward
Europe and embraced the push for a Common Market. After France was
twice condemned by the ECJ for violating European Community directives
(in cases concerning administrative decisions whose legality had been upheld
by the Conseil d'Etat), the Mitterrand government demonstrated its commitment to Europeanization by removing the Conseil d'Etat's jurisdiction over
competition lawsuits brought by foreign firms (Plötner 1998, 66). At the same
time, the Mitterrand government also opened the door for French litigants to
bring individual appeals to the ECHR, and in 1986 the Strasbourg Court duly
rendered its first judgment against France.

In the face of accelerating Europeanization, the Conseil d'Etat at the end
of the 1980s switched to a more proactive strategy. A new generation of judges,
some of whom had experience in European institutions, pushed their colleagues to adopt a pragmatic stance toward European engagement. As one of
them would later recall, "It wasn't so much that we were enthusiastically taking up the European cause ... rather that we had worked out that Community
law existed and that there was no good reason for the Conseil d'Etat to be on
the outside" (Mangenot 2005, 91). In its 1989 *Nicolo* decision, the Conseil
d'Etat abandoned the *loi-écran* doctrine and announced that the constitution
contained an implicit authorization for judges to give direct effect to international treaties and to do so even when national law called for a different
result.[33] In doing so, it asserted its willingness to engage with other high courts,

at both the national and European level, in the collective development of juridical principles and standards carried out in the common language of fundamental rights. The Conseil d'Etat sought to hold its own in what Mitchel Lasser pithily terms the frantic and disorganized "legal arms race" unleashed by these Franco-European judicial interactions (Lasser 2009, 301).[34]

Given their wide-ranging importance, it should come as no surprise that, beginning in the 1990s, these developments gradually had an impact on French immigration jurisprudence. With the door now open to arguments framed in terms of the ECHR's fundamental rights jurisprudence, cases filed by individual foreigners seeking to avoid expulsion measures increasingly found their way to the Strasbourg Court.[35] Although the Conseil d'Etat attempted to forestall European judicial intervention by asserting its own interpretations of European human rights law, it was overruled by the ECHR in the 1992 *Beldjoudi* decision.[36] Contrary to the Conseil d'Etat's analysis, the Strasbourg Court determined that the expulsion measure against a longtime permanent resident whose parents had been Algerian colonial subjects was in fact a violation of Article 8 of the European Convention on Human Rights, concerning the right to respect for private and family life. Less than three years after the *Nicolo* decision, Franco-European judicial engagement had resulted in the integration of a more protective reading of foreigners' right to family life. The *Beldjoudi* decision was an early sign that the context for immigrant rights legal activism was shifting. As discussed in the next section, the relevance for legal activists of European law and European legal institutions has expanded and deepened during the first decades of the twenty-first century.

Before turning to examine the impact of these deepening Franco-European judicial interactions on legal activism, it is important to make one final point. From the perspective of the Conseil d'Etat, although its members would undoubtedly prefer to handle immigration matters without European courts forcing their hand, they see their most urgent task at the current moment as preserving the separate system of administrative law that is distinct to France. In their view, the Conseil d'Etat's distinct procedures allow the administrative judge to "make the symbolic link between the citizens and the state."[37] They recognize that they will need to compromise in order to maintain French administrative law's signal features, so that "even if the French system has changed, we will still have a French system." Among the features considered to be essential to the French system is the Conseil d'Etat's unique process of decision making, including the involvement of the *commissaire du gouvernement* in the court's nonpublic deliberations, which in recent years has come under threat from European jurisdictions (Lasser 2009, 105–15). Just as concerted use of the *recours pour excès de pouvoir* resulted in the extension of the Conseil d'Etat's influence within the administration, so too immigrant rights legal activism potentially provides a resource to French judges in the expanded game of Franco-European judicial interaction. Senior judges recognize that immigrant rights legal activism has been at the origin of an elevated number of decisions that created jurisprudence. As they see it, not only does this suggest that immigrant rights litigation has been of consequence, but it also usefully illustrates the efficacy of the administrative jurisdiction. In the words of Judge Bruno Genevois, "The *recours pour excès de pouvoir* is a good instrument for collective action *à la française*" (Genevois 2009, 74). Judge Bernard Stirn, who succeeded Genevois as president of the Conseil d'Etat's *Section des Contentieux*, similarly expresses pride in the court's advanced jurisprudence in immigration matters and mentions associations defending the cause of immigrants alongside associations active on behalf of the environment as regular litigants before the Conseil d'Etat.[38] In other words, legal activism in the area of immigration policy is useful to the Conseil d'Etat as it seeks to expand its institutional influence. From the perspective of the Conseil d'Etat, legal activists' use of the *recours pour excès de pouvoir* offers an opportunity for French administrative law to take jurisprudential initiative and thereby regain control over jurisprudential developments propelled by assertive judicial interventions at the European level. There is also a sense that the regular appearance of social justice associations before the Conseil d'Etat might usefully demonstrate the effectiveness of the French system of administrative law, particularly in the matter of upholding basic standards of procedural fairness, a question with which the ECHR has recently been concerned.[39] In this respect, the Conseil d'Etat's willingness to leverage the claims of civil society associations for its own doctrinal and institutional purposes represents an instantiation of the type of strategic behavior observed in the literature on comparative judicial politics.[40] To the extent that they feature in judicial calculations, legal activists are seen as helpful junior partners in the Conseil d'Etat's current project to maintain the French system of administrative law.

LEGAL ACTIVISM TURNS TO EUROPE: CONTINUITY AND CHANGE

If the Conseil d'Etat has been primarily concerned with preserving its status amidst the contemporary intrajudicial palace wars, Franco-European judicial interactions are nevertheless gradually altering the context of immigrant rights adjudication. Immigrant rights legal activists are becoming more familiar with European law and European courts, in keeping with a more general expansion of civil society engagement with European institutions on matters related to immigration politics (Guiraudon 2011). European courts are at the center of a deepening body of immigrant rights jurisprudence, and there is a sense among French immigrant rights legal activists that the frequency of their engagements with European law has significantly accelerated in the past decade. While it is still too soon to see the full potential of these shifting dynamics, at the current moment they are occurring along at least four distinct dimensions.

First, the ratcheting up of fundamental rights engendered through Franco-European judicial interaction offers those organizing *recours pour excès de pouvoir* a larger toolkit of devices for formulating legal claims. Although legal activists in the 1970s and 1980s had been aware of the potential of the European Convention on Human Rights for defending noncitizens, they were discouraged from developing these arguments by what they saw as the Conseil d'Etat's "total scorn" for European law.[41] However, after the *Nicolo* decision in 1989 opened the door to arguments based on supranational law, legal activists could use this extended legal repertoire interchangeably with arguments based on fundamental principles deduced from national legal sources. They were pushed to explore these possibilities as quickly as possible because legislative changes initiated by Minister of Interior Charles Pasqua in 1993 called into question many of the core immigration policy principles that they had worked for several decades to secure within French law. Because the Conseil d'Etat does not have the power to review enacted legislation, legal activists had no mechanism for challenging the legality of these statutes. In this context, international conventions presented the "sole rampart" against strongly restrictionist changes in immigration policy making, such as the government's move to prevent third-country nationals from accessing public assistance programs to which French citizens and European Union (EU) nationals had access.[42] Through the *recours pour excès de pouvoir* mechanism, GISTI was successful in challenging the legality of a circular implementing the 1993 Pasqua legislation that tacitly dissuaded administrators from providing state-funded disability assistance to migrants from states with whom the European Community had signed cooperation accords guaranteeing reciprocal access to such programs.[43] As the restrictionist trend continued in the first decade of the twenty-first century, propelled by Minister of Interior and then President Nicolas Sarkozy, GISTI repeatedly incorporated arguments based on the jurisprudence of the ECHR into its *recours pour excès de pouvoir* challenging – with mixed success – the regulations implementing these laws.

Second, in addition to augmenting the plausible arguments that might be presented to the Conseil d'Etat, the increased willingness of French judges to refer EU legal questions to the ECJ for an advisory opinion means that proceedings before the Conseil d'Etat can bring legal activists directly before the

Luxembourg Court. Of course, as a court against which there is no appeal, the Conseil d'Etat is formally obligated to refer cases raising issues of European law to the ECJ. However, as a practical matter, and as every sophisticated player in these matters fully understands, the ECJ's elaboration of a set of conditions under which no referral is necessary means that even national jurisdictions against which there is no appeal, such as the Conseil d'Etat, retain some control over referral decisions.[44] Thus, despite the increasing influence of European legal norms, the Conseil d'Etat operates as a gatekeeper for legal activists seeking to access the ECJ. Nonetheless, should the Conseil d'Etat choose to seek a legal opinion from the ECJ on a point of EU law, then legal activists have the opportunity to go to Luxembourg to plead their case. In September 2012, GISTI and the Cimade for the first time saw their names attached to a decision that had arrived at the Luxembourg Court through this referral mechanism. The ECJ vindicated their arguments that a policy that restricted the eligibility of some asylum seekers for temporary public assistance was incompatible with a 2003 EU Council Directive laying down minimum standards for the reception of asylum seekers.[45] As the EU continues to take an active hand in setting minimal standards for member state immigration and asylum policies, this referral mechanism is likely to engage the ECJ's involvement in *recours pour excès de pouvoir* with increasing frequency.

Third, French legal activists have begun to explore the possibilities for applying their experience with abstract review proceedings to initiate such cases directly before European institutions. Starting in 2003, GISTI has collaborated with international partners in the newly established "Migreurop" network to lobby the European Parliament to initiate a challenge before the ECJ to the legality of the EU Council Directive on the right to family reunification, which advocates view as insufficiently protective (Rodier 2009). When the European Parliament did eventually bring the case, GISTI supplied a memoire containing legal arguments alleging the directive was enacted through improper procedures as well as substantive arguments based on the EU's commitment to fundamental rights as expressed implicitly in ECJ case law. In other words, they applied the model of the *recours pour excès de pouvoir*, thereby extending French public law's unique hybrid of administrative legality and fundamental principles to the European level. Although the ECJ dismissed the substantive arguments, it admitted the procedural validity of a proceeding initiated by the European Parliament. GISTI's legal activists were encouraged by the decision, seeing it as "a defeat that opens paths for the future" (Rodier 2009, 170). Nevertheless, they recognize that organizing direct appeals before the ECJ is "a path filled with obstacles," as illustrated by a subsequent unsuccessful effort to compel the European Commission to bring a case before the European Court of First Instance concerning the Italian government's expulsions of irregular migrants from Lampedusa to Libya.

Finally, a new generation of French legal activists increasingly feels that abstract review, of the type exemplified by the *recours pour excès de pouvoir*, may no longer be the single best way to effect policy change. All things equal, appeals to the ECHR of cases concerning individual noncitizens are relatively more likely to compel policy change within the administration than successfully appealing these cases to the Conseil d'Etat. Moreover, at the level of symbolism, there is the additional embarrassment to the French government of being condemned in an international forum whose procedures are much more public. A new generation of legal activists is eager to use the ECHR's emergency procedures to bring cases directly to the Strasbourg Court. In a 1996 decision in a case brought by immigrant advocates, the ECHR demonstrated a willingness to hear individual cases that raised legal questions about administrative policies restricting access to the asylum system for migrants detained at points of entry, a decision more important as a harbinger of change than for its outcome, as the European Court's decision came after the government had already tweaked its policies concerning retention at points of entry.[46] Subsequent cases have propelled further substantive policy changes by compelling the French government to guarantee suspensive appeal procedures even when asylum applicants are detained at points of entry and fast-tracked for removal.[47]

These victories have led some within the new generation of French legal activists to declare that European judges have replaced the Conseil d'Etat as the ultimate judicial forum for compelling policy change. In the words of attorney Christophe Pouly to readers of GISTI's newsletter, "Even if, at the political level, Europe is constructing a fortress against migrants, its judges nevertheless constitute a rampart against the insidious wearing-down of foreigners' rights by the legislatures of member states."[48] Another younger jurist with substantial experience organizing cases before the Conseil d'Etat, Serge Slama, insists that it is now more interesting to bring cases in European courts, where some of the individual judges are both approachable and sympathetic to immigrant rights advocates.[49] Other members of the younger generation of French legal activists are less sanguine. Jean-Eric Malabre, who previously directed *L'Association Nationale d'Assistance aux Frontières pour les Etrangers* and who also has substantial experience litigating before French and European jurisdictions, notes that it has become more difficult in recent years to win cases before the ECHR. In his view, it is the ECHR's substantive norms that are seen as most useful: "The ECHR is like a nuclear weapon; it is much stronger if you don't use it, but you always put European Convention arguments into the Conseil d'Etat petitions."[50]

The dynamics of French immigrant rights legal activism are clearly in a state of flux. The opening of the French legal system to Europe has created new possibilities for legal activism, both substantively and procedurally. Yet it is not clear whether these new options will fundamentally alter the French way of bringing immigration issues to the courts or rather, as in the case of attempts to organize abstract challenges before European jurisdictions, allow an expansion of the French approach at the European level. Even those who are most critical of the Conseil d'Etat for its hesitancy to apply its fundamental rights jurisprudence against the recent restrictionist turn in immigration policy making nevertheless continue to draw upon the *recours pour excès de pouvoir* to contest newly enacted regulations. The form of these proceedings has undergone some revisions, most notably through the introduction of the *référé* procedure and various constitutional and supranational referral procedures. Yet the nonpublic nature and high formality of proceedings before the Conseil d'Etat remains substantially unchanged and appears unlikely to undergo radical revision.[51] At this point, the most that can be said is that there are signs that new forms of legal activism are being explored, but that the *recours pour excès de pouvoir* is unlikely to be fundamentally altered or abandoned anytime soon.

CONCLUSION

Throughout France's first three postwar decades, immigration policy making operated as a zone where the principles and values of *Etat de droit* were much less visible than in other domains of policy making. Starting in the late 1970s, however, routinized judicial engagement with immigration issues – propelled by sustained legal activist efforts – has brought immigration administrators into regularized dialogue with the Conseil d'Etat at multiple points in the policy implementation process. In what we can label a version of court-propelled juridification, the operative language of the Conseil d'Etat, has come to be mirrored in the language and processes by which immigration regulations are formulated by bureaucratic agents. On one level, this has had the effect of making immigration governance a relatively more legalistic – and thus publically acceptable – apparatus for the exercise of state authority. Yet these developments have occurred through engagement with France's distinctly formalistic system of administrative justice. The judicial appropriation of ministerial functions that some have associated with the "rights revolution" (Epp 1998) is noticeably absent from this civil law context.

It is important to emphasize that the civil law's tradition of austere formality does not necessarily mean that the power of law is not at work. In his study of the contribution of the ECJ to the project of European integration, Joseph Weiler points to the importance of formalism as an explanation for the "compliance pull" of that jurisdiction (Weiler 1994). Legal formalism's power, in this analysis, lies in its language of reasoned interpretation, systemic and temporal coherence, and logical deduction, as well as in the appearance of a judicial process resting above politics. National courts, particularly those at the lower levels of the judicial hierarchy, responded to ECJ decisions by willingly cooperating in the administration of European Community law, while the political branches of national governments adopted a relatively deferential posture toward the ECJ and its output, in part due to the performance of a neutral and apolitical judicial process. Regardless of whether legal outputs in reality conformed to formalistic ideals, it was the performance of formalism that contributed to the ECJ's power to impose its terms of discourse on policy making by national governments, who could have easily acted to reduce its powers, curtail its jurisdiction, or control its personnel, but did not do so.

This chapter has highlighted the pull of formalism in the context of the French system of administrative justice. Rather than amplifying adversarialism, repeated interactions between administrators, litigants, and judges enact conflicts over immigration policy in an abstract and dispassionate legal register. Challenges to government policies are played out on a stage that offers no opportunity for confrontation and where those petitioning the court are relegated to a background role. The association of judicial activity with partisanship, so prevalent in immigration litigation in the United States, has not taken place in the French system of administrative review, whose formalistic register is materially and theoretically distanced from policy implementation and where decisions are framed as a correction of administrative legality rather than a victory for activist litigators.

At the same time that formalism has minimized the visibility of litigants, it has nevertheless encouraged administrators to explain, justify, and defend their policies in juridical terms. The highly stylized deductive logic of the Conseil d'Etat's decisions, with their scrupulous adherence to the vocabulary of the hierarchy of norms, has infused the regulatory drafting process with a heightened sensitivity to aesthetic and rhetorical conventions of legal form. From the perspective of immigrant rights advocates, however, this process of juridification has produced disappointing results. They are well aware that the marked shift in the forms and processes through which administrative rule making is enacted has not been accompanied by an equally potent impact at the level of substantive immigration policy making. In the concluding chapter, I examine how those who have devoted their professional careers to the practice of immigrant rights legal activism in the United States and France assess their efforts as they reflect back on four decades of contesting immigration policy in court.

Conclusion: Legal Activism and Its Radiating Effects

Immigration policy making has emerged as one of the most important and contentious areas of contemporary political life. It is an area in which courts have traditionally limited their interventions in the name of deference to sovereign authority. At the same time, irregular migrants are uniquely in need of law's protection because their legal entitlements are very low and their social vulnerability makes the struggle for the enforcement of rights particularly challenging. This tension between territorial sovereignty principles and legal rights defines contemporary immigration governance. What this means for immigration law is that those engaged in efforts to enlist courts in a program of broad policy change face a uniquely daunting task.

This book began by asking what difference law makes in immigration policy making. Contrary to the conventional wisdom that law has little impact on immigration policy matters, the preceding chapters have demonstrated the multiple paths by which activity in court has contributed to reshaping how policy makers approach immigration issues. I make the argument that the power of juridical activity in this domain stems not from its coercive or regulatory authority but rather from the capacity of legal frames, narratives, and performances to construct identities and meanings. Moreover, I suggest that legal activism offers a window for observing law's culturally productive role because it has intentionally reformulated immigration debates as questions of law. By untangling the webs of translations through which legal activists have brought immigration into association with law and by exploring the radiating political effects of this legal meaning-making – the approach advanced in this study – we can more fully appreciate law's constitutive role in immigration policy matters. This concluding chapter first clarifies the key findings of the study before examining their implications for research regarding law and the politics of social reform.

THE MECHANICS OF BRINGING IMMIGRATION
INTO ASSOCIATION WITH LAW

What does it mean to associate an area of policy making with law? A central insight of constructivist sociolegal scholarship is that juridical activity is an important site for assembling and reassembling social reality. The frames, narratives, and performances forged through action in court are *constitutive* to the extent that they do not merely regulate antecedently existing behavior but rather configure the very nature of politics. The present study builds on this insight by distinguishing the specific legal instruments and mechanisms that are at work in concrete engagements with law. By tracing the differing paths for bringing a particular domain of social life – immigration policy making – into association with law, the comparison of the United States and France highlights the distinct epistemic features of liberal legality at work in these efforts to invoke rights on behalf of irregular migrants.

We observed one set of culturally productive legal devices in the rights-oriented jurisprudential regimes formulated by liberal courts in the 1960s and 1970s. In the United States, the vibrant legacy of the Warren Court's civil rights jurisprudence offered a repertoire of instruments for groups to acquire expansive rights protections if they could show that they had faced historical discrimination. By contrast, in France, the repertoire of administrative legality that emerged in the early 1970s placed little emphasis on the characteristics of those claiming rights and instead predicated judicial intervention on a showing of policy makers' autocratic tendencies. By framing immigration matters in terms of these existing sets of categories, immigrant defense efforts in both countries were able to move their claims onto the terrain of formal law, even as these discursive framings took on strikingly different forms in each national setting.

The organizational models of institutionalized legal practice present a second set of devices for bringing immigration into association with law. In the United States, institutionalizing their efforts allowed aspiring legal activists to cement alliances with the support structures that had developed around public interest law. In France, by contrast, the institutionalization of legal activism was a more trial-and-error process. On the one hand, repeated high-profile litigation facilitated the association of immigrant defense efforts with the civil society mobilizations of France's institutional Left. On the other hand, the process of repeatedly petitioning the Conseil d'Etat gradually incorporated immigrant rights legal activism into the orbit of this institution, reinforcing advocates' investment in the language of legal integrity and coherence. In both countries, attachments to locally based mobilizations became more attenuated as claims making shifted toward the terrain of official lawmaking, yet this shift was mediated by nationally distinct norms concerning the political roles of lawyers and legal organizations.

We see a third set of devices at work in the informal protocols that developed around legal activists' semiritualized usage of distinctly American and French procedural avenues for invoking judicial oversight of immigration administration. In the United States, a steady stream of immigration class action lawsuits focused attention on the pathologies of a particular administrative agency and its informal practices, producing a highly adversarial set of interactions between litigators and their administrative counterparts. In France, by contrast, immigrant rights legal activism developed a ritualized reliance on petitioning the Conseil d'Etat to exercise its power of abstract review, a mode of legal interaction notable for its austere and highly formalized register. In both settings, litigators and their administrative counterparts were configured by the roles they enacted in court, although these litigation rituals assumed very different modalities.

It is hard to miss the striking differences between the paths selected in the United States and in France for associating immigration and law. Beyond empirical observation, the comparative optic offers an important reminder for sociolegal scholars, namely that we should not assume what kind of entities, forms of being, or structures of existence are inevitable features of legality. Sociolegal scholars in the United States have made important contributions by identifying "the American way of law" with adversarial legalism (Kagan 2001) or with identity politics (Brigham 1996). Yet examination of how legal activism has operated in France shows that neither adversarialism nor liberal pluralism is an inevitable feature of legality. As we saw in France, contesting immigration policy in court has meant associating immigration issues with a rarefied mode of enunciation concerned with normative coherence and integrity. For the burgeoning sociolegal scholarship on legal mobilization, bringing this distinct modality of law into focus offers a reminder that studying the constitutive power of rights rhetoric is only scratching the surface of this phenomenon. As this study has shown, rights may be invoked through a variety of juridical frames and procedures and the particularities of these forms are worthy of close attention.

Certainly, nationally based comparisons have their limits; it would be incorrect to draw the conclusion that all U.S legal processes are necessarily pluralist in their politics and adversarial in their procedures or that legality in France is always and at all times austere and abstract. Indeed, my analysis has repeatedly emphasized the historically contingent nature of the cultural assemblages constructed through immigration-centered legal activist efforts, and also the fact that the very meaning of immigrant rights legal activism as a professional project is likewise a moving target. As the preceding chapters emphasized, the strategies developed by legal activists were assembled from repertoires of elements available to them at a particular place and at a particular time. In each country, these repertoires contained a mix of long-established elements as well as legal forms of more recent vintage, and substantial creativity was involved in applying them to the immigration policy domain. The argument that I have developed throughout this book is that we need to look at the way that action in court unfolds without any *a priori* assumptions and with sensitivity to all conditions of the case at hand. Sociolegal scholar Mariana Valverde makes a similar point about the importance of concrete analyses when she writes, "Understanding the politics – including the knowledge of politics – of the situated present among which each of us circulates requires a fresh start every time" (Valverde 2003, 229). The comparative optic brings into sharp focus this call for concrete analysis of the arrangement and relationship of different local configurations and the registers among them.

LAW'S RADIATING EFFECTS

The U.S. and French variants of immigrant rights legal activism, despite their different forms, were initially propelled by a common faith in the power of legality to produce policy change with widespread impact. In both countries, the project of contesting immigration policy in court emerged during the 1970s, not only a moment when immigration policy turned to restrictionism but also a moment when narratives of the triumph of rights over politics were ascendant. In the United States, legal liberalism developed a mythical narrative of the *Brown v. Board of Education* litigation, identifying the Supreme Court's holding as proof that rules and remedies achieved through planned litigation offered the principal mechanisms for achieving policy reform. Participants in the rapidly expanding field of public interest litigation in the 1970s felt no reason to doubt that law and lawyers could play a part in building a better society. In the words of women's rights activist Janet Beals, "Everyone assumed that when the Supreme Court made its decision ... that we'd got what we wanted and the battle was over" (cited in Rosenberg 1991, 339). Legal scholar Derek Bell memorably evokes a narrative of biblical salvation when discussing the hopes of civil rights advocates that litigation would bring about fundamental social change (Bell 1987, 70). This narrative of litigation as salvation was less developed in France, where legal activism was a more recent phenomenon, yet many young professionals belonging to France's 1968 generation were seduced by "the notion that the juridical protection of public liberties constituted an essential objective of political action" (Agrikoliansky 2005, 326).

As we saw in Chapter 3, the breakthrough immigrant rights decisions of the late 1970s and early 1980s were understood at the time according to this paradigm of optimism concerning the potential of litigation-propelled policy reform. Immigrant rights litigators in the United States shared the optimism of legal scholars who interpreted their victories as signs of a forthcoming "transformation of immigration law" (Schuck 1984) and who predicted that it was only a matter of time before the plenary power doctrine would be expressly rejected (Motomura 1990). In France, the jubilant tone with which *Groupe d'Information et de Soutien des Immigrés* (GISTI) announced its victories before the Conseil d'Etat reveals a similar optimism on the part of litigators that courts were on the verge of definitively abandoning their self-imposed historical deference to the executive on matters of immigration policy. French legal scholars likewise heralded the landmark 1978 *GISTI* decision as charting a new course for the rights of noncitizens with potentially far-reaching doctrinal consequences (Hamon 1979).

With time, however, this enthusiasm turned to disappointment. At a conference marking the thirtieth anniversary of GISTI's legal activism, veteran litigators lamented that the group's overall record was "mostly negative" and was characterized by "repeated defeats interspersed with victories that encourage perseverance" (Lochak 2009, 63). Members of GISTI's legal network likewise spoke of repeated "stolen victories," instances when judicially enunciated principles that promised to protect the rights of foreigners were given scant attention in subsequent policy-making initiatives or were substantially narrowed by later judicial readings (Ferré 2009, 233–6). Even with the new *référé* procedure, which offers the potential to target informal administrative practices, French legal activists express frustration that they lack the litigation capacity to prompt fundamental changes in practice (Alaux 2009). From this perspective, the project of contesting immigration policy in court seems to have produced only marginal and sporadic changes in policy making.

U.S. immigrant rights advocates express similar disappointment with what they see as the persistently inhumane tendency of legislative policy making on immigration matters over the past two decades. The landmark 1982 *Plyler* decision has not been overturned, despite legislative attempts to do so, but neither has it generated a jurisprudence with far-reaching effects. Scholars have determined it to be *sui generis*, "not so much limited to its facts but possessing weak doctrinal force and little constitutional significance" (Olivas 2012, 92). Cumulative assessments likewise suggest that migrant rights remain "indirect and oblique" (Motomura 2008, 1729), and that the immigration bar's relatively

expanded use of appellate litigation in recent years has as yet produced primarily "highly technical" statutorily based decisions that rarely enunciate broad
rights-protective principles (Law 2010, 226). In this regard, it is notable that
the Supreme Court's 2001 decision in *Zadvydas v. Davis*, which went further
than most in dissecting immigration policy making, nevertheless shied away
from explicit constitutional review and was careful to emphasize that statutory review "must take appropriate account of the greater immigration-related
expertise of the Executive Branch ... and the Nation's need to 'speak in one
voice' in immigration matters."[1] Veteran litigators lament that migrant interdiction policies and expedited removal procedures, both of which have sur-
vived legal challenge, now prevent many recent migrants from having access
to the systemic reforms achieved in earlier litigation.

In short, after more than four decades of efforts to systematically contest
immigration policy in court, legal activists express disappointment that judicial engagement with immigration matters – while numerically voluminous –
remains doctrinally curtailed. For veteran litigators who pioneered the project
of immigrant rights legal activism, the record of the past four decades of efforts
to contest immigration policy in court offers little to sustain any narrative
of litigation-based salvation. They recognize that there are few instances in
which the rules or remedies produced through action in court have placed
insurmountable obstacles in the way of policy makers who are determined to
act. These retrospective assessments are generally similar to the observations
of political scientists who have noted the tendency of immigration policy makers to "contain" their compliance with rights-expansive judicial interventions
through a combination of forum shopping and narrow application (Conant
2002, Guiraudon 2002).

Without contesting these observations about the limited potency of judicial rules and remedies to coerce immigration policy makers into abandoning
restrictionism, this study examines law's engagement with migration through
a different analytical lens. I suggest that we can conceptualize activity in court
not only as a generator of official rules but also as a process of meaning-making.
My contention is that this conceptual shift allows us to explore the relationship between the juridical world and the domain of immigration policy making as a set of dynamic and never fully settled interactions. In this way of
seeing things, activity in court holds the potential to forge collectively held
understandings about what is real. Describing this culturally productive role
of law, Sally Merry writes that courts "provide *performances* in which problems are named and solutions determined" (Merry 1995, 14). Rather than considering legal activity in terms of the potency with which it constrains policy
making, we can instead conceptualize law's power in terms of its ability to

frame issues and stage political interactions. Doing so allows us to chart the effects of these legal constructions as they are taken up by social actors in ways that cannot be predicted in advance. Particularly in the case of high-profile litigation, as John Brigham emphasizes, legally generated constructions enter into the broader political environment and thereby "join with a configuration of defined interests and values operating around institutions, doctrines, and perceptions of what is possible" (Brigham 1987, 208). Law's radiating effects at the level of policy making may be indirect and indeterminate, while nonetheless constitutive of political identities and meanings.

We saw one such radiating effect in the discussion in Chapter 3 of the political mobilizations assembled around early litigation campaigns. As scholars of legal mobilization have demonstrated, legal frames and narratives, particularly when they evoke the language of rights, can have a catalytic effect on social movement activity (McCann 1994, NeJaime 2011). In the immigration policy domain, this catalytic dynamic was especially evident in the early 1980s, a moment when the legislative politics of immigration was in flux in the United States and France. In this political context, the process of high-profile litigation offered receptive audiences something around which to mobilize, crystallizing a political agenda for those seeking to challenge the materialist frame that dominated immigration policy making. In the United States, legal interventions on behalf of Haitian asylum seekers during this period, even as they ultimately failed to develop a new constitutionally based precedent, solidified the epistemic foundations of a civil rights–based immigration reform coalition, modeled on the Leadership Conference on Civil Rights, which left a lasting imprint on legislative policy making during the 1980s and beyond. In France, the very fact of challenging immigration regulations before France's highest administrative jurisdiction reconfigured immigration control measures from individualized penalties into political acts that could be contested, energizing local protest activities that brought together foreign migrants of diverse backgrounds. Although these decisions asserted no constraining authority over legislative policy making, they reinforced a narrative of postwar immigrant workers as permanent members of the French polity, a paradigm that strongly colored the French Left's approach to immigration legislation in succeeding years.

At the same time that it contributed to constructing the legislative politics of immigration, the process of contesting policies in court also changed how immigrant rights litigators viewed their own work. In the United States, as immigrant rights legal activism became a branch of public interest law, litigators who had started their careers in close contact with local protest movements became more specialized in focus and more reliant on dialogue and

engagement with state institutions. In France, this process of institutionalization and specialization was less dramatic, yet the effects of persistent juridical
engagement are nonetheless visible in GISTI's relative shift away from contact with locally based immigrant movements and in the group's more regular
association with legal elites. The concept of a "legal complex" (Karpik and
Halliday 2011) extending inside and outside of the state is helpful for understanding these developments. In both countries, judicial recognition has
propelled immigrant rights litigators toward the sphere of formal law while
providing members of each country's legal complex with a cultural resource
to claim expertise in public affairs.

Finally, legal activism has generated important effects in the domain of
immigration-related administrative policy making. Not only has regular
engagement with sources of legal authority repositioned those responsible
for initiating immigrant rights litigation, reinforcing their identity as elite
technicians, but it has also left an imprint on the activities of their administrative interlocutors. By focusing attention on the pathologies of agency
practices, immigration class action lawsuits reinforced the defensive disposition of administrative officials and inserted litigators and their activities into
debates over immigration policy. We do not see this politicization of law in
France, but legal activists' repeated litigation of immigration issues has had
its own set of indirect and unforeseen effects. In particular, as discussed in
Chapter 6, ritualized consultation of the Conseil d'Etat has heightened the
visibility of France's highest administrative jurisdiction within immigration
administration and has also provided it with a means to increase its jurisprudential authority in relation to other jurisdictions. In both countries, immigrant rights legal activism has contributed indirectly to the "juridification"
of policy administration, in the sense that legal forms and legally generated
dispositions are now more apparent within the sphere of immigration-related
policy administration even as the direction of policy making on immigration
matters remains restrictionist.

In sum, if policy makers today exhibit a determination to act on immigration matters, then the nature of that determination and the target of their
actions are both in part constructed by the process of high-profile legal contestation. For instance, when scholars observe that "the modern view [since the
1980s] within the labor and civil rights communities is that workers' rights and
civil rights are indistinguishable" in the context of U.S. immigration debates
(Gimpel and Edwards 1999, 306), they demonstrate the potency of the pluralist narrative of immigration politics that legal contestation had a hand in constructing. Similarly, if legal activist efforts have sustained themselves in both
countries for more than four decades, then this reflects not only the ongoing

need for immigrant rights to be defended but also the success of a project to define court-centered strategies as an appropriate response to immigration restrictionism. The multiple epistemic assemblages instantiated by the development of immigrant rights legal activism attest to the dynamic interrelationship between the legal and political spheres in this domain. A practice-based approach that is attentive to both the constructive and constructed nature of legal contestation helps us to more fully understand how law matters in the politics of immigration.

CONTESTING IMMIGRATION POLICY IN COURT: THE PATH AHEAD

This attentiveness to both the constructive and constructed nature of legal contestation is all the more important in the current moment, when immigration governance is "positioned within a vortex of globalization" (Dauvergne 2008, 28) characterized by the increased integration of first world economies, their heightened dominance over world economic processes, and their increasing reliance on Third World labor. Within such a system, "immigration is like a mirror" exposing how lawmaking in liberal democracies coexists with – and legitimizes – conditions of extreme material inequality (Calavita 2005, 160). Immigrant rights legal activism arose with the turn to restrictionist immigration politics during the 1970s, a moment when global economic recession provided the context for heightened border control. Four decades later, this restrictionist paradigm remains largely unchanged even as hundreds of thousands of people are put on the road to migration by forces at work in the global economy. For undocumented migrant workers, refugees, and other vulnerable migrants, the process of neoliberal globalization is implicated in a "reterritorialization" of social relations, as states reify immigration status as the sole determinant of political membership (Santos 1995, 298).

If anything, the beginning of the twenty-first century has witnessed a further heightening of immigration restrictionism. After 9/11, the philosophy known as "enforcement first" became the de facto prism through which legislators and administrators responded to irregular migration, with the consequence that changes to the immigration system focused almost entirely on building enforcement programs and improving their performance (Meissner et al. 2013, 1). Over the past two decades, policy makers have made the systems for deporting migrants for postentry criminal conduct more efficient, less discretionary, and substantially more rigid, in what has been described as a "dramatic convergence between the deportation system and an earlier declared 'war' against crime" (Kanstroom 2007, 10). As one of the few windows for legal admission, asylum processing continues to come under criticism as a system prone to abuse, prompting ongoing experiments on the part of policy makers to tighten access to asylum procedures (Walters 2002, Junker 2006, Bohmer and Shuman 2008). At the same time that postentry controls have been tightened, strategies of militarization and "control through deterrence" have placed important new limits on the rights of irregular migrants intercepted at or near the border (Nevins 2002, Feldman 2012), cementing a marginalization of racialized migrant populations that in turn justifies harsh measures to prevent their entry and settlement (Provine and Doty 2011). Extraterritorial interdiction has likewise expanded, as policy makers have aimed to preempt irregular migrants from entering into the national territory and availing themselves of legal protections (Brouwer and Kumin 2003). Recent executive actions to defer deportation for some irregular migrants notwithstanding, the overall global trend remains one of border closure and restrictionism.

For jurists who have devoted their professional lives to the project of expanding immigrant rights, these are all very discouraging developments. Legal activists in the United States and France would agree with the assessment of the UN Special Rapporteur on the Human Rights of Migrants that the current moment is one in which immigration enforcement policies raise "serious concerns" that the rights of migrants are not respected.[2] GISTI's current president, Stéphane Maugendre, poses these developments as a paradox, writing:

> If litigating the rights of foreigners has seen an exponential development and consequently has attracted the attention of jurists, if 30 years after the first "grand arrêt" GISTI the rights of foreigners need more than ever to be defended, it is surely because they are not respected.
>
> Maugendre 2009, 2.

Clearly, legal activists are fully aware that activity in court does not exist in a vacuum and that it fits into a larger political context.

Such adverse circumstances call for legal efforts that are not only technically adept but also creative. These might take a variety of forms. For instance, we see the pragmatic tendencies of U.S. immigrant rights legal activism being put to good use in recent attempts to coordinate individual lawsuits challenging alleged administrative illegalities in the context of removal hearings. The aim, though not yet realized, is to create a de facto substitute for curtailed class action lawsuits, one that offers comparable potential to generate media coverage. French legal activists have demonstrated a similarly creative approach in their recent initiatives to formulate arguments based on the claim that national policies fall short of the minimal standards set by European Union (EU) treaties and directives. European guidelines in this area originally emerged as part of a "venue shopping" strategy on the part of control-oriented officials seeking to achieve their policy goals unencumbered by domestic political or legal obstacles (Guiraudon 2002). However, creative legal argumentation has found in EU directives and other supranational norms an additional legal avenue for organizing abstract challenges to national immigration policy making (Lochak 2011).

Beyond these technical innovations, the current moment may call for a creative rethinking of the division of labor that has developed between *immigration* lawyering and *immigrant* lawyering. As scholar-activist Frances Ansley emphasizes, in the context of free trade, unchained global capital, and the dispossession of labor in the Global South, careful and long-term thought and outreach – especially efforts to build solidarity between immigrants and citizens who are similarly excluded from the global economy – are very much in order for those who care about reform in the immigration policy domain and social justice more broadly (Ansley 2005). Along these lines, a number of recent initiatives have combined expertise in immigration law with a range of other legal tools as part of a broader strategy to resist inegalitarian globalization (Gordon 2005, Ansley 2010). These efforts run in parallel with a broader trend among liberal-oriented groups in the United States to explore "multidimensional strategies" that combine legal activism with other tactics in an effort to adapt to an increasingly conservative judicial climate (Chen and Cummings 2012, 511–39). At the same time, the ambitions of legally trained immigrant community organizers are not limited to reform of official law, but rather aim to develop the broad-based alliances and shared conception of systemic harm necessary for what critical legal theorist Boaventura de Sousa Santos refers to as "counter-hegemonic globalization" (Santos 2005). To adopt this perspective is to recognize that activity centered in state institutions – including courts – can be part of a social justice mobilization, while emphasizing that legal expertise cannot work alone and must be put into dialogue with localized forms of legal knowledge.

One final point: if mobilizations built on the fusion of subaltern and institutional law hold emancipatory potential in part through their capacity to rethink dominant legal categories, then perhaps looking beyond any single national setting can also contribute to shaking up categories of governance that have come to be taken for granted. In the case of immigrant rights advocacy, the process of translating one set of cultural categories into the terms of another, and vice versa, highlights how advocates across national settings respond to a common systemic harm that is manifested in, but that also exceeds, the politics of restrictionism. Bringing this common threat into focus, while also showing points of difference among advocates' responses, can potentially unsettle unconscious assumptions about the limits of what is possible. In this way, comparison prevents any single strategy from becoming too settled in the guise of a pre-given natural or functional adaptation.

Immigrant rights legal activism has successfully sustained itself, in the United States and France, for more than three decades. In recent years, those who pioneered these efforts and who have maintained the field's notable institutional continuity are gradually transitioning away from organizational leadership positions. Immigrant rights legal activism is now increasingly steered by members of a new generation of law school graduates who gravitated toward this specialized area of professional practice. Indeed, as it enters its fourth decade, the project has attracted both new litigators and new organizations. In the United States, emergent groups such as the American Immigration Council's Legal Action Center have joined existing law reform organizations in coordinating impact litigation on immigration issues. Similarly in France, members of a new generation of legal activists have familiarized themselves with immigration law's architecture and now engage in targeted litigation on a regular basis. By all accounts, there are more lawyers than ever before working in this area and more case law with which they can work.

As a hybrid legal-political project, immigrant rights legal activism has built its claims by developing creative extensions of existing legal avenues and applying them to new policy initiatives in the immigration domain. Yet even in high-profile cases, judicial holdings offered only a starting point; more lasting influence resulted from the political mobilizations catalyzed by the *process* of legal contestation. Because there is no red herring of assertive constitutional review in immigration matters, this domain of legal engagement encourages an approach that looks beyond compliance with official case dispositions so as to multiply the dimensions along which we trace the passage of law. Even in the immigration policy domain where, as critical legal theorist Catherine Dauvergne argues, migrant rights always simultaneously conjure the more forceful rights of the state to create illegality based on immigration status (Dauvergne 2008, 27–8), the process of deploying nationally distinct juridical instruments has had important effects. As we have seen, legal action can catalyze social movements, but it can also increase the power of elite technicians. The identities and meanings constructed through activity in court enter into a political environment where they join in unforeseen ways with existing assemblages of values and interests of varying authority.

Focusing on the actual practices set in motion by high-profile legal contestation allows us to see these translations in all of their fragility and specificity. Law matters less than the content of rights-expansive decisions would indicate, but law matters more than an examination of compliance with official case dispositions would suggest. The findings of the present study demonstrate that scholars of immigration politics should take law seriously, while recognizing that it is possible to do so without reproducing a narrative that presents litigation as a salvation for groups engaged in political struggle. Understanding the constructive potential of law, while appreciating the wide array of culturally productive associations set in motion by activity in court, advances the project of breaking down rigidified borders, whether territorial or conceptual.

Notes

1 What Difference Does Law Make in Immigration Policy Making?

1   *Harisiades v. Shaughnessy*, 342 U.S. 580, 587 (1952).
2   *Harisiades v. Shaughnessy*, 342 U.S. at 588.
3   For an exception to this focus on doctrinally significant cases, see Susan Sterett, "Caring about Individual Cases: Immigration Lawyering in Britain," in *Cause Lawyering: Political Commitments and Professional Responsibilities*, ed. Austin Sarat and Stuart A. Scheingold (New York: Oxford University Press, 1998), 293–316.
4   French legal activists were the first in Europe to successfully litigate fundamental rights for noncitizens. See Virginie Guiraudon, "The Constitution of a European Immigration Policy Domain: A Political Sociology Approach," *Journal of European Public Policy* 10, no. 2 (2003): 268–70.
5   The Ford Foundation archives are catalogued by grant number, and I requested all files related to the "refugees and migrants rights" subject heading, although files related to grants that were ongoing or that had closed within the past ten years were not available for viewing. Journals and reports produced by the American Bar Association and the American Immigration Lawyers Association also provided useful data documenting the role played by the private bar as an additional benefactor of U.S. immigrant rights lawyering. I made an effort to view the administrative archives of the U.S. government divisions most closely involved with defending the government against immigrant rights lawsuits, and was able to do so to a limited extent. However, the records generated by the U.S. Department of Justice over the past fifty years, held at the National Archives at College Park, are currently largely inaccessible to researchers. In France, at the National Archives at Fontainebleau, I was able to examine the 1972–99 archived files of the DPLAJ concerning the regulation of residence for noncitizens as well as the 1984–96 archived files of the DPM relating to immigration and asylum policy. In addition, at the Archives d'Histoire Contemporaine at Sciences Po, Paris, I examined the 1981–4 archived papers of Patrick Weil, containing immigration-related files of the DPM.

2 A New Area of Legal Practice

1   Sbicca Legal Defense Team, "INS Raids Sbicca Shoes – Mass Defense and Action Center Organized," *Immigration Newsletter*, November–December 1987, 6.

2   Bruce Bowman, "Sbicca Workers Winning – I.N.S. Reshuffling Deck," *Immigration Newsletter*, November 1978–February 1979, 5.

3   Sbicca Legal Defense Team, "INS Raids Sbicca Shoes – Mass Defense and Action Center Organized," *Immigration Newsletter*, November–December 1987, 6.

4   The case began as *Vallejo v. Sureck*, CV No. 78-1912 (C.D.Cal. December 27, 1978). At the time it was settled, it carried the name *Lopez v. INS*, CV. No. 78-1912-WB(xJ) (C.D.Cal. June 4, 1992).

5   The founding members of GISTI reminisced about the group's early years during a "Journée Histoire et Mémoire" held in on December 8, 2000 in Paris. I refer to the text of the transcript of these proceedings held in GISTI's archives as an original source and cite it accordingly. Although the transcript identifies the speakers by name, I follow the practice of other scholars in not revealing the names of these individuals so as to respect the anonymity requested by those among GISTI's founders who pursued careers in public service. The proceedings were originally transcribed by legal sociologist Liora Israel, who attended the conference and who drew on these discussions in a published article. Liora Israel, "Faire Emerger Le Droit Des Etrangers En Le Contestant, Ou L'histoire Paradoxale Des Premieres Annees Du Gisti," *Politix* 16, no. 62 (2003): 115–44.

6   As political scientist Aristide Zolberg explains, "The term 'back door' was itself coined [in the 1930s] by frustrated cultural restrictionists, who sought in vain to limit the growing Mexican immigration by subjecting it to a quota." Aristide R. Zolberg, *A Nation by Design: Immigration Policy in the Fashioning of America* (Cambridge, MA: Harvard University Press, 2006), 256.

7   During the 1920s and 1930s, governments in the United States and France adopted restrictive measures that limited foreigners' access to work authorization, and administrators in both countries demonstrated a repressive zeal in ensuring the departure of hundreds of thousands of foreign workers. These aggressive removal campaigns applied state authority in ways that were certainly legally questionable. In the United States, immigration agents conducted "scarehead" campaigns involving mass round ups in public parks and the barricading of entire Mexican neighborhoods. In France, indigènes whose work contracts had expired were marched under armed guard to ships in the port of Marseille that would return them to the other side of the Mediterranean. On U.S. Depression-era repatriations, see Abraham Hoffman, *Unwanted Mexican Americans in the Great Depression; Repatriation Pressures, 1929–1939* (Tucson: University of Arizona Press, 1974), 56–7; Francisco E. Balderama and Raymond Rodriguez, *Decade of Betrayal: Mexican Repatriation in the 1930s* (Albuquerque: University of New Mexico Press, 1995), 56–60. On French interwar repatriations, see Mary Dewhurst Lewis, *The Boundaries of the Republic: Migrant Rights and the Limits of Universalism in France, 1918–1940* (Stanford, CA: Stanford University Press, 2007), 190–1.

8   The Wickersham Report focused on improving systems of internal accountability and raising the caliber of immigration field personnel. U.S. National Commission on Law Observance and Enforcement, *Report on the Enforcement of Deportation*

Laws of the United States (Washington, D.C.: Government Printing Office, 1931), 177.

9 Several of the attorneys did mention that they were drawn to the cause of immigrants in part because their parents or grandparents had come to the United States from Europe after World War II. Peter Schey, who is South African by birth, is the only legal activist that I met who immigrated to the United States.

10 Gary Silbiger, interview by the author, September 5, 2006, by telephone.

11 The Haitian Refugee Center had previously been administered by the National Council of Churches, an ecumenical organization with close links to the civil rights movement. Jeffrey Sterling Kahn, "Islands of Sovereignty: Haitian Migration and the Borders of Empire," PhD diss. (University of Chicago, 2013), 65.

12 Larry Kleinman, interview by the author, November 22, 2011, by telephone.

13 Ibid.

14 Steve Hollopeter and Cynthia Whitham, "NLG Convention Opposes Carter Plan," *Immigration Newsletter*, July 1977, 1.

15 Ira Kurzban, interview by the author, April 6, 2006, by telephone.

16 "Courts Deny Haitian Fascism," *Immigration Newsletter*, March 1977, 25.

17 Ira Kurzban, interview by the author, April 6, 2006, by telephone.

18 Adam Green, "Manzo Victory: All Charges Dropped," *Immigration Newsletter*, March 1977, 6.

19 Attorneys for the Legal Services for the Elderly Poor Project of the Center on Social Welfare Policy and Law were closely involved in the Supreme Court's decision in *Graham v. Richardson*, 403 U.S. 365 (1971), which overturned state laws restricting the eligibility of legal permanent residents to public assistance. A subsequent Supreme Court case, *Matthews v. Diaz*, 426 U.S. 67 (1976), seeking to extend this analysis to federal restrictions on access to welfare programs, was litigated by attorneys from Legal Services of Greater Miami. Somewhat relatedly, the litigation campaign organized by the San Francisco Neighborhood Legal Assistance Foundation targeted restrictions on permanent residents' employment in the civil service and resulted in the Supreme Court's decision in *Hampton v. Wong*, 426 U.S. 88 (1976).

20 The leaders of the farmworker movement had participated in the efforts to end the Bracero Program a decade earlier, and they did not initially envision including more recently arrived immigrants within the movement's ethnic framing of civil rights struggle, concentrating instead on mobilizing farmworkers who by the 1960s thought of themselves as American workers rather than as immigrants. On the farmworker movement, see Marshall Ganz, *Why David Sometimes Wins: Leadership, Organization, and Strategy in the California Farm Worker Movement* (New York: Oxford University Press, 2009).

21 *AILA Celebrates 50 Years: Reflections of Past Presidents* (Washington, D.C.: American Immigration Lawyers Association, 1996), 8.

22 In addition to serving as general counsel to the American Committee for the Protection of the Foreign Born, Gollobin was also a member of the National Emergency Civil Liberties Committee. Both of these organizations gave their support to early litigation efforts to defend Haitian asylum seekers during the 1970s. The former organization was created in 1933 by Roger Baldwin to assist in the defense of noncitizen rights and worked closely with the American Civil Liberties

Union (ACLU) and the International Labor Defense. The latter was a leftist organization created in response to the ACLU's purging of suspected Communist Party members during the McCarthy era. The papers of the American Committee for the Protection of the Foreign Born are housed in the Tamiment Labor Archives at New York University.

23 Lory Rosenberg, interview by the author, May 24, 2006, by telephone.

24 Gary Silbiger, interview by the author, September 5, 2006, by telephone.

25 Ibid.

26 "Finally … a Practical Immigration Defense Manual," *Immigration Newsletter*, March 1977, 1.

27 "Target: Area Controls," *Immigration Newsletter*, May 1979.

28 The case was *Bocanegra-Leos v. Dahlin*, No. 78–313 (D.Or. Apr. 7, 1978). Advocate Larry Kleinman represented the plaintiff and circulated the decision through the National Lawyers Guild's National Immigration Project Brief Bank. Larry Kleinman, interview by the author, November 22, 2011, by telephone.

29 "News from Legal Services," *Immigration Newsletter*, November 1979, 20.

30 Carolyn Patty Blum, "Note to Our Readers," *Immigration Newsletter*, March 1979, 17.

31 May 1968 has been the subject of numerous historical accounts. For those seeking to get a sense of the diverse interpretations given to these events, see Kristin Ross, *May '68 and Its Afterlives* (Chicago: University of Chicago Press, 2002); Hervé Hamon and Patrick Rotman, *Génération: Tome 1* (Paris: Seuil, 2008).

32 For a detailed examination of the Group d'Information sur les Prisons and its project, see Benedikte Zitouni, "Michel Foucault et Le Groupe D'information Sur Les Prisons," *Les Temps Modernes* 62, no. 645 (2007): 268–307.

33 Extensive documentation on MAJ and its work between 1970 and 1977 can be found in the papers of founding attorney Jean-Jacques de Felice, which are archived at the BDIC, Nanterre.

34 Transcript, GISTI Journée Histoire et Mémoire, December 8, 2000. For a detailed account of GISTI's early years, see Liora Israel, "Faire émerger le droit des étrangers en le contestant, ou l'histoire paradoxale des premières années du GISTI," *Politix* 16, no. 62 (2003): 115–44.

35 The book in question was *Bidonvilles: L'Enlisement*, written by Monique Hervo and Marie-Ange Charras and originally published by Maspero in 1971.

36 The Director of the Cimade's migrant sector was André Legouy, a former prison chaplain, who had first been attracted to the struggles of France's foreign population through his contacts with imprisoned Algerian independence activists during the period of the Algerian War. He was joined by social workers Patrick Mony and Pauline Boutron, who both also had connections to Catholic social justice work and to reformist currents during the 1970s within the CFDT labor federation. See "Défendre Sans Relâche Les Droits Fondamentaux," *Plein Droit*, July 2009, 40–1.

37 GISTI's name bears similarities to the names of two contemporaneous groups. On the one hand, GISTI appears to have borrowed parts of its moniker from the *Associations de Solidarité avec les Travailleurs Immigrés*, whose volunteers were involved in philanthropic work within immigrant communities during this period. On the other hand, Michel Foucault's *Group d'Information sur les Prisons* clearly inspired and provided a rationale for GISTI's aspiration to support collective struggle through juridical expertise, as several of GISTI's founders have suggested in their historical recollections. See

Transcript, GISTI Journée Histoire et Mémoire, December 8, 2000. It is important to note, however, that GISTI's énarque-influenced approach was somewhat more top-down than Foucault's project, whose premise was that contre-expertise could be generated by synthesizing the prisoners' own expressed vindications. See Zitouni, "Michel Foucault et Le Groupe d'Information sur Les Prisons," 270.

38 Hélène Trappo, "De la Clandestinité à la Reconnaissance: Entrevue avec Said Bouziri et Driss El Yazami," *Plein Droit*, July 1990, 18–20.

39 Patrick Mony, interview by the author, January 30, 2007, Paris.

40 For more on the "alphabetization" movement, see Collectif d'Alphabétisation, *Alphabétisation, Pédagogie et Luttes* (Paris: Maspero, 1972).

41 "Communiqué," October 31, 1980, GISTI Papers, n.p.

42 "Pour la Defense Juridique des Droits des Travailleurs Immigrés," June 10, 1976, GISTI Papers, n.p.

43 "Declaration de 5 Organisations de Juristes en Réponse à la Direction de la SONACOTRA," July 10, 1979, GISTI Papers, n.p. The five organizations included Association Française des Juristes Démocrates, GISTI, MAJ, Syndicat de la Magistrature, and Syndicat des Avocats de France.

44 "Communiqué," December 5, 1979, GISTI Papers, n.p.

45 Christian Bourguet, interview by the author, February 15, 2007, Paris.

46 Philippe Waquet, interview by the author, June 12, 2007, Paris.

47 In 1973, at its congress in Nantes, the CFDT enacted a resolution on immigration that called on all workers to struggle against all discriminations that accost immigrant workers, so as to strengthen and unify the working class. However, only a few CFDT trade unionists seem to have been actively engaged in immigration defense efforts during this period. On the CFDT's position on immigration, see Anne-Sophie Bruno, "Solidarité Avec Les Travailleurs Immigrés," *Plein Droit*, March 2011, 37–40.

48 "Communiqué: Pour La Defense Juridique des Droits des Travailleurs Immigrés," June 10, 1976, GISTI Papers, n.p.

49 Letter from Jean-Jacques Massard to André Legouy, December 20, 1973, GISTI Papers.

50 "Luttes des Sans-Papiers," February 1975, GISTI Papers, n.p.

51 Correspondence, December 1976, GISTI Papers.

52 Clippings of advertisements placed in *Libération*, March 16, 1978 and March 30, 1978, GISTI Papers.

53 "Le Sursis à l'Exécution des Mesures de Refoulement," October 1978, GISTI Papers, n.p.

54 Invitation from Groupe Européen d'Action Juridique et de Defense des Immigrés (GEAJDI) to André Legouy, June 5, 1979, GISTI Papers.

55 "Raisons de Refus et Actions du GISTI," December 1, 1979, GISTI Papers, n.p.

3 Formalization of Immigrant Rights

1 For more on the plenary power doctrine in the immigration context and its foundational cases, see Stephen H. Legomsky, "Immigration Law and the Principle of Plenary Congressional Power," *The Supreme Court Review* 84 (1984): 255–307. T. Alexander Aleinikoff, *Semblances of Sovereignty: The Constitution, the State, and American Citizenship* (Cambridge, MA: Harvard University Press, 2002), 151–81;

Lucy E. Salyer, *Law Harsh as Tigers: Chinese Immigrants and the Shaping of Modern Immigration Law* (Chapel Hill: The University of North Carolina Press, 1995), 117–216.

2 See CE, November 26, 1954, *Ministre de l'Intérieur v. van Peborgh*, Leb 627; CE, December 23, 1954, *Wygoda*, Leb 697.

3 The National Lawyers Guild's National Immigration Project named its award for outstanding immigrant rights lawyering after Carol King, the founder of the American Committee for the Protection of the Foreign Born who had led the legal defense in the *Harisiades* case.

4 In attending to the role of human agency in generating new ideas and institutions, my analysis takes inspiration from the work of public law scholars of Supreme Court decision making, who conceptualize a jurisprudential regime in terms of "a key precedent, or a set of related precedents, that structures the way in which the Supreme Court justices evaluate key elements of cases in arriving at decisions." Mark J. Richards and Herbert M. Kritzer, "Jurisprudential Regimes in Supreme Court Decision Making," *American Political Science Review* 96 (2002), 308.

5 *U.S. v. Carolene Products Company*, 304 U.S. 144 (1938). The politics of the New Deal provides the context for this footnote to a decision upholding a federal law regulating commerce in "filled milk" in the name of public health and safety. As part of its move toward an accommodation with the expansion of the welfare state, the Supreme Court abandoned scrutiny of policies allegedly biased in favor of a particular economic class. However, the Court did not abandon assertive judicial review of government policies that allegedly violated individual rights. Instead of using rights to protect economic classes, federal judges directed their scrutiny toward legislation that discriminated against core New Deal constituencies, whose racial or religious characteristics arguably made them particularly vulnerable to abuses of governmental power. Michael J. Klarman, *From Jim Crow to Civil Rights: The Supreme Court and the Struggle for Racial Equality* (New York: Oxford University Press, 2004), 195–6.

6 *Brown v. Board of Education of Topeka*, 347 U.S. 483 (1954) and 349 U.S. 294 (1955).

7 *Cisneros v. Corpus Christi Independent School District*, 324 F. Supp. 599 (S.D. Tex., 1970); *Lau v. Nichols*, 414 U.S. 563 (1974).

8 *Swann v. Charlotte-Mecklenburg Board of Education*, 402 U.S. 1 (1971).

9 The Supreme Court did ultimately limit the applicability of this device through its decision in *San Antonio School District v. Rodriguez*, 411 U.S. 1 (1973), holding that the invocation of searching judicial review on the basis of inequality in the funding of school districts was inoperable in the absence of a clearly established link to state-sponsored racial discrimination.

10 426 U.S. 67, 78 (1976).

11 MALDEF Appellee Brief to the U.S. Supreme Court in *Plyler v. Doe*, 1980 WL 339676, 17.

12 Interestingly, this testimony is also revealing in so far as it points to the lack of distinction for both the advocates and their witnesses between "Mexican Americans" and undocumented immigrants. The state did not distinguish between members of the same racial group, and neither did defenders of immigrant civil rights.

13 MALDEF Appellee Brief to the U.S. Supreme Court in *Plyler v. Doe*, 1980 WL 339676, 8.

14 *In re Alien Children Education Litigation*, 501 F. Supp. 544, 573 (S.D. Tex. 1980).

15 NCIR Appellee Brief to the U.S. Supreme Court in *Plyler v. Doe*, 1981 WL 389636, 24.

16 NCIR Appellee Brief to the U.S. Supreme Court in *Plyler v. Doe*, 1981 WL 389636, 40.

17 458 F. Supp. 569, 589 (E.D. Tex. 1978).

18 *Plyler v. Doe*, 628 F.2d 448 (5th Cir. 1980).

19 *In re Alien Children Education Litigation*, 501 F. Supp. 544, 583 (S.D. Tex. 1980).

20 *Plyler v. Doe*, 457 U.S. 202 (1982).

21 *Plyler v. Doe*, 457 U.S. at 253.

22 *Plyler v. Doe*, 457 U.S. at 219.

23 *Plyler v. Doe*, 457 U.S. at 222.

24 Congress incorporated the 1967 Bellagio Protocol to the Geneva Convention on Refugees into U.S. law in 1968. Starting in 1972, federal policy granted unadmitted foreign migrants, such as those arriving unauthorized by sea, an opportunity to have their claims for asylum status heard before INS District Directors, who had the discretion to apply these international standards to individual cases.

25 Jeffrey Kahn provides a similar and more detailed recounting of these events. See Jeffrey Sterling Kahn, "Islands of Sovereignty: Haitian Migration and the Borders of Empire," PhD diss. (University of Chicago, 2013), 66–7.

26 *Haitian Refugee Center v. Civiletti*, 503 F.Supp. 442, 451 (S.D.Fla. 1980).

27 *Haitian Refugee Center v. Civiletti*, 503 F.Supp. at 519.

28 *Haitian Refugee Center v. Civiletti*, 503 F.Supp. at 451.

29 *Louis v. Nelson*, 544 F.Supp. 973, 982 (S.D. Fla. 1982).

30 *Louis v. Nelson*, 544 F.Supp. at Note 1.

31 *Jean v. Nelson*, 711 F.2d 1455 (11th Cir. 1983).

32 *Jean v. Nelson*, 727 F.2d 957 (11th Cir. 1984).

33 Brief for Petitioners, 1985 WL 670048, Note 3.

34 Brief for Petitioners, 1985 WL 670048, Note 21.

35 Brief for Petitioners, 1985 WL 670048, 44.

36 *Jean v. Nelson*, 427 U.S. 846, 852–7 (1985).

37 As Gabriel Chin points out, lawmakers likely did not anticipate that ending race-based admissions quotas would have the effect of allowing non-European sources of immigration to expand as rapidly as they did. Gabriel J. Chin, "The Civil Rights Revolution Comes to Immigration Law: A New Look at the Immigration and Nationality Act of 1965," *North Carolina Law Review* 75, no. 273 (1996): 273–345.

38 Larry Daves, interview by Virginia Marie Raymond, May 28, 2008. Institute of Oral History, University of Texas, El Paso.

39 The connection between legal activists and the Hesburgh Commission was sufficiently strong that litigator Peter Schey was eventually hired into a legal research position with the Hesburgh Commission. The commission's report, eventually released in March 1981, advocated controlling unauthorized migration but doing so in a way that protected alien rights. U.S. Select Commission on Immigration and Refugee Policy, *U.S. Immigration Policy and the National Interest* (Washington, D.C.: Government Printing Office, 1981).

40 Rick Swartz, interview by the author, June 2, 2006, by telephone.

41 *Louis v. Nelson*, 544 F.Supp. 1004, 1005 (SD Fla. 1982).

42 "U.S. Immigration Policy," C-Span Video Library, July 6, 1986, http://www.c-span
.org/video/?123478-1/US-immigration-policy.

43 Rick Swartz, interview by the author, June 2, 2006, by telephone.

44 "U.S. Immigration Policy," C-Span Video Library, July 6, 1986, http://www.c-span
.org/video/?123478-1/US-immigration-policy.

45 On the politics of the Constitutional Council's review, see Alec Stone, *The Birth of
Judicial Politics in France* (New York: Oxford University Press, 1992); Louis Favoreu,
La politique saisie par le droit (Paris: Economica, 1988). For a sociological study
of the Constitutional Council, see Dominique Schnapper, *Une sociologue au
Conseil Constitutionnel* (Paris: Galimard, 2010).

46 The Conseil d'Etat had already paved the way in this direction in a 1936 decision
which invoked "principles enjoying constitutional status" (*principes à valeur
constitutionelle*). CE, February 7, 1936, *Arrighi*, Leb 966.

47 CE, May 28, 1971, *Ville Nouvelle-Est*, Recueil Lebon 409. See also CE, July 25,
1975, *Syndicat CFDT des Marins-Pêcheurs de la Rade de Brest.*

48 CE, May 28, 1971, *Damasio*, Leb 391.

49 This jurisprudence was based on an interpretation of the administrative tribunal
code's provision concerning "jurisdiction over decisions concerning public order"
and the 1945 ordinance governing immigration, which had given the Minister
of Interior the authority to pronounce expulsions in the name of public order.
See CE, November 26, 1954, *Ministre de l'Intérieur v. van Peborgh*, Leb 627; CE,
December 23, 1954, *Wygoda*, Leb 697.

50 "Mémoire ampliatif en défense à la requête de M. Da Silva" from J. G. Nicolas for
the CFDT to the Conseil d'Etat, January 4, 1974, Archives Nationales, 19990260,
box 1, Ministry of Interior Papers.

51 "Mémoire ampliatif en défense à la requête de M. Da Silva" from Philippe Waquet
to the Conseil d'Etat, April 6, 1973, Archives Nationales, 19990260, box 1, Ministry
of Interior Papers.

52 CE, January 13, 1975, *Da Silva et CFDT*, Leb 16.

53 Quoted in Liora Israel, "Philippe Waquet, au coeur de la 'fabrique du droit,'" *Plein
Droit*, June 2008, 50.

54 CE, November 24, 1978, CGT, *Association Culturelle des Travailleurs Africains en
France, l'Union Générale des Travailleurs Sénégalais en France, l'Union Nationale
des Etudiants du Cameroun, GISTI, et autres;* CE, November 24, 1978, CGT,
Bocar, GISTI; CE, November 24, 1978, *MRAP.*

55 The government had initially suspended family immigration in July 1974 by
circular, but had then reopened family migration using a decree in April 1976
that stipulated that the spouse and minor children of labor migrants were to
be granted a residence permit if they fulfilled the conditions of stability of
employment and residence, suitable housing, and a medical check. The government's decision to revisit the policy reflected a recognition that the abrupt
closure of formal channels for family migration was responsible for the spike
in applications from family members for postentry regularization. Although
the Minister of Labor initially drafted a decree aiming to shift family migration
entirely toward formal channels, an advisory opinion of the Conseil d'Etat's
Social Section ensured that the April 1976 decree allowed for the possibility of

postentry regularization. For a detailed analysis of these internal discussions, see Saskia Bonjour, "Courts in Control? The Impact of the Judiciary on the Making of Family Migration Policies in France, Germany and the Netherlands," paper presented at the Annual Meeting of the American Political Science Association, Washington, D.C., August 2014.

56 GISTI had close contacts with the Conseil d'Etat's inner sanctum because one of its founding members held a prestigious law clerk position within the Documentation Center. The group was thus well placed to carry the issue across the Conseil d'Etat's internal organizational divisions so that the adjudicatory section could consider the matter.

57 Transcript, "*Journée Histoire et Mémoire*," December 8, 2000, 8.

58 CE, December 8, 1978, *GISTI, CFDT, et CGT*, Leb 67.

59 These conclusions situate the decision within the court's jurisprudence and they are read by public commentators alongside the published decision. See L. Neville Brown and John Bell, *French Administrative Law* (Oxford: Clarendon Press, 1998), 104–6. Since February 2009, the position formerly titled *commissaire du gourverne-ment* has been given the new title of *rapporteur public*.

60 Conclusions of CDG Dondoux, *GISTI*, December 8, 1978, *Droit Social*, 1979, 17.

61 Conclusions of CDG Dondoux, *GISTI*, 25.

62 Conclusions of CDG Dondoux, *GISTI*, 26.

63 Even before their annulment, the circulars' registration requirements had proved difficult to apply and, as a result, the government abandoned its effort and allowed the regularization of approximately fifty thousand immigrant workers in the latter half of 1973. Patrick Weil, *La France et ses etrangers: L'aventure d'une politique de l'immigration, de 1938 à nos jours* (Paris: Calmann-Lévy, 2004), 99.

64 "Pour le Droit au Travail des Ouvriers Immigrés," *La Voix Immigré*, January 1973, Carton 7, Saïd Bouziri Papers, Association Génériques, Paris.

65 Léo Hamon, "Note: GISTI, December 8, 1978," *Recueil Dalloz Sirey*, 1979, 661–5.

66 Note from GISTI to Prefects and Departmental Directors of Labor and Employment, "Portée administrative des récentes décisions du Conseil d'Etat," January 24, 1979, Archives Nationales, 19990260, box 1, Ministry of Interior Papers.

67 Letter from Minister of Interior to Préfet de la Loire, February 6, 1979, Archives Nationales, 19990260, box 1, Ministry of Interior Papers.

68 "110 Propositions pour la France," L'Office Universitaire de Recherche Socialiste, April-May 1981, http://www.lours.org/default.asp?pid=307.

4 Institutionalizing Legal Innovation

1 According to an announcement in the *Immigration Newsletter*, the conference in August 1981 would "bring together the leadership of 'grass-roots community organizations' involved in immigration advocacy to allow for information exchange and the development of advocacy strategies on issues of labor and immigration, INS enforcement, refugee and asylum matters, and social services." "National Consultation on Immigration and Refugee Issues," *National Immigration Project Newsletter*, July 1981, 1.

2 In 1976, the newly created Council for Public Interest Law listed seventy-two "public interest law firms" in operation. See *Balancing the Scales of Justice: Financing Public Interest Law in America* (Washington, D.C.: Council for Public Interest Law, 1976). Two years later, a study by a multidisciplinary team of scholars, supported by a grant from the Ford Foundation, uncovered an additional fourteen public interest law firms using a more abstract and theoretically motivated set of criteria. Burton Weisbrod, "Conceptual Perspective on the Public Interest: An Economic Analysis," in *Public Interest Law: An Economic and Institutional Analysis*, ed. Burton Weisbrod (Berkeley: University of California Press, 1978), 4–29. Public interest law has remained a touchstone of the contemporary American legal scene. For a recent and comprehensive survey of the field, see Alan Chen and Scott L. Cummings, *Public Interest Lawyering: A Contemporary Perspective* (New York: Aspen Publishers).

3 This lobbying from the liberal legal network was not the sole factor contributing to the enactment of fee-shifting legislation. As Sean Farhang shows, conflict between legislative and executive preferences encouraged Congress to rely upon private litigation as a means to implement its statutes. Sean Farhang, *The Litigation State: Public Regulation and Private Lawsuits in the U.S.* (Princeton, NJ: Princeton University Press, 2010).

4 Michael S. Teitelbaum, A Proposed Foundation-Wide Program on Immigration and Refugees, November 1979, Report #76811, Ford Foundation Grant Files.

5 Legal organizations featured prominently among the program's recipients. See "Human Rights and Social Justice Program Refugee and Migrant Rights FY 1982–FY 1986 Grants List," November 1987, 011006, Ford Foundation Grant Files.

6 Conservative critics were particularly irked by the impact litigation organized by legal services attorneys on behalf of undocumented migrants. In 1983, the LSC restricted the use of its funds to activities that assisted "aliens who are lawfully admitted for permanent residence; those who are married to, parents of, or unmarried children under 21 of a citizen; those who have filed an adjustment of status to permanent resident; those who are refugees or who have been granted political asylum; or those who have had deportation withheld." John A. Dooley and Alan W. Houseman, *Legal Services History* (Washington, D.C.: Management Project of the NLADA, 1984), 54.

7 Patty Blum, "To Our Readers," *National Immigration Project Newsletter*, March 1979, 17.

8 "Recommendation for Grant/FAP Action," April 23, 1987. USIAP-124, Ford Foundation Grant Files.

9 Leah Wortham and Robert Dinerstein, "Report to the Ford Foundation on Legal Services Support Centers," November 1989, 20–1. Report #012588, Ford Foundation Grant Files.

10 Scott Slonim, "Freedom Flotilla from Cuba," *ABA Journal*, July 1980, 825.

11 "Human Rights and Social Justice Program Refugee and Migrant Rights FY 1982-FY 1986 Grants List," November 1987, 011006, Ford Foundation Grant Files.

12 "Recommendation for Grant/FAP Action," July 2, 1987, USIAP-193, 87–727, Ford Foundation Grant Files.

13 National Center for Immigrants' Rights, "Board Meeting and Agenda of October 8, 1984," 83-71, Ford Foundation Grant Files.

14 "A Proposal to the Ford Foundation to Support the ACLU Foundation Immigrants' Rights Project," June 27, 1996, 830-0810-5, Ford Foundation Grant Files.

15 The Ford Foundation declined to support the activities of immigrant rights litigator Peter Schey, despite his central involvement in key immigrant rights litigation successes, telling him that there were insufficient funds in the immigrant rights program to support new projects. "Request for Grant Action," May 17, 1983, Report # 84–827, Ford Foundation Grant Files. Schey applied in 1983 for foundation funds for his newly created "National Center for Immigrants Rights, Inc." after a difficult separation from the original National Center for Immigrants Rights that involved a dispute over attorneys' fees. His move to market his skills on his own and his reputation for having an "abrasive" and entrepreneurial litigation style were viewed with both disapproval and consternation by Ford Foundation grant makers. Amy S. Vance, "Preliminary Recommendation Regarding Support for the LSC National Back-Up Centers," March 22, 1982, 840-0827, Ford Foundation Grant Files.

16 Peter Schey, interview by the author, May 2, 2006, by telephone.

17 In 1982, the National Immigration Project's Subcommittee on Refugees compiled 710 pages of documentation materials to assist attorneys litigating cases involving Central American asylum seekers. See "Publications Available," *Immigration Newsletter*, January–February 1982, 20. For background on the Sanctuary Movement, see Susan Coutin, *The Culture of Protest: Religious Activism and the U.S. Sanctuary Movement* (Boulder, CO: Westview Press, 1993).

18 Carolyn Patty Blum, interview by the author, June 19, 2006, New York.

19 Letter from Maureen O'Sullivan, National Immigration Project Director, to Diana Morris, Ford Foundation, November 6, 1984, 17–946, Ford Foundation Grant Files.

20 "Announcements," *Immigration Newsletter*, December 1984, 3.

21 "Recommendation for a Delegated-Authority Grant," January 23, 1989, Request No. USIAP-81, Ford Foundation Grant Files.

22 "Recommendation for Grant/FAP Action," July 2, 1987, USIAP-193, 87–727, Ford Foundation Grant Files.

23 Leah Wortham and Robert Dinerstein, "Report to the Ford Foundation on Legal Services Support Centers," November 1989, 012588, Ford Foundation Grant Files.

24 Lucas Guttentag, interview by the author, July 31, 2006, by telephone.

25 "Recommendation for Grant/FAP Action," July 2, 1987, USIAP-193, 87–727, Ford Foundation Grant Files.

26 National Center for Immigrants' Rights, "Recommendation for Grant/FAP Action," April 27, 1989, 840-0827, Ford Foundation Grant Files.

27 "Recommendation for Grant/FAP Action," April 23, 1987, USIAP-124, Ford Foundation Grant Files.

28 National Immigration Law Center, "Final Narrative and Financial Report," November 1991, 840-0827B, Ford Foundation Grant Files.

29 ACLU Immigration and Aliens' Rights Task Force, "Report on Project Activities," August 31, 1991, 830-0810-2, Ford Foundation Grant Files.

30 National Immigration Law Center, "Final Narrative and Financial Report," November 1991, 840-0827B, Ford Foundation Grant Files.

31 ACLU Immigrants' Rights Project, "Report to the Ford Foundation," August 31, 1993, 830-0810-3, Ford Foundation Grant Files.

32 William Reece Smith Jr., "The Refugee Crisis: Solving the Problems," *ABA Journal*, November 1981, 1465.

33 *AILA Celebrates 50 Years: Reflections of Past Presidents* (Washington, D.C.: American Immigration Lawyers Association, 1996), 50–1.

34 ACLU Immigrants' Rights Project, "A Narrative and Financial Report," August 31, 1992, 830-0810-3, Ford Foundation Grant Files.

35 High-profile class action lawsuits in which corporate firms contributed pro bono assistance included *American Baptist Churches v. Thornburgh*, 760 F. Supp. 796 (N.D. Cal. 1991), *Haitian Centers Council v. McNary*, 789 F.Supp. 541 (1992), and *Walters v. Reno*, 145 F.3d 1032 (9th Cir. 1998). These litigation campaigns are discussed more fully in Chapter 5.

36 Omnibus Consolidated Rescissions and Appropriations Act, Public Law No. 104–134, 110 Stat 1321 (1996). The "poison pill" restriction on LSC-funded programs extended existing federal funding restrictions on representing undocumented immigrants or migrant workers so as to limit all activities conducted on behalf of these clients by LSC programs, even when these were funded by non-LSC funds. Following the act's enactment, recipients of LSC funds were permitted to provide legal assistance only to permanent residents and immigrants admitted as refugees or asylees or granted withholding of deportation pursuant to section 243(h) of the Immigration and Nationality Act.

37 Chris Nugent, interview by the author, June 28, 2006, Washington, D.C.

38 Interview with Dan Kesselbrenner, National Immigration Project of the National Lawyers Guild, January 20, 2012.

39 For a list of these early publications, see GISTI, *La Petite Livre Des Travailleurs Immigrés* (Paris: Editions Maspéro, 1975).

40 "Communiqué," May 11, 1981, GISTI Papers, n.p.

41 Letter from André Legouy to Pierre Bérégovoy, May 19, 1981, GISTI Papers.

42 "Compte rendu de la réunion," Meeting of February 25, 1982, GISTI Papers, n.p.

43 Transcript, GISTI Journée Histoire et Mémoire, December 8, 2000, 51, GISTI Papers.

44 These challenges were partially successful, insofar as the Conseil d'Etat overturned some requirements in the ministerial circular that limited foreigners' protections against immediate repatriation. See Conseil d'Etat, September 27, 1985, *GISTI*.

45 "Note sur la Jurisprudence de la Cour de Cassation Relative au Controle d'Identité des Etrangers," May 1985, GISTI Papers, n.p. The campaign was engineered by attorneys Didier Liger and Gérard Tcholakian, who had both recently joined GISTI's legal network.

46 Yves Jouffa, "L'Intégration: Une Vieille Question," November 19, 1986, Box 17, Yves Jouffa Papers, Centre de Recherche en Histoire Contemporaine. Fondation Nationale des Sciences Politiques, Paris.

47 "Compte Rendu de la Réunion," September 25, 1986, GISTI Papers. GISTI also prepared a brochure with legal analysis and practical advice for associations assisting foreigners impacted by the new laws.

48 Founded in 1970 as a member-based association, France Terre d'Asile opened a permanent office in 1976 as public funding for assisting asylum seekers became available. During the early 1980s, it created its own newsletter and established a juridical commission that brought together representatives of GISTI, the Cimade,

and the Ligue des Droits de l'Homme. Interview with François Julien-Laferrière, March 6, 2007.

49 Maurice Peyrot, "Le Procès des 'Zones de Non-Droit,'" *Le Monde*, February 28, 1992. The lawsuit was brought before the Tribunal de Grande Instance of Paris on behalf of six asylum seekers detained at Roissy in November 1991.

50 "Correspondants du GISTI," circa 1973/1974, GISTI Papers, n.p.

51 "Compte rendu de la réunion," February 27, 1986, GISTI Papers, n.p.

52 Letter from Pauline Boutron, Responsable de Formation, to Batonnier de l'Ordre des avocats du barreau de Seine Saint-Denis, July 25, 1995, GISTI Papers.

53 "Compte rendu de la réunion," February 27, 1986, GISTI Papers, n.p.

54 Letter from Gerold de Wangen to Gérard Moreau, February 3, 1986, Cote 19990260, Box 26, Ministry of Interior Papers.

55 Transcript, GISTI Journée Histoire et Mémoire, December 8, 2000, 45.

56 See, e.g., Letter from Gérard Moreau to André Legouy, December 29, 1992, GISTI Papers.

57 "Compte rendu de la réunion," September 25, 1986, GISTI Papers, n.p.

58 GISTI did participate in the launch in 2001 of a national campaign on this issue, sponsoring the screening of a film about the *double-peine* in the French Senate, but collaboration with grassroots activists around this issue was marked by accusations that more established associations had adopted a condescending attitude toward locally based groups. See Lilian Mathieu, "Mouvements Sociaux et Recours au Droit: Le Cas de la Double Peine," Terra Network, http://terra.rezo.net/article339.html.

59 There is evidence that this divergence between grassroots social movements and Left Bank intellectuals has continued in the early twenty-first century. Bernard Dréano, "In Paris, the Global Place Is No More Saint-Germain-Des-Prés," in *Exploring Civil Society*, ed. Marlies Glasius (New York: Routledge, 2004), 82–8.

60 "Communiqué: Une Entreprise Xénophobe de Désintégration," May 4, 1993, GISTI Papers, n.p.

61 Jean-Pierre Alaux, "Contre L'Extrême Droit, La Liberté de Circulation," *Plein Droit*, July 1996, 3–9.

62 "L'Auteur de 'Rapport Weil' Face à Une Militante du Droit des Immigrés: Débat entre Patrick Weil et Danièle Lochak," *Le Monde*, September 23, 1997, 1.

63 Nathalie Ferré, "Résistance à L'Immigration Jetable," *Plein Droit*, December 2006, 3–6.

64 In France, legal aid has been available since 1991 for petitions brought to the Conseil d'Etat and the Cour de Cassation but it is relatively difficult to apply for these funds. Moreover, the small number of lawyers qualified to practice before these jurisdictions reduces the relevance of legal aid for this type of legal work. For a history of legal aid in France, see Jacques Faget, "L'accès au droit: logiques de marché et enjeux sociaux," *Droit et Société*, 30–1 (1995): 367–78.

65 Danièle Lochak recounts how she came into contact with the group only through a chance meeting at a 1982 conference on immigrant rights in Marseille, having been unable to locate them in Paris because GISTI functioned at the time as a small, almost clandestine group. Danièle Lochak, interview by the author, March 2, 2007, Paris.

66 The Conseil d'Etat has granted an audience in every case that GISTI has filed. Bruno Genevois, "Le GISTI: Requérant d'Habitude? La Vision du Conseil

d'Etat," in *Défendre La Cause des Etrangers en Justice*, ed. GISTI (Paris: Dalloz, 2009), 68.

67 Letter to GISTI members, September 11, 1992, GISTI Papers.

68 Transcript, GISTI Journée Histoire et Memoire, December 8, 2000, 57.

69 Serge Slama, interview by the author, February 10, 2007, Paris.

70 Jean-Pierre Alaux, interview by the author, January 26, 2007.

71 I was introduced to members of this new generation of legal activists, many of whom are Professor Lochak's former students, at a gathering sponsored by GISTI at its Paris office in June 2009.

72 A search of all Conseil d'Etat cases since 1972 revealed only six in which the court heard cases related to immigration issues that were brought by other associations without the participation of GISTI.

73 See, e.g., Craig L. Hymowitz, "The Birth of a Nation: At the Ford Foundation Ethnicity Is Always Job 1," *American Patrol*, http://www.americanpatrol.com/REFERENCE/MALDEF-LA_RAZA-Hymowitz.html.

5 Enacting Adversarial Legalism through Class Action Lawsuits

1 IIRIRA, Public Law No. 104–208, 110 Stat. 3009 (1996). The relevant provision was codified as 8 U.S.C.A. Section 1252(F). A few months later, legislators hammered in their intention to disable activist lawyering by barring attorneys receiving funding from the Legal Services Corporation from litigating class action cases of any type. Omnibus Consolidated Rescissions and Appropriations Act, Public Law No. 104–134, 110 Stat 1321 (1996).

2 For a comprehensive summary of the jurisdiction stripping provisions, see Lucas Guttentag, "The 1996 Immigration Act: Federal Court Jurisdiction – Statutory Restrictions and Constitutional Rights," *Interpreter Releases*, 74 (February 1997): 245–60.

3 Statement of Senator Simpson, September 28, 1996, 142 Congressional Record S11, 711.

4 Patrick J. McDonnell, "New Law Could End Immigrants' Amnesty Hopes," *Los Angeles Times*, October 9, 1996, A1.

5 Lamar Smith, "Letter to the Editor: Nothing to Fear in Immigration Legislation," *New York Times*, September 25, 1996, A20.

6 The 1980s saw a notable increase in the number of affirmative legal challenges of immigration agency practices, with many of these "impact cases" organized or supported by public interest law firms. Peter Schuck and Theodore Hsien Wang, "Continuity and Change: Patterns of Immigration Litigation in the Courts, 1979–1990," *Stanford Law Review* 45, no. 115 (1992): 155.

7 National Center for Immigrants' Rights, "Board Meeting and Agenda," October 8, 1984, 83-71 (Ford Foundation Archives).

8 In 1984, the legal activists who had organized the class action challenging the Carter administration's handling of Haitian asylum seekers were awarded attorneys' fees in excess of the regular limit, with the judge citing the contribution of attorneys Ira Kurzban, Peter Schey, and Rick Swartz and the difficulties they faced in bringing the first class action in the immigration context. *Louis v. Nelson*, 644 F.Supp. 382, 391 (S.D. Fla 1984).

9　"International Molders v. Nelson: Enjoining Unconstitutional Sweeps after Delgado," *Immigration Newsletter*, January 1986, 8.

10　For background on the Sanctuary Movement, see Susan Coutin, *The Culture of Protest: Religious Activism and the U.S. Sanctuary Movement* (Boulder, CO: Westview Press, 1993); Robert S. Kahn, *Other People's Blood: U.S. Immigration Prisons in the Reagan Decade* (Boulder, CO: Westview Press, 1996).

11　See Lucas Guttentag, "A Brief Introduction to Judicial Review in Relation to IRCA Legislation," Yale Law School Workshop Series Readings, Fall 2009, http://www .law.yale.edu/documents/pdf/Clinics/Immigration_Readings.pdf

12　For a detailed recounting of these litigation campaigns, see Niels Frenzen, "U.S. Migrant Interdiction Practices in International and Territorial Waters," in *Extraterritorial Immigration Control*, ed. Bernard Ryan and Valsamis Mitsilegas (Leiden, The Netherlands: Koninklijke Brill NV, 2010); Lory Diana Rosenberg, "The Courts and Interception: The United States' Interdiction Experience and Its Impact on Refugees and Asylum Seekers," *Georgetown Immigration Law Journal* 17 (2003): 99–219; Brandt Goldstein, *Storming the Court: How a Band of Yale Law Students Sued the President – and Won* (New York: Scribner, 2005).

13　While the vast majority of immigrant rights legal activism during this period targeted federal immigration policies, there are nevertheless some exceptions. Most prominently, in 1994, the immigrant rights national legal organizations discussed in this chapter collaborated in organizing a successful consolidated federal lawsuit challenging the State of California's Proposition 187, which barred undocumented immigrants from access to public social services, nonemergency health care, and schools. See "CA's Anti-Immigrant Proposition 187 is Voided, Ending State's Five-Year Battle with ACLU, Rights Groups," ACLU Press Release, July 29, 1999, https://www.aclu.org/immigrants-rights/cas-anti-immigrant-proposition -187-voided-ending-states-five-year-battle-aclu-righ.

14　So as to meet the threshold for certification of a national class, litigators must show that administrative practices are widespread and must paint a sufficiently detailed picture of these practices to allow the case to go forward.

15　"Update," *Immigration Newsletter*, September 1981, 3.

16　Haitian Refugee Center Brief to the U.S. Supreme Court in *McNary v. Haitian Refugee Center*, 1990 WL 511339, 10–11.

17　Cheryl Little, interview by the author, June 6, 2006, by telephone.

18　Dan Kesselbrenner, interview by the author, January 20, 2012, Boston.

19　Marita Hernandez, "L.A.'s Oldest Catholic Parish Declares Itself a Sanctuary for Latin Refugees," *Los Angeles* Times, December 13, 1985, 1; George Ramos, "U.S. Jurists Pressure State Department for Data on Salvadoran Death Squads," *Los Angeles Times*, December 13, 1985, 1.

20　*Haitian Centers Council v. Sale*, 823 F. Supp. 1028, 1038 (E.D. NY 1993).

21　Peter Schey, interview by the author, May 2, 2006, by telephone.

22　U.S. Department of Homeland Security, Office of Immigration Litigation, senior attorney #2, interview by the author, January 17, 2012, Washington, D.C.

23　"We had a compelling narrative and we didn't let formal legal obstacles stop us," recalled litigator Dan Kesselbrenner of the strategy developed by the coalition of advocates organizing the *ABC* class action, "Sometimes you fling things at windmills and it works." Dan Kesselbrenner, interview by the author, January 20, 2012, Boston.

24 *Orantes-Hernandes v. Meese*, 685 F. Supp. 1495 (1988).

25 In the years since the injunction was issued, changing circumstances brought to light issues the injunction didn't specifically address. For instance, detention centers replaced pay phones with a cell phone system, making it prohibitively expensive for some detainees to contact counsel. Immigrant rights legal activists twice negotiated a modification to the injunction with the agency and also returned to court to present evidence for why the injunction should be maintained after the government in 2005 sought to have it dissolved. Linton Joaquin, interview by the author, June 14, 2006, by telephone.

26 Memo from Carolyn Patty Blum to ABC Litigation Team, October 2, 1990, CARDF Papers, Private Collection of Carolyn Patty Blum, New York.

27 Lucas Guttentag, interview by the author, July 31, 2006, by telephone.

28 Letter from Debbie Smith, ABC Settlement Coordinator, to Francesco Isgro, Office of Immigration Litigation, Department of Justice, July 2, 1992, National Immigration Project Papers.

29 "An Aggressive and Effective Approach to Litigation," *INS Reporter*, Fall-Winter 1983–4, 22.

30 U.S. Department of Homeland Security, Office of Immigration Litigation, senior attorney #2, interview by the author, January 17, 2012, Washington, D.C. In addition to asking for injunctions, litigators sued agency officials (including Associate Attorney General Rudolph Giuliani) in their personal capacities for damages. Giuliani and others felt that they needed a stronger defense team.

31 Dick Joyce, INS Acting Deputy Counsel, cited in "The L.A. 8 Case," *Immigration Newsletter*, July 1987.

32 U.S. Department of Homeland Security, Office of Immigration Litigation, senior attorney #1, interview by the author, January 17, 2012, Washington, D.C.

33 Raymond M. Momboisse, General Counsel, Immigration and Naturalization Service, "Annual State of the Office Report," February 5, 1988; Legal Services Corporation (Immigration); Office of the Attorney General, Subject Files of the Assistants to the Attorney General, Henry G. "Hank" Barr, 1988–9; General Records of the Department of Justice, Record Group 60, National Archives at College Park, College Park, MD.

34 Grover Joseph Rees III, General Counsel, to Regional Counsel and District Counsel, "Litigation of Asylum Claims," November 30, 1992, National Immigration Project Papers.

35 U.S. Department of Justice, Immigration and Naturalization Service, Office of General Counsel, senior attorney #2, interview by the author, June 20, 2006, by telephone.

36 Raymond M. Momboisse, INS General Counsel, to All GENCO Attorneys, "The National Lawyers Guild Conference, 25 May 1987," June 5, 1987, National Immigration Project Papers.

37 Momboisse Memo, June 5, 1987, National Immigration Project Papers.

38 *Interpreter Releases*, Vol. 64, No. 39 (October 9, 1987). The case in question was *LULAC v. INS*, Civ. No. 87-4757-WDK (C.D. Cal. 1988).

39 More recently, immigrant rights legal advocates marked the twentieth anniversary of the ABC litigation by celebrating an "amazing settlement agreement" that

continues to provide rights and benefits. Trina Realmuto, "ABC v. Thornburgh: 20 Years Later," National Immigration Project, January 31, 2011, http://www.nationalimmigrationproject.org/legalresources/practice_advisories/cd_pa_ABC%20-%2020%20Years%20Later%20-%20amended.pdf.

40 The *Lopez* settlement in July 1992 required the agency to hand arrested persons a "Notice of Rights" form advising them of their right to speak with an attorney as well as their right to apply for asylum and other defenses to deportation available under federal law.

41 U.S. Department of Justice, Immigration and Naturalization Service, Office of General Counsel, senior attorney #1, interview by the author, June 16, 2006, by telephone.

42 U.S. Department of Homeland Security, Office of Immigration Litigation, senior attorney #1, interview by the author, January 17, 2012, Washington, D.C.

43 Statement of Doris M. Meissner, Commissioner of the INS on Cuban-Haitian Refugee Policy, July 31, 1981, Hearings on S.1761 Before the Subcommittee on Immigration and Refugee Policy of the Senate Committee on the Judiciary, 97th Congress, 1st Session. Cited in Ira J. Kurzban, "Restructuring the Asylum Process," *San Diego Law Review* 19 (1981): 91–117.

44 "The Reagan Immigration Proposals," *Immigration Newsletter*, November 1981, 1.

45 David Johnston, "Government Is Quickly Using Power of New Immigration Law," *New York Times*, October 22, 1996, 20.

46 Quoted in Louis Freedberg, "Feds Move to Limit Migrants' Challenges," *Denver Post*, October 22, 1996, A5.

47 U.S. Department of Homeland Security, Office of Immigration Litigation, senior attorney #1, interview by the author, January 17, 2012, Washington, D.C.

48 Linda Greenhouse, "How Congress Curtailed the Courts' Jurisdiction," *New York Times*, October 27, 1996, A5.

49 Anthony Lewis, "Mean and Petty," *New York Times*, April 12, 1996, A31.

50 Lucas Guttentag, "Obama Administration Takes on Immigration Reform," *Daily Kos*, April 15, 2009, http://www.dailykos.com/storyonly/2009/4/15/720361/-Obama-AdministrationTakes-on-Immigration-Reform.

51 Dan Kesselbrenner, interview by the author, January 20, 2012, Boston.

52 Lory Rosenberg, interview by the author, August 17, 2014, by telephone. For a description of the class action lawsuit filed in the fall of 2014 on behalf of Central Americans placed in immigration detention, see "RILR v. Johnson," ACLU Immigrants' Rights Project, December 6, 2014, http//www.aclu.org/immigrants-rights/rilr-v-johnson.

53 *INS v. St. Cyr*, 533 U.S. 289 (2001).

54 *Zadvydas v. Davis*, 533 U.S. 678 (2001).

55 U.S. Department of Homeland Security, Office of Immigration Litigation, senior attorney #1, interview by the author, January 17, 2012, Washington, D.C.

56 Attorney General John Ashcroft's attempt in 2002 to "streamline" the immigration court system had the unanticipated effect of shifting review of determinations by agency adjudicators to judges on the federal courts of appeals. Faced with this influx of individual immigration appeals – whose numbers were further expanded by the fact that larger numbers of individuals were being placed in removal hearings due

to the 1996 legislative changes – judges in some circuits repeatedly came to the conclusion that administrative decision making in immigration matters was faulty and irrational. For an overview of the streamlining program and its institutionally specific effects, see Anna O. Law, *The Immigration Battle in American Courts* (New York: Cambridge University Press, 2010), 144–87; Rebecca Hamlin, *Let Me Be a Refugee* (New York: Oxford University Press, 2014), 73–81.

57 Proposals in Congress in the wake of the *St. Cyr* and *Zadvydas* decisions to enact statutory overrides of either decision were ultimately removed from the final legislation. Nancy Morawetz suggests that this indicates recognition on the part of congressional leaders of the serious constitutional issues raised by foreclosing judicial review of immigration matters. Nancy Morawetz, "INS v. St. Cyr," in *Immigration Stories*, ed. David A. Martin and Peter H. Schuck (New York: Foundation Press, 2005), 279–310.

58 "U Visa Litigation Update," Center for Human Rights and Constitutional Law, May 3, 2008, http://lawprofessors.typepad.com/immigration/2008/05/u-visa-litigati.html.

59 "Detention, Deportation and Mental Disabilities," ACLU Immigrants' Rights Project, October 1, 2012, https://www.aclu.org/immigrants-rights/detention-deportation-and-mental-disabilities.

60 Hotel and Restaurant Employees Union v. Smith, 594 F. Supp. 502 (1984).

61 U.S. Department of Justice, Executive Office for Immigration Review, senior attorney, interview by the author, January 10, 2012, Washington, D.C.

62 U.S. Department of Homeland Security, Office of Immigration Litigation, senior attorney #1, interview by the author, January 17, 2012, Washington, D.C.

63 *Valle del Sol v. Whiting*, 2013 U.S. App. Lexis 20474 (9th Cir. 2013). Following the Supreme Court's decision in a companion case brought by the U.S. Department of Justice, the class action lawsuit was subsequently modified to focus on provisions of the state law that criminalize the solicitation of work by immigrant day laborers.

64 For a list of these lawsuits, see Michael A. Olivas, "State and Federal Immigration Litigation and Legislation Concerning Higher Education, 2004–2015," Institute for Higher Education Law and Governance, January 18, 2015, http://law.uh.edu/ihelg/documents/StateandFederalImmigrationLitigationandLegislation.asp.

65 E.g., in its cases focusing on immigration marriage fraud, the ACLU challenged not agency implementation of immigration statutes but rather the constitutionality of statutory provisions. See *Manwani v. U.S. Department of Justice*, 736 F.Supp. 1367 (1990).

66 Peter Schey, interview by the author, May 2, 2006, by telephone.

67 Dan Kesselbrenner, interview by the author, January 20, 2012, Boston.

68 Order Approving Settlement of Class Action, U.S. District Court, Eastern Division of California, Case No. Civ S-86-1343-LKK, January 21, 2004, National Immigration Project Papers.

69 Peter Schey, interview by the author, May 2, 2006, by telephone.

70 U.S. Department of Homeland Security, Office of Immigration Litigation, senior attorney #1, interview by the author, January 17, 2012, Washington, D.C.

71 Lucas Guttentag, "Obama Administration Takes on Immigration Reform," *Daily Kos*, April 15, 2009, http://www.dailykos.com/storyonly/2009/4/15/720361/-Obama-AdministrationTakes-on-Immigration-Reform.

6 Performing Legal Activism before the Conseil d'Etat

1 The law of February 8, 1995 created for the first time a type of public law injunction remedy. After the review of the Code of Administrative Justice in 2000, it became possible to obtain injunctions in cases deemed to be urgent, expanding the efficacy of the injunctive power. However, the application of the *référé administratif* in the immigration law context has been restrictive. "There is for the most part a presumed absence of urgency when demanding the suspension of decisions concerning the entry and sojourn of foreigners in irregular situation." Matthias Guyomar and Patrick Collin, "Chronique De Jurisprudence," *Actualité Juridique Droit Administratif* (2001): 467.

2 These themes were echoed in recent parliamentary debates preceding the establishment through legislation in February 2014 of a limited form of class action (*actions de groupe*) in the area of consumer rights. There is currently no discussion of extending this mechanism to encompass lawsuits against the state. See Cécile Prudhomme, "La France s'ouvre à l'action de groupe," *Le Monde*, May 3, 2013, 6.

3 In her study of judicial dialogues in the United Kingdom, Susan Sterett observes a somewhat similar phenomenon in a national context where constitutionally based judicial review has traditionally been similarly circumscribed. According to Sterett, the British Law Lords' initial moves to elaborate principles of legality and to assert jurisdiction over a wider range of administrative acts remained deferential to central government policies, but this shift in judicial review nevertheless had the effect of encouraging civil society groups to adopt the language of legality when framing criticisms of the government. Susan Sterett, *Creating Constitutionalism* (Ann Arbor: University of Michigan Press, 1997), 115–45.

4 As of February 2009, this position has been renamed the *rapporteur public*.

5 Gerard Sadik, interview by the author, July 2, 2009, Paris.

6 Philippe Waquet, interview by the author, June 12, 2007, Paris.

7 The Constitutional Council does have the authority to review the constitutionality of legislation prior to its enactment, but this review does not take place at the request of private litigants. In 2009, the Constitution of the Fifth Republic was modified to allow ordinary judges to refer constitutional questions concerning previously enacted legislation to the Constitutional Council for an advisory opinion through the *question prioritaire de constitutionnalité* procedure. However, the decision to refer a question lies within the discretion of the judges and has been used very sparingly. For an example, see CE, November 25, 2011, *Mouvement Democrate Sciences Po*.

8 Waquet, interview, June 12, 2007.

9 Ibid.

10 Danièle Lochak, interview by the author, March 2, 2007, Paris.

11 Letter from André Legouy to Georgina Dufoix sent to *Le Monde* newspaper, "Réponse à Madame Georgina Dufoix," October 24, 1984, GISTI papers, n.p.

12 "Requête et Mémoire pour l'Association GISTI contre le décret 84–1080 and le décret 84–1078," February 4, 1985, GISTI Papers, n.p.

13 Gerard Sadik, interview by the author, July 2, 2009, Paris.

14 "Requête et Memoire pour l'Association GISTI contre le décret 84–1078 du Ministre de l'Intérieur du 4 décembre 1984," February 4, 1985, GISTI Papers, n.p.

15 "La Bataille Perdue des Associations," *Plein Droit*, October 1992, 29.
16 "Argumentaire contre la circulaire du 25 Juin 1998," GISTI's Asylum Litigation, May 15, 2001, http://www.gisti.org/doc/argumentaires/2000/asile/recours.html.
17 Letter from Marceau Long, Vice-Président du Conseil d'Etat, to Danièle Lochak, GISTI President, September 10, 1992, GISTI Papers.
18 Bruno Latour describes this cultivated style on the part of Conseil d'Etat adjudicators as a "hexis of indifference" signaling a combination of distance and precision (Latour 2002, 214). The procedure for hearing a *référé* (injunction) is slightly more informal, with a single member of the Conseil d'Etat sitting at the head of a table at which representatives of the parties and the reporter are also seated.
19 CE, April 21, 1997, *GISTI*.
20 "Les Rafistolages du Conseil d'Etat," *Plein Droit*, February 1988, 51.
21 CE, April 21, 1997, *GISTI*.
22 Waquet, interview, June 12, 2007.
23 Sylvia Zappi, "Le Conseil d'Etat Annule Plusieurs Dispositions d'Une Circulaire sur Le Droit d'Asile Territorial," *Le Monde*, January 28, 2000, 10.
24 Sylvia Zappi, "Bercy Veut Limiter Le Coût des Pensions des Anciens Combattants Etrangers," *Le Monde*, January 5, 2002, 9.
25 Bertrand Bissuel, "Le Conseil d'Etat Annule l'Arrêté du Ministre de l'Intérieur Créant le Fichier Eloi," *Le Monde*, March 14, 2007, 10.
26 Ministère de l'Intérieur, Direction des Libertés Publiques et des Affaires Juridiques, senior legal advisor, interview by the author, February 21, 2007, Paris.
27 Note from Jean Duliège, Direction de la Population et des Migrations, to Christian Nguyen, Conseiller Technique au Ministre des Affaires Sociales, September 22, 1984, box 26, Patrick Weil Papers, Centre de Recherche en Histoire Contemporaine. Fondation Nationale des Sciences Politiques, Paris.
28 Note from Christian Nguyen, Conseiller Technique au Ministre des Affaires Sociales, to Georgina Dufoix, Ministre des Affaires Sociales, September 22, 1984, box 26, Patrick Weil Papers.
29 Conseil d'Etat, Section Sociale, senior member, interview by the author, May 23, 2007, Paris.
30 Ministère de l'Intérieur, Direction des Libertés Publiques et des Affaires Juridiques, senior legal advisor, interview by the author, March 8, 2007, Paris.
31 E.g., the member of the Conseil d'Etat seconded to the Ministry of Interior recognized the ingenuity of interpreting the penal code's requirement of "a good chance of social re-insertion," as applicable only to the country of origin for migrants repatriated following their release from incarceration. Notes of meeting between the Ministries of Interior and Justice on the application of *reconduites à la frontière*, January 21, 1986, Archives Nationales, 19990260, box 31, Ministry of Interior Papers.
32 Letter from Claire Waquet to André Legouy, July 6, 1990, GISTI Papers.
33 CE, October 20, 1989, *Nicolo*, Recueil Lebon 190.
34 This phenomenon of intercourt competition is not confined to competition among France's various jurisdictions. According to Karen Alter, intercourt competition between courts at different levels of the national judicial hierarchy has been a major driver of the penetration of European legal principles into the jurisprudence of national courts. See Karen Alter, *Establishing the Supremacy of European Law* (New York: Oxford University Press, 2003).

35 This area of immigration governance had not been accessible to challenge through *recours pour excès de pouvoir* because it had not been the subject of written policy regulations and had instead been left to a case-by-case balancing of equities against state interest.

36 ECHR, March 26, 1992, *Beldjoudi v. France*, 12083/86.

37 Conseil d'Etat, Section des Contentieux, senior member, interview by the author, July 11, 2007.

38 Bernard Stirn, interview by the author, February 20, 2007, Paris.

39 As the ECHR was preparing to hear a case challenging the Conseil d'Etat's revised decision-making procedures, which renamed the *commissaire du gouvernement* the *"rapporteur public"* but otherwise kept the process substantially the same, senior judges organized a meeting with French civil society associations who are frequent litigants, including GISTI, asking them to write a letter to the Strasbourg Court in support of the new procedures. Although GISTI had no strong opinion on the new procedures, it ultimately decided that writing such a letter might undermine its reputation with the ECHR. Interview with Serge Slama, August 2012 in Paris.

40 E.g., according to Alter and Vargas, the European Commission has actively encouraged women's groups and labor unions to use its procedures, with the aim of increasing its institutional power by persuading national governments to embrace European law. Karen Alter and Jeanette Vargas, "Explaining Variation in the Use of European Litigation Strategies: EC Law and UK Gender Equality Policy," *Comparative Political Studies* 33, no. 4 (2000): 452–82. Rachel Cichowski's study of legal activism at the European level suggests that NGOs have also been useful to the European Court of Justice in its efforts to institutionalize European legal norms. Rachel A. Cichowski, *The European Court and Civil Society* (New York: Cambridge University Press, 2007).

41 Waquet, interview, June 12, 2007.

42 Patrick Mony, interview by the author, January 30, 2007, Paris.

43 CE, January 14, 1998, *GISTI.*

44 According to the ECJ's *CILFIT* decision, no referral is necessary if the answer to the EU legal question can in no way affect the outcome of the case, if the question raised is materially identical with a question that has already been the subject of a preliminary ruling in a similar case, if previous decisions of the ECJ have already dealt with the point of law in question, or if the correct application of EU law is obvious. See ECJ, October 6, 1982, *Srl CILFIT and Lanificio di Gavardo SpA v Ministry of Health*, 283/81. As a legal matter, should the Conseil d'Etat abuse its power to decide whether these exceptions apply by refusing to refer legitimate EU legal questions, France would be subject to legal action before the ECJ. I thank Mitchel Lasser for clarifying this point.

45 ECJ, September 27, 2012, *Cimade and GISTI*, C-179/11.

46 ECHR, June 25, 1996, *Amuur v. France*, 19776/92.

47 ECHR, April 26, 2007, *Gebremedhin v. France*, 25389/05; ECHR, February 2, 2012, *I.M. v. France*, 9152/09.

48 Christophe Pouly, "Le Juge Européen: L'Ultime Recours," *Plein Droit*, March 2012, 31.

49 Serge Slama, interview by the author, February 10, 2007, Paris.

50 Jean-Eric Malabre, interview by the author, February 9, 2007, Paris.

51 This is particularly the case following a June 2013 decision in which the Conseil d'Etat's revised procedures maintaining a privileged role for the CDG, now renamed the *rapporteur public*, received the ECHR's official blessing. ECHR, June 4, 2013, *Marc-Antoine v. France*, 54984/09.

Conclusion: Legal Activism and Its Radiating Effects

1 533 U.S. 678, 700 (2001).
2 UN Human Rights Council, "Report of the UN Special Rapporteur on the Human Rights of Migrants, Jorge Bustamente," Mission to the United States of America, April 30–May 18, 2007, A/HRC/7/12/Add.2. New York: United Nations, 2008; UN Human Rights Council, "Report of the UN Special Rapporteur on the Human Rights of Migrants, François Crépeau," Regional Study: Management of the External Borders of the EU and Its Impact on the Human Rights of Migrants, A/HRC/23/46. New York: United Nations, 2013.

Archival and Other Primary Sources

U.S. Manuscript Collections

American Civil Liberties Union, New York
Immigrants' Rights Project Papers

National Archives at College Park, College Park, MD
U.S. Department of Justice, Record Group 60

National Immigration Project of the National Lawyers Guild, Boston
Immigration Newsletter
National Immigration Project Papers

Private Collection of Carolyn Patty Blum, New York
Central American Refugee Defense Fund Papers

Rockefeller Archive Center, Sleepy Hollow, NY
Ford Foundation Grant Files

Tamiment Library, New York
Ira Gollobin Papers

University of Texas, Institute for Oral History, El Paso

France Manuscript Collections

Archives Nationales, Centre des Archives Contemporaines, Fontainebleau
Ministry of Interior Papers
Ministry of Social Affairs Papers

Association Génériques, Paris.

Saïd Bouziri Papers

Bibliothèque de Documentation Internationale Contemporaine, Nanterre

Jean-Jacques De Felice Papers

Centre de Recherche en Histoire Contemporaine. Fondation Nationale des Sciences Politiques, Paris

Yves Jouffa Papers
Patrick Weil Papers

Groupe d'Information et de Soutien des Immigrés, Paris

GISTI Papers
Plein Droit

U.S. Interviews and Oral Histories

Deborah Anker, interview by the author, January 2, 2011, by telephone.
Carolyn Patty Blum, interview by the author, June 19, 2006, New York.
Larry Daves, interview by Virginia Marie Raymond, May 28, 2008. Institute of Oral History, University of Texas, El Paso.
Steven Forester, interview by the author, February 25, 2005, by telephone.
Adam Green, interview by the author, August 29, 2006, by telephone.
Lucas Guttentag, interview by the author July 31, 2006, by telephone.
Linton Joaquin, interview by the author, June 14, 2006, by telephone.
Dan Kesselbrenner, interview by the author, January 20, 2012, Boston.
Larry Kleinman, interview by the author, November 22, 2011, by telephone.
Ira Kurzban, interview by the author, April 6, 2006, by telephone.
Cheryl Little, interview by the author, June 6, 2006, by telephone.
Doris Meissner, interview by the author, April 13, 2006, by telephone.
Bruce A. Morrison, interview by the author, June 15, 2006, by telephone.
Karen Musalo, interview by the author, January 20, 2006, San Francisco.
Burt Newborne, interview by the author, June 16, 2006, New York.
Chris Nugent, interview by the author, June 28, 2006, Washington, DC.
Judy Rabinovitz, interview by the author, May 25, 2006, by telephone.
Lory Rosenberg, interview by the author, May 24, 2006 and August 17, 2014, by telephone.
Gary Silbiger, interview by the author, September 5, 2006, by telephone.
Rick Swartz, interview by the author, June 2, 2006, by telephone.
Peter Schey, interview by the author, May 2, 2006, by telephone.
U.S. Department of Homeland Security, Office of Immigration Litigation, senior attorneys #1 and #2, interviews by the author, January 17, 2012, Washington, DC.
U.S. Department of Justice, Asylum Office, senior attorney, interview by the author, February 25, 2005, Washington, DC.

U.S. Department of Justice, Executive Office for Immigration Review, senior attorney, interview by the author, January 10, 2012, Washington, DC.
U.S. Department of Justice, Immigration and Naturalization Service, Office of General Counsel, senior attorney #1, interview by the author, June 16, 2006, by telephone.
U.S. Department of Justice, Immigration and Naturalization Service, Office of General Counsel, senior attorney #2, interview by the author, June 20, 2006, by telephone.
U.S. Department of Justice, Immigration and Naturalization Service, Office of General Counsel, senior attorney #3, interview by the author, July 20, 2006, by telephone.
Michael Wishnie, interview by the author, May 2, 2005, New York.
Carol Wolchok, interview by the author, June 1, 2006, by telephone.

France Interviews and Oral Histories

Jean-Pierre Alaux, interview by the author, January 26, 2007.
Bernard Aubrée, interview by the author, June 22, 2009, Paris.
Jean-Michel Belorgey, interview by the author, November 29, 2006, Paris.
Christian Bourguet, interview by the author, February 15, 2007, Paris.
Commission des Recours des Refugiés, senior judge, interview by the author, February 28, 2007, Paris.
Conseil d'Etat, Section Sociale, senior member, interview by the author, May 23, 2007, Paris.
Conseil d'Etat, Section des Contentieux, senior member, interview by the author, July 11, 2007.
Benjamin Demagny, interview by the author, June 22, 2009, Paris.
Nathalie Ferré, interview by the author, January 2, 2011, Paris.
Hélène Gacon, interview by the author, July 29, 2005, Paris.
Marie Hénocq, interview by the author, June 22, 2009, Paris.
François Julien-Laferrière, interview by the author, March 6, 2007, Paris.
Henri Leclerc, interview by the author, June 4, 2007, Paris.
Danièle Lochak, interview by the author, March 2, 2007, Paris.
Jean-Eric Malabre, interview by the author, February 9, 2007, Paris.
Hélène Masse-Dessen, interview by the author, June 27, 2007, Paris.
Ministère de l'Intérieur, Direction des Libertés Publiques et des Affaires Juridiques, senior legal advisor, interview by the author, February 21, 2007, Paris.
Ministère de l'Intérieur, Direction des Libertés Publiques et des Affaires Juridiques, senior legal advisor, interview by the author, March 8, 2007, Paris.
Patrick Mony, interview by the author, January 30, 2007, Paris.
Claire Rodier, interview by the author, June 26, 2007, Paris.
Vanina Rocchioli, interview by the author, June 22, 2009, Paris.
Gérard Sadik, interview by the author, July 2, 2009, Paris.
Bernard Schmid, interview by the author, June 24, 2009, Paris.
Serge Slama, interview by the author, February 10, 2007 and August 6, 2012, Paris.
Bernard Stirn, interview by the author, February 20, 2007, Paris.
Maxime Tandonnet, interview by the author, December 5, 2011, Paris.
Frédéric Tiberghien, interview by the author, June 20, 2010, Paris.

Transcript, GISTI Journée Histoire et Mémoire, transcribed by Liora Israel, December
    8, 2000. Groupe d'Information et de Soutien des Immigrés, Paris.
Philippe Waquet, interview by the author, June 12, 2007, Paris.

Newspapers, Periodicals, and Serial Publications

Congressional Record
INS Reporter
Interpreter Releases
Le Monde
Libération
Los Angeles Times
New Republic
New York Times

Published Government Documents

UN Human Rights Council. "Report of the UN Special Rapporteur on the Human
    Rights of Migrants, Jorge Bustamente," Mission to the United States of America,
    April 30–May 18, 2007, A/HRC/7/12/Add.2. New York: United Nations, 2008.
UN Human Rights Council. "Report of the UN Special Rapporteur on the Human
    Rights of Migrants, François Crépeau," Regional Study: Management of the
    External Borders of the EU and Its Impact on the Human Rights of Migrants, A/
    HRC/23/46. New York: United Nations, 2013.
U.S. Congress. Senate. Committee on the Judiciary. "Proposals to Reform U.S.
    Immigration Policy." Hearing, 103rd Congress, 2nd Session. Washington,
    DC: Government Printing Office, 1994.
U.S. National Commission on Law Observance and Enforcement. *Report on
    the Enforcement of Deportation Laws of the United States*. Washington,
    DC: Government Printing Office, 1931.
U.S. Select Commission on Immigration and Refugee Policy. *U.S. Immigration Policy
    and the National Interest*. Washington, DC: Government Printing Office, 1981.

Bibliography

Abdelgawad, Elizabeth Lambert, and Ann Weber. 2008. "The Reception Process in France and Germany." In *A Europe of Rights: The Impact of the ECHR on National Legal Systems*, ed. Helen Keller and Alec Stone Sweet, 107–64. Oxford: Oxford University Press.

Abel, Richard L. 1985. "Lawyers and the Power to Change." *Law and Policy* 7 (1): 5–18.

1995. *Politics by Other Means*. New York: Routledge.

Agrikoliansky, Eric. 2002. *La Ligue Française des Droits de l'Homme et du Citoyen depuis 1945: sociologie d'un engagement civique*. Paris: Harmattan.

2005. "'Liberté, liberté chérie...': la gauche et la protection des libertés publiques dans les années 1970." In *Sur la portée sociale du droit*, ed. Liora Israel, Guillaume Sacriste, Antoine Vauchez, and Laurent Willemez, 325–40. Paris: Presses Universitaires de France.

Alaux, Jean-Pierre. 2009. "Asile: des décisions assez peu productrices de 'droit'." In *Défendre la cause des étrangers en justice*, ed. GISTI, 259–64. Paris: GISTI.

Aleinikoff, T. Alexander. 2002. *Semblances of Sovereignty: The Constitution, the State, and American Citizenship*. Cambridge, MA: Harvard University Press.

Alter, Karen J. 2003. *Establishing the Supremacy of European Law: The Making of an International Rule of Law in Europe*. New York: Oxford University Press.

Alter, Karen J., and Sophie Meunier-Aitsahalia. 1994. "Judicial Politics in the European Community: European Integration and the Pathbreaking Cassis de Dijon Decision." *Comparative Political Studies* 26 (4): 535–61.

Alter, Karen, and Jeanette Vargas. 2000. "Explaining Variation in the Use of European Litigation Strategies: EC Law and UK Gender Equality Policy." *Comparative Political Studies* 33 (4): 452–82.

Anderson, Ellen. 2006. *Out of the Closets and into the Courts: Legal Opportunity Structure and Gay Rights Litigation*. Ann Arbor: University of Michigan Press.

Ansley, Fran. 2005. "Local Contact Points at Global Divides: Labor Rights and Immigrant Rights as Sites for Cosmopolitan Legality." In *Law and Globalization from Below: Towards a Cosmopolitan Legality*, ed. Boaventura de Sousa Santos and César A. Rodriguez-Garavito, 158–80. New York: Cambridge.

2010. "Constructing Citizenship without a License: The Struggle of Undocumented Immigrants in the USA for Livelihoods and Recognition." *Studies in Social Justice* 4 (2): 165–78.

Applebaum, David. 2003. "The Syndicat de la Magistrature 1968–1978: Elements in the History of French White Collar Professional Unionism." In *Lawyers and Vampires: Cultural Histories of Legal Professions*, ed. W. Wesley Pue and David Sugarman, 269–89. New York: Oxford University Press.

Auerbach, Jerold. 1976. *Unequal Justice*. London: Oxford University Press.

Balderama, Francisco E., and Raymond Rodriguez. 1995. *Decade of Betrayal: Mexican Repatriation in the 1930s*. Albuquerque: University of New Mexico Press.

Bell, Derrick A. 1976. "Serving Two Masters: Integration Ideals and Client Interests in School Desegregation Litigation." *Yale Law Journal* 85 (4): 470–516.

Bennett, Michael, and Cruz Reynoso. 1972. "California Rural Legal Assistance (CRLA): Survival of a Poverty Law Practice." *Chicano Law Review* 1 (1): 1–79.

Berrey, Ellen, Steve G. Hoffman, and Laura Beth Nielsen. 2012. "Situated Justice: A Contextual Analysis of Fairness and Inequality in Employment Discrimination Litigation." *Law and Society Review* 46 (1): 1–36.

Beyer, Gregg A. 1992. "Establishing the United States Asylum Officer Corps: A First Report." *International Journal of Refugee Law* 1 (4): 455–85.

2000. "Striking a Balance: The 1995 Asylum Reforms." Paper presented at the INS Symposium and Celebration on the Fifth Anniversary of the 1995 Asylum Reforms, Washington, D.C., January.

Blanc-Chaléard, Marie-Claude. 2010. "Face à l'immigration." In *Comprendre la Ve République*, ed. Jean Garrigues, Sylvie Guillaume, and Jean-François Sirinelli, 481–98. Paris: Presses Universitaires de France.

Blum, Carolyn Patty. 1991. "The Settlement of *American Baptist Churches v. Thornburgh*: Landmark Victory for Central American Asylum-Seekers." *International Journal of Refugee Law* 3 (2): 347–56.

Bohmer, Carol, and Amy Shuman. 2008. *Rejecting Refugees: Political Asylum in the 21st Century*. New York: Routledge.

Bonjour, Saskia. 2014. "Courts in Control? The Impact of the Judiciary on the Making of Family Migration Policies in France, Germany and the Netherlands." Paper presented at the American Political Science Association Annual Meeting, Washington, D.C., August 28–31.

Bouziri, Said. 2005. "Itinéraire d'un militant dans l'immigration." *Migrance* 25: 118–33.

Brigham, John. 1987. *The Cult of the Court*. Philadelphia: Temple University Press.

1996. *The Constitution of Interests: Beyond the Politics of Rights*. New York: New York University Press.

Brouwer, Andrew, and Judith Kumin. 2003. "Interception and Asylum: When Migration Control and Human Rights Collide." *Refuge*: 6–24.

Brown, L. Neville, and John Bell. 1998. *French Administrative Law*. Oxford: Clarendon Press.

Burke, Thomas F., and Jeb Barnes. 2012. "Making Way: Legal Mobilization, Organizational Response, and Wheelchair Access." *Law and Society Review* 46 (1): 167–98.

Calavita, Kitty. 1992. *Inside the State: The Bracero Program, Immigration, and the I.N.S.* New York: Routledge.

2005. *Immigrants at the Margins: Law, Race, and Exclusion in Southern Europe.* New York: Cambridge University Press.

2010. *Invitation to Law and Society: An Introduction to the Study of Real Law.* Chicago: University of Chicago Press.

Cassia, Paul. 2009. *Robert Badinter: un juriste en politique.* Paris: Fayard.

Chavez, Ernesto. 2002. *"Mi Raza Primero!": Nationalism, Identity, and Insurgency in the Chicano Movement in Los Angeles, 1966–1978.* Berkeley: University of California Press.

Chen, Alan, and Scott L. Cummings. 2012. *Public Interest Lawyering: A Contemporary Perspective.* New York: Aspen Publishers.

Chevallier, Jacques. 1989. "Changement politique et droit administratif." In *Les usages sociaux du droit,* ed. Centre Universitaire de Recherches Administratives et Politiques de Picardie, 293–326. Paris: Presses Universitaires de France.

1993. "Les interprètes du droit." In *La doctrine juridique,* ed. Centre Universitaire de Recherches Administratives et Politiques de Picardie, 259–82. Paris: Presses Universitaires de France.

1999. *L'Etat de Droit.* Paris: Montchrestien.

Chin, Gabriel J. 1996. "The Civil Rights Revolution Comes to Immigration Law: A New Look at the Immigration and Nationality Act of 1965." *North Carolina Law Review* 75: 273–345.

Chua, Lynette. 2014. *Mobilizing Gay Singapore.* Philadelphia: Temple University Press.

Cichowski, Rachel A. 2007. *The European Court and Civil Society.* New York: Cambridge University Press.

Comaroff, John, and Simon Roberts. 1981. *Rules and Processes: The Cultural Logic of Dispute in an African Context.* Chicago: University of Chicago Press.

Commaille, Jacques, Laurence Demoulin, and Cécile Robert. 2000. *La juridicisation du politique: leçons scientifiques.* Paris: LGDJ.

Conant, Lisa. 2002. *Justice Contained: Law and Politics in the European Union.* Ithaca, NY: Cornell University Press.

Coombe, Rosemary J. 2000. "Contingent Articulations: A Critical Studies of Law." In *Law in the Domains of Culture,* ed. Austin Sarat and Thomas Kearns, 21–64. Ann Arbor: University of Michigan Press.

Cooper, Bo. 1997. "Procedures for Expedited Removal and Asylum Screening under the Illegal Immigration Reform and Immigrant Responsibility Act of 1996." *Connecticut Law Review* 29: 1501–24.

Coutin, Susan. 1993. *The Culture of Protest: Religious Activism and the U.S. Sanctuary Movement.* Boulder, CO: Westview Press.

2000. *Legalizing Moves: Salvadoran Immigrants' Struggle for U.S. Residency.* Ann Arbor: University of Michigan Press.

2006. "Cause Lawyering and Political Advocacy: Moving Law on Behalf of Central American Refugees." In *Cause Lawyers and Social Movements,* ed. Austin Sarat and Stewart Scheingold, 101–19. Stanford, CA: Stanford University Press.

2011. "The Rights of Noncitizens in the United States." *Annual Review of Law and Social Science* 7: 289–308.

Cummings, Scott L. 2007. "The Internationalization of Public Interest Law." *Duke Law Journal* 57: 891–959.

Cummings, Scott L., and Louise G. Trubek. 2008. "Globalizing Public Interest Law." *UCLA Journal of International Law and Foreign Affairs* 13: 1–53.

Dauvergne, Catherine. 2008. *Making People Illegal: What Globalization Means for Migration and Law*. New York: Cambridge University Press.

DeBenedictis, Don J. 1992. "INS in a Mood to Settle." *American Bar Association Journal* 78: 36.

De Felice, Jean-Jacques. 2002. "Etre avocat pendant la guerre d'Algerie." In *Des Français contre la terreur d'Etat*, ed. Sidi Mohammed Barkat, 149–58. Paris: Editions Reflex.

Dooley, John A., and Alan W. Houseman. 1984. *Legal Services History*. Washington, D.C.: Center for Law and Social Policy.

Dréano, Bernard. 2004. "In Paris, the Global Place Is No More Saint-Germain-des-Prés." In *Exploring Civil Society*, edited by Marlies Glasius, 82–8. New York: Routledge.

Ducamin, Bernard. 1981. "The Role of the Conseil d'Etat in Drafting Legislation." *International and Comparative Law Quarterly* 30 (4): 882–901.

Ellermann, Antje. 2009. *States against Migrants: Deportation in Germany and the United States*. New York: Cambridge University Press.

Epp, Charles R. 2009. *Making Rights Real: Activists, Bureaucrats, and the Creation of the Legalistic State*. Chicago: University of Chicago Press.

Epstein, Lee. 1985. *Conservatives in Court*. Knoxville: University of Tennessee Press.

Escafré-Dublet, Angéline. 2014. *Culture et immigration: De la question sociale à l'enjeu politique*. Paris: Presses Universitaires de Rennes.

Ewick, Patricia, and Susan S. Silbey. 1998. *The Common Place of Law: Stories from Everyday Life*. Chicago: University of Chicago Press.

Faget, Jacques. 1995. "L'accès au droit: logiques de marché et enjeux sociaux." *Droit et Société* 30–1: 367–78.

Family, Jill E. 2008. "Threats to the Future of the Immigration Class Action." *Washington University Journal of Law and Policy* 27: 71–122.

Favier, Pierre, and Michel Martin-Roland. 1997. *La décennie Mitterrand*. Paris: Editions du Seuil.

Favoreu, Louis. 1988. *La politique saisi par le droit*. Paris: Economica.

Feldman, Gregory. 2012. *The Migration Apparatus: Security, Labor, and Policymaking in the European Union*. Stanford, CA: Stanford University Press.

Ferré, Natalie. 2009. "Victoires volées." In *Défendre la cause des étrangers en justice*, ed. GISTI, 227–38. Paris: GISTI.

Fournier, Jacques. 2014. "Le Conseil d'Etat précurseur du droit à la vie familiale." *Actualité Juridique Droit Administratif* 2: 95–6.

Frenzen, Niels. 2010. "U.S. Migrant Interdiction Practices in International and Territorial Waters." In *Extraterritorial Immigration Control*, ed. Bernard Ryan and Valsamis Mitsilegas, 375–96. Leiden, The Netherlands: Koninklijke Brill NV.

Gabel, Peter, and Paul Harris. 1982. "Building Power and Breaking Images: Critical Legal Theory and the Practice of Law." *NYU Review of Law and Social Change* 11: 369–411.

Galanter, Marc. 1983. "The Radiating Effects of Courts." In *Empirical Theories of Courts*, ed. Keith D. Boyum and Lynn M. Mather, 117–42. New York: Longman.

1990. "Case Congregations and Their Careers." *Law and Society Review* 24 (2): 371–96.

Ganz, Marshall. 2009. *Why David Sometimes Wins: Leadership, Organization, and Strategy in the California Farm Worker Movement*. New York: Oxford University Press.

Gaxie, Daniel, ed. 1995. *Rapport sur l'analyse secondaire des enquêtes d'opinion relatives à l'immigration et à la présence étrangère en France.* Paris: APRED.

Geddes, Andrew. 2003. *The Politics of Migration and Immigration in Europe.* London: Sage Publications.

Geertz, Clifford. 1968. *Islam Observed.* Chicago: University of Chicago Press.

Genevois, Bruno. 2009. "Le GISTI: requérant d'habitude? La vision du Conseil d'Etat." In *Défendre la cause des étrangers en justice,* ed. GISTI, 65–79. Paris: Dalloz.

Gillman, Howard. 2006. "Party Politics and Constitutional Change: The Political Origins of Liberal Judicial Activism." In *The Supreme Court and American Political Development,* ed. Ken Kersch and Ronald Kahn, 138–68. Lawrence: University Press of Kansas.

Gimpel, James, and James Edwards. 1999. *The Congressional Politics of Immigration Reform.* Boston: Allyn and Bacon.

Ginesy-Galand, Mireille. 1984. *Les immigrés hors la cité: Le système d'encadrement dans les foyers.* Paris: Editions l'Harmattan.

Ginger, Ann Fagan. 1993. *Carol Weiss King: Human Rights Lawyer, 1895–1952.* Niwot: University of Colorado Press.

GISTI. 1975. *Le petit livre des travailleures immigrés.* Paris: Editions Maspéro.

1992. *Guide de la nationalité française.* Paris: La Découverte.

Gleeson, Shannon. 2013. *Conflicting Commitments: The Politics of Enforcing Immigrant Worker Rights in San Jose and Houston.* Ithaca, NY: Cornell University Press.

Goldstein, Brandt. 2005. *Storming the Court: How a Band of Yale Law Students Sued the President – And Won.* New York: Scribner.

Gomes, Charles. 2000. "Les limites de la souveraineté." *Revue Française de Science Politique* 50 (6): 422–33.

Gordon, Jennifer. 2005. *Suburban Sweatshops: The Fight for Immigrant Rights.* Cambridge, MA: Harvard University Press.

2006. "A Movement in the Wake of a New Law: The United Farm Workers and the California Agricultural Labor Relations Act." In *Cause Lawyers and Social Movements,* ed. Austin Sarat and Stewart Scheingold, 277–301. Cambridge, MA: Harvard University Press.

Graham, Hugh Davies. 2003. *Collision Course: The Strange Convergence of Affirmative Action and Immigration Policy in America.* New York: Oxford University Press.

Grelet, Stany, Philippe Margeot, Victoire Patouillard, and Isabelle Saint-Saens. 2001. "Vingt ans après: Entretien avec Assane Ba." *Vacarme* 16 (Summer): 4–14.

Grillo, R. D. 1985. *Ideologies and Institutions in Urban France: The Representation of Immigrants.* New York: Cambridge University Press.

Guiraudon, Virginie. 2000a. "European Courts and Foreigners' Rights: A Comparative Study of Norms Diffusion." *International Migration Review* 34 (4): 1088–125.

2000b. *Les politiques d'immigration en Europe: Allemagne, France, Pays-Bas.* Paris: L'Harmattan.

2002. "European Integration and Migration Policy: Vertical Policy-Making as Venue Shopping." *Journal of Common Market Studies* 38 (2): 251–71.

2011. "Mobilization, Social Movements and the Media." In *Sociology of the European Union,* ed. Virginie Guiraudon and Adrian Favell, 128–49. London: Palgrave.

Gutierrez, David G. 1995. *Walls and Mirrors: Mexican Americans, Mexican Immigrants, and the Politics of Ethnicity.* Berkeley: University of California Press.

Halliday, Terence C., and Lucien Karpik. 1997. *Lawyers and the Rise of Western Political Liberalism*. Oxford: Clarendon Press.

Halliday, Terence C., Lucien Karpik, and Malcolm Feeley. 2007. "The Legal Complex and Struggles for Political Liberalism." In *Fighting for Political Freedom: Comparative Studies of the Legal Complex and Political Liberalism*, ed. Terence C. Halliday, Lucien Karpik, and Malcolm Feeley, 1–41. Oxford: Hart Publishing.

Hamlin, Rebecca. 2014. *Let Me Be a Refugee: Administrative Justice and the Politics of Asylum in the United States, Canada, and Australia*. New York: Oxford University Press.

Handler, Joel. 1978. *Social Movements and the Legal System: A Theory of Law Reform and Social Change*. New York: Academic Press.

Handler, Joel F., Betsy Ginsberg, and Arthur Snow. 1978. "The Public Interest Law Industry." In *Public Interest Law: An Economic and Institutional Analysis*, ed. Burton Weisbrod, 42–79. Berkeley: University of California Press.

Handler, Joel, Elizabeth Hollingsworth, and Howard Erlanger. 1978. *Lawyers and the Pursuit of Legal Rights*. New York: Academic Press.

Haney-López, Ian. 2003. *Racism on Trial: The Chicano Fight for Justice*. Cambridge, MA: Belknap Press of Harvard University Press.

Harrington, Christine B., and Sally Merry. 1988. "Ideological Production: The Making of Community Mediation." *Law and Society Review* 22 (4): 709–32.

Harrison, Gordon, and Sanford M. Jaffe. 1973. *The Public Interest Law Firm: New Voices for New Constituencies*. New York: The Ford Foundation.

Haus, Leah A. 2002. *Unions, Immigration, and Internationalization: New Challenges and Changing Coalitions in the United States and France*. New York: Palgrave Macmillan.

Helton, Arthur C. 1984/1985. "The Most Ambitious Pro Bono Ever Attempted." *Human Rights* 12: 18–48.

Hilbink, Thomas. 2006. "Constructing Cause Lawyering: Professionalism, Politics, and Social Change in 1960s America." PhD diss., Institute for Law and Society, New York University.

Hing, Bill Ong. 2000. "The Emma Lazarus Effect: A Case Study in Philanthropic Revitalization of the Immigrant Rights Community." *Georgetown Immigration Law Journal* (Fall): 47–97.

Hoffman, Abraham. 1974. *Unwanted Mexican Americans in the Great Depression; Repatriation Pressures, 1929–1939*. Tucson: University of Arizona Press.

Hollifield, James F. 1992. *Immigrants, Markets, and States: The Political Economy of Postwar Europe*. Cambridge, MA: Harvard University Press.

  2004. "The Emerging Migration State." *International Migration Review* 38 (3): 885–906.

Hunt, Alan. 1985. "The Ideology of Law: Advances and Problems in Recent Applications of the Concept of Ideology to the Analysis of Law." *Law and Society Review* 19 (11): 11–38.

Israel, Liora. 2003. "Faire émerger le droit des étrangers en le contestant, ou l'histoire paradoxale des premières années du GISTI." *Politix* 16 (62): 115–44.

Jacobson, David. 1996. *Rights across Borders: Immigration and the Decline of Citizenship*. Baltimore, MD: Johns Hopkins University Press.

Jacobson, David, and Galya Ruffer. 2003. "Courts across Borders." *Human Rights Quarterly* 25 (1): 74–93.

Joppke, Christian. 1998. *Immigration and the Nation-State: The United States, Germany, and Great Britain.* New York: Oxford University Press.

Junker, Barry. 2006. "Burden Sharing or Burden Shifting? Asylum and Expansion in the European Union." *Georgetown Immigration Law Journal* 20: 293–322.

Kagan, Robert A. 2001. *Adversarial Legalism: The American Way of Law.* Cambridge, MA: Harvard University Press.

Kahn, Jeffrey Sterling. 2013. "Islands of Sovereignty: Haitian Migration and the Borders of Empire." PhD diss., University of Chicago.

Kalman, Laura. 1996. *The Strange Career of Liberal Legalism.* New Haven, CT: Yale University Press.

Kanstroom, Dan. 2007. *Deportation Nation: Outsiders in American History.* Cambridge, MA: Harvard University Press.

Karpik, Lucien. 1999. *French Lawyers: A Study in Collective Action.* New York: Clarendon Press.

Karpik, Lucien, and Terence C. Halliday. 2011. "The Legal Complex." *Annual Review of Law and Social Science* 7: 217–36.

Kawar, Leila, and Mark Fathi Massoud. 2012. "Symposium: New Directions in Comparative Public Law." *American Political Science Association Law and Courts Section Newsletter* 22 (3): 32–6.

Keleman, R. Daniel. 2008. "The Americanisation of European Law? Adversarial legalism à la européenne." *European Political Science* 7: 32–40.

Kelly, Tobias. 2012. *This Side of Silence: Human Rights, Torture, and the Recognition of Cruelty.* Philadelphia: University of Pennsylvania Press.

Kenney, Sally J., William M. Reisinger, and John C. Reitz, eds. 1999. *Constitutional Dialogues in Comparative Perspective.* New York: St. Martin's Press.

Kersch, Ken I. 2006. "The New Deal Triumph as the End of History?" In *The Supreme Court and American Political Development,* ed. Ronald Kahn and Ken I. Kersch, 169–226. Lawrence: University Press of Kansas.

Klarman, Michael J. 2004. *From Jim Crow to Civil Rights: The Supreme Court and the Struggle for Racial Equality.* New York: Oxford University Press.

Knorr Cetina, Karin. 1999. *Epistemic Cultures: How the Sciences Make Knowledge.* Cambridge, MA: Harvard University Press.

Koopmans, Tim. 2003. *Courts and Political Institutions: A Comparative View.* New York: Cambridge University Press.

Kurzban, Ira J. 1981. "Restructuring the Asylum Process." *San Diego Law Review* 19 (1): 91–117.

Laham, Nicholas. 2000. *Ronald Reagan and the Politics of Immigration Reform.* Westport, CT: Praeger.

Lamont, Michèle. 1992. *Money, Morals, and Manners: The Culture of the French and the American Upper-Middle Class.* Chicago: University of Chicago Press.

Lascoumes, Pierre. 2009. "Changer le droit, changer la société: Le moment d'un retournement." *Genèses* 77: 110–23.

Lasser, Mitchel. 2009. *Judicial Transformations: The Rights Revolution in the Courts of Europe.* Oxford: Oxford University Press.

Latour, Bruno. 1993. *We Have Never Been Modern*. Translated by Catherine Porter. Cambridge, MA: Harvard University Press.

    1999. *Pandora's Hope: Essays on the Reality of Science Studies*. Cambridge, MA: Harvard University Press.

    2002. *La fabrique du droit. Une ethnographie du Conseil d'Etat*. Paris: La Découverte.

    2004a. "Note brève sur l'écologie du droit saisi comme énonciation." *Cosmopolitique* 8: 34–40.

    2004b. "Scientific Objects and Legal Objectivity." In *Law, Anthropology, and the Constitution of the Social*, ed. Alain Pottage and Martha Mundy, 73–114. New York: Cambridge University Press.

Law, Anna O. 2010. *The Immigration Battle in American Courts*. New York: Cambridge University Press.

Law, John. 2004. *After Method: Mess in Social Science Research*. London: Routledge.

    2009. "Actor Network Theory and Material Semiotics." In *The New Blackwell Companion to Social Theory*, ed. Bryan S. Turner, 141–58. Malden, MA: Wiley-Blackwell.

Leclerc, Henri. 1994. *Un combat pour la justice*. Paris: La Découverte.

Leclerc, Henri, and Michel Blum. 1970. "Crise de la justice." *Après-Demain* 122 (March): 4–6.

Legomsky, Stephen H. 1984. "Immigration Law and the Principle of Plenary Congressional Power." *The Supreme Court Review* 84: 255–307.

    1987. *Immigration and the Judiciary: Law and Politics in Britain and America*. New York: Oxford University Press.

Levi, Ron, and Mariana Valverde. 2008. "Studying Law by Association: Bruno Latour goes to the Conseil d'Etat." *Law and Social Inquiry* 33 (Summer): 805–25.

Levin, Leslie C. 2009. "Guardians at the Gate: The Backgrounds, Career Paths, and Professional Development of Private US Immigration Lawyers." *Law and Social Inquiry* 34 (2): 399–436.

Lewis, Mary Dewhurst. 2007. *The Boundaries of the Republic: Migrant Rights and the Limits of Universalism in France, 1918–1940*. Stanford, CA: Stanford University Press.

Lochak, Danièle. 1985. *Etrangers: de quel droit?* Paris: Presses Universitaires de France.

    1987. "Code de la nationalité: la logique de l'exclusion." *Les Temps Modernes* 490 (May): 54–104.

    1993. "Quelle legitimité pour le juge administratif?" In *Droit et Politique*, ed. Centre Universitaire de Recherches Administratives et Politiques de Picardie, 141–57. Paris: Presses Universitaires de France.

    2009. "Trente ans de contentieux à l'initiative du GISTI." In *Défendre la cause des étrangers en justice*, ed. GISTI, 43–64. Paris: Dalloz.

    2011. "Des droits fondamentaux sacrifiés." In *Liberté de circulation: un droit, quelles politiques?*, 10–23. Paris: GISTI.

Loescher, Gill, and John A. Scanlan. 1986. *Calculated Kindness: Refugees and America's Half-Open Door, 1945 to the Present*. New York: Free Press.

Lynch, Michael. 1997. "Preliminary Notes on Judges' Work: The Judge as a Constituent of Courtroom 'Hearings'." In *Law in Action: Ethnomethodological and Conversation Analytic Approaches to Law*, ed. Max Travers and John F. Manzo, 99–130. Brookfield, VT: Ashgate.

Mack, Kenneth W. 2005. "Rethinking Civil Rights Lawyering and Politics in the Era Before Brown." *Yale Law Journal* 115: 256–354.

Madsen, Mikael Rask. 2005. "L'émergence d'un champ des droits de l'homme dans les pays européens: Enjeux professionnels et stratégies d'Etat au carrefour du droit et de la politique." PhD diss., Sociology, Ecole des Hautes Etudes en Sciences Sociales.

Mangenot, Michel. 2005. "The Conseil d'Etat and Europe." In *French Relations with the European Union*, ed. Helen Drake, 142–78. New York: Routledge.

Marshall, Anna-Maria, and Daniel Crocker Hale. 2014. "Cause Lawyering." *Annual Review of Law and Social Science* 10: 301–20.

Martin, David A. 2002. "Behind the Scenes on a Different Set: What Congress Needs to Do in the Aftermath of St. Cyr and Nguyen." *Georgetown Immigration Law Journal* 16: 313–38.

Massot, Jean, Olivier Fouquet, and Jacques-Henri Stahl. 2001. *Le Conseil d'Etat, juge de cassation*. 3rd ed. Paris: Berger-Levrault.

Mather, Lynn, and Barbara Yngvesson. 1980. "Language, Audience, and the Transformation of Disputes." *Law and Society Review* 15 (3): 775–822.

Mathieu, Lilian. 2006. "La double peine. Histoire d'un lutte inachevée." La Dispute. http://terra.rezo.net/article339.html.

Maugendre, Stéphane. 2009. "Présentation." In *Défendre la cause des étrangers en justice*, ed. GISTI, 2–3. Paris: Dalloz.

Mauger, Gérard. 1994. "Gauchisme, contre-culture et néo-libéralisme: pour une histoire de la génération de mai 1968." In *L'identité politique*, ed. Centre Universitaire de Recherches Administratives et Politiques de Picardie, 206–26. Paris: Presses Universitaires de France.

McCann, Michael W. 1986. *Taking Reform Seriously: Perspectives on Public Interest Liberalism*. Ithaca, NY: Cornell University Press.

1994. *Rights At Work: Pay Equity Reform and the Politics of Legal Mobilization*. Chicago: University of Chicago Press.

McCann, Michael, and Helena Silverstein. 1998. "Rethinking Law's 'Allurements': A Relational Analysis of Social Movement Lawyers in the United States." In *Cause Lawyering: Political Commitments and Professional Responsibilities*, ed. Austin Sarat and Stewart Scheingold, 261–90. New York: Oxford University Press.

McClymont, Mary, and Stephen Golub. 2000. *Many Roads to Justice: The Law-Related Work of Ford Foundation Grantees around the World*. New York: Ford Foundation.

McGee, Kyle. 2014. *Bruno Latour: The Normativity of Networks*. New York: Routledge.

McKinley, Michelle. 1997. "Life Stories, Disclosure and the Law." *PoLAR* 20 (2): 70–82.

Meissner, Doris, Donald M. Kerwin, Muzaffar Chishti, and Claire Bergeron. 2013. *Immigration Enforcement in the United States: The Rise of a Formidable Machinery*. Washington, D.C.: Migration Policy Institute.

Melnick, R. Shep. 1994. *Between the Lines: Interpreting Welfare Rights*. Washington, D.C.: The Brookings Institution.

Menkel-Meadow, Carrie. 1998. "The Causes of Cause Lawyering: Toward an Understanding of the Motivation and Commitment of Social Justice Lawyers." In *Cause Lawyering: Political Commitments and Professional Responsibilities*, ed. Austin Sarat and Stewart Scheingold, 31–68. New York: Oxford University Press.

Menz, Georg. 2009. *The Political Economy of Managed Migration: Nonstate Actors, Europeanization, and the Politics of Designing Migration Policies.* New York: Oxford University Press.

Merry, Sally Engle. 1995. "Resistance and the Cultural Power of Law." *Law and Society Review* 29 (1): 11–26.

1999. *Colonizing Hawai'i.* Princeton, NJ: Princeton University Press.

Mezey, Susan Gluck. 2007. *Queers in Court: Gay Rights Law and Public Policy.* Lanham, MD: Rowman and Littlefield Publishers.

Michel, Claude. 2004. *Les vingt ans du SAF, 1972–1992.* Paris: Syndicat des Avocats de France.

Minami, Dale. 2000. "Speech: Asian Law Caucus: Recognizing Twenty-Five Years of Struggle." *UCLA Asian Pacific American Law Journal* 6: 50–4.

Morag-Levine, Noga. 2003. "Partners No More: Relational Transformation and the Turn to Litigation in Two Conservationist Organizations." *Law and Society Review* 37: 457.

Morawetz, Nancy. 2005. "INS v. St. Cyr." In *Immigration Stories,* ed. David A. Martin and Peter H. Schuck, 279–310. New York: Foundation Press.

2011. "Counterbalancing Distorted Incentives in Supreme Court Pro Bono Practice: Recommedations for the New Supreme Court Pro Bono Bar and Public Interest Practice Communities." *New York University Law Review* 86: 131–206.

Moreau, Gérard. 2009. "Circulaires et droit." In *Défendre la cause des étrangers en justice,* ed. GISTI, 241–5. Paris: Dalloz.

Morris, Milton D. 1984. *Immigration – The Beleaguered Bureaucracy.* Washington, D.C.: Brookings Institution.

Motomura, Hiroshi. 1990. "Immigration Law after a Century of Plenary Power: Phantom Norms and Statutory Interpretation." *Yale Law Journal* 100: 545–613.

2008. "The Rights of Others: Legal Claims and Immigration Outside the Law." *Duke Law Journal* 59: 1723–62.

Naquet, Emmanuel. 2009. "Ligue des Droits de l'Homme, syndicalisme et syndicats dans le premier XXe siècle." In *Etre dreyfusard hier et aujourd'hui,* ed. Gilles Manceron and Emmanuel Naquet, 371–80. Rennes, France: Presses Universitaires de Rennes.

NeJaime, Douglas. 2011. "Winning through Losing." *Iowa Law Review* 96: 941.

Nelken, David. 2010. *Comparative Criminal Justice: Making Sense of Difference.* London: Sage.

Nelken, David, ed. 1997. *Comparing Legal Cultures.* Hants, UK: Dartmouth Publishers.

Nevins, Joseph. 2002. *Operation Gatekeeper.* New York: Routledge.

Newton, Lina. 2008. *Illegal, Alien, or Immigrant: The Politics of Immigration Reform.* New York: New York University Press.

Ngai, Mai. 2005. *Impossible Subjects: Illegal Aliens and the Making of Modern America.* Princeton, NJ: Princeton University Press.

Nielsen, Laura Beth, and Catherine R. Albiston. 2006. "What Do We Know about Lawyers' Lives? The Organization of Public Interest Practice, 1975–2004." *North Carolina Law Review* 84: 1591–1621.

Noblecourt, Michel. 1990. *Les syndicats en questions*. Paris: Les Editions Ouvrières.

Noiriel, Gérard. 2001. *Etat, nation et immigration*. Paris: Gallimard.

2010. *Dire la vérité au pouvoir. Les intellectuels en question*. Paris: Agone.

Olivas, Michael A. 2005. "Plyler v. Doe, the Education of Undocumented Children, and the Polity." In *Immigration Stories*, ed. Peter H. Schuck and David A. Martin, 197–220. New York: Foundation Press.

2012. *No Undocumented Child Left Behind*. New York: New York University Press.

Olson, Susan. 1995. "Comparing Women's Rights Litigation in the Netherlands and the United States." *Polity* 28: 189–215.

Péchu, Cécile. 2006. *Droit au Logement: genèse et sociologie d'une mobilisation*. Paris: Dalloz.

Pitti, Laure. 2006. "Une matrice algérienne? Trajectoires et recompositions militantes en terrain ouvrier, de la cause de l'indépendance aux grèves d'OS des années 1968–1975." *Politix* 76: 143–66.

2010. "Experts 'bruts' et médecins critiques: ou comment la mise en débats des savoirs médicaux a modifié la définition du saturnisme en France durant les années 1970." *Politix* 23 (91): 103–32.

Plötner, Jens. 1998. "Report on France." In *The European Court and the National Courts*, ed. Anne-Marie Slaughter, Alec Stone Sweet, and Joseph H. H. Weiler, 41–76. Oxford: Hart Publishing.

Polletta, Francesca. 2000. "The Structural Context of Novel Rights Claims: Southern Civil Rights Organizing, 1961–1966." *Law and Society Review* 34 (2): 367–406.

Provine, Doris Marie, and Roxanne Lynn Doty. 2011. "The Criminalization of Immigrants as a Racial Project." *Journal of Contemporary Criminal Justice* 27 (3): 261–77.

Rabin, Robert. 1975. "Lawyers for Social Change: Perspectives on Public Interest." *Stanford University Law Review* 28: 207–61.

Redish, Martin H. 2009. *Wholesale Justice: Constitutional Democracy and the Problem of the Class Action Lawsuit*. Stanford, CA: Stanford University Press.

Revon, Christian, ed. 1978. *Boutiques de droit*. Paris: Editions Solin.

Rhode, Deborah L. 2008. "Public Interest Law: The Movement at Midlife." *Stanford Law Review* 60: 2027–78.

Richards, Mark J., and Herbert M. Kritzer. 2002. "Jurisprudential Regimes in Supreme Court Decision Making." *American Political Science Review* 96 (June): 305–20.

Riles, Annelise. 1998. "Infinity within the Brackets." *American Ethnologist* 25 (3): 378–98.

2006. "[Deadlines]: Removing the Brackets on Politics in Bureaucratic and Anthropological Analysis." In *Documents: Artifacts of Modern Knowledge*, ed. Annelise Riles, 71–94. Ann Arbor: University of Michigan Press.

2011. *Collateral Knowledge: Legal Reasoning in the Global Financial Markets*. Chicago: University of Chicago Press.

Rodier, Claire. 2009. "Saisir la Cour de Justice des Communautés Europénnes: une route semée d'obstacles." In *Défendre la cause des étrangers en justice*, ed. GISTI, 165–76. Paris: Dalloz.

Rosenau, Neal. 1989. "From the Barrio to the Boardroom." *ABA Journal* 75: 60–4.

Rosenberg, Gerald N. 1991. *The Hollow Hope: Can Courts Bring about Social Change?* Chicago: University of Chicago.

Rosenberg, Lory Diana. 2003. "The Courts and Interception: The United States' Interdiction Experience and Its Impact on Refugees and Asylum Seekers." *Georgetown Immigration Law Journal* 17: 199–219.

Ross, Kristin. 2002. *May '68 and Its Afterlives*. Chicago: University of Chicago Press.

Roussel, Violaine. 2002. *Affaires de juges: les magistrats dans les scandales politiques en France*. Paris: La Découverte.

Salyer, Lucy E. 1995. *Laws Harsh as Tigers: Chinese Immigrants and the Shaping of Modern Immigration Law*. Chapel Hill: The University of North Carolina Press.

San Miguel, Guadelupe. 1987. *Let All of Them Take Heed: Mexican Americans and the Campaign for Educational Equality in Texas, 1910–1981*. Austin: University of Texas Press.

Santos, Boaventura de Sousa. 1995. *Toward a New Common Sense: Law, Science and Politics in the Paradigmatic Transition*. New York: Routledge.

———. 2005. "Beyond Neoliberal Governance: The World Social Forum as SUbaltern Cosmopolitan Politics and Legality." In *Law and Globalization from Below: Towards a Cosmopolitan Legality*, ed. Boaventura de Sousa Santos and César A. Rodriguez-Garavito, 29–63. New York: Cambridge.

Sarat, Austin, and Stewart Scheingold, eds. 1998. *Cause Lawyering: Political Commitments and Professional Responsibilities*. New York: Cambridge University Press.

———. eds. 2001. *Cause Lawyering and the State in a Global Era*. New York: Oxford University Press.

———. eds. 2008. *The Cultural Lives of Cause Lawyers*. New York: Cambridge University Press.

Schain, Martin A. 2008. *The Politics of Immigration in France, Britain, and the United States*. New York: Palgrave MacMillan.

Scheingold, Stewart. 1998. "The Struggle to Politicize Legal Practice: A Case Study of Left-Activist Lawyering in Seattle." In *Cause Lawyering: Political Commitments and Professional Responsibilities*, ed. Austin Sarat and Stewart Scheingold, 118–50. New York: Cambridge University Press.

Scheppele, Kim Lane. 2004. "Constitutional Ethnography: An Introduction." *Law and Society Review* 38 (3): 389–406.

Schnapper, Dominique. 2010. *Une sociologue au Conseil Constitutionnel*. Paris: Galimard.

Schuck, Peter H. 1983. *Suing Government: Citizen Remedies for Official Wrongs*. New Haven, CT: Yale University Press.

———. 1984. "The Transformation of Immigration Law." *Columbia Law Review* 84 (1): 1–90.

Schuck, Peter, and Theodore Hsien Wang. 1992. "Continuity and Change: Patterns of Immigration Litigation in the Courts, 1979–1990." *Stanford Law Review* 45: 115–76.

Shamir, Ronen, and Sarah Chinsky. 1998. "Destruction of Houses and Construction of a Cause: Lawyers and Bedouins in Israeli Courts." In *Cause Lawyering: Political Commitments and Professional Responsibilities*, ed. Austin Sarat and Stewart Scheingold, 227–92. New York: Cambridge University Press.

Shapiro, Martin M. 1988. *Who Guards the Guardians? Judicial Control of Administration*. Athens: University of Georgia Press.

———. 1990. "Judicial Review in France." *Journal of Law and Politics* 6: 531–48.

Silbey, Susan. 1981. "Case Processing: Consumer Protection in an Attorney General's Office." *Law and Society Review* 15 (3–4): 849–910.

Silverstein, Gordon. 2009. *Law's Allure: How Law Shapes, Constrains, Saves, and Kills Politics*. New York: Cambridge University Press.

Siméant, Johanna. 1998. *La cause des sans-papiers*. Paris: Presses de Sciences Po.

Skrentny, John D. 2002. *The Minority Rights Revolution*. Cambridge, MA: Harvard University Press.

Slama, Serge, and Nicolas Ferran, eds. 2014. *Défendre en justice la cause des personnes détenues*. Paris: La Documentation Française.

Soennecken, Dagmar. 2008. "The Growing Influence of the Courts over the Fate of Refugees." *Review of European and Russian Affairs* 4 (2): 55–88.

Soysal, Yasemin Nuhoglu. 1994. *Limits of Citizenship: Migrants and Postnational Membership in Europe*. Chicago: University of Chicago Press.

Sterett, Susan. 1997. *Creating Constitutionalism*. Ann Arbor: University of Michigan Press.

Stirn, Bernard. 1991. *Le Conseil d'Etat: Son Rôle, Sa Jurisprudence*. Paris: Hachette.

Stone, Alec. 1989. "Legal Constraints to Policy-Making: The Constitutional Council and the Council of State." In *Policy-Making in France from De Gaulle to Mitterand*, ed. Paul Godt, 28–41. New York: Pinter Publishers.

1992. *The Birth of Judicial Politics in France*. New York: Oxford University Press.

Stone Sweet, Alec. 2000. *Governing with Judges: Constitutional Politics in Europe*. Oxford and New York: Oxford University Press.

Taylor, Margaret H. 2002. "Behind the Scenes of St. Cyr and Zadvydas: Making Policy in the Midst of Litigation." *Georgetown Immigration Law Journal* 16: 271–312.

Teles, Steven. 2008. *The Rise of the Conservative Legal Movement: The Battle for Control of the Law*. Princeton, NJ: Princeton University Press.

Tichenor, Daniel J. 2002. *Dividing Lines: The Politics of Immigration Control in America*. Princeton, NJ: Princeton University Press.

Trubek, Louise. 2011. "Public Interest Law: Facing the Problems of Maturity." *University of Arkansas Little Rock Law Review* 33: 417–33.

Tushnet, Mark. 1997. "Symobic Statutes and Real Laws: The Pathologies of Antiterrorism and Effective Death Penalty Act and The Prison Litigation Reform Act." *Duke Law Journal* 47: 1–86.

2006. "The Supreme Court and the National Political Order: Collaboration and Confrontation." In *The Supreme Court and American Political Development*, ed. Ronald Kahn and Ken I. Kersch, 117–37. Lawrence: University Press of Kansas.

Tushnet, Mark V. 2004. *The NAACP's Legal Strategy against Segregated Education, 1925–1950*. Chapel Hill: University of North Carolina Press.

Valverde, Mariana. 2003. *Law's Dream of a Common Knowledge*. Princeton, NJ: Princeton University Press.

Vanhala, Lisa. 2011. *Making Rights a Reality? Disability Rights Activists and Legal Mobilization*. Cambridge Disability Law and Policy Series. New York: Cambridge University Press.

Vauchez, Antoine, and Laurent Willemez. 2007. *La justice face à ses réformateurs*. Paris: Presses Universitaires de France.

Viet, Vincent. 1998. *La France immigré: Construction d'une politique, 1914–1997.* Paris: Fayard.

Volpp, Leti. 2000. "Court-Stripping and Class-Wide Relief: A Response to Judicial Review in Immigration Cases After AADC." *Georgetown Immigration Law Journal* 14: 463–79.

Voss, Kim, and Irene Bloemraad. 2011. *Rallying for Immigrant Rights: The Fight for Inclusion in 21st Century America.* Berkeley: University of California Press.

Wadhia, Shoba Sivaprasad. 2013. "The Immigration Prosecutor and the Judge: Examining the Role of the Judiciary in Prosecutorial Discretion Decisions." *Harvard Latino Law Review* 16: 39–78.

Walters, William. 2002. "Deportation, Expulsion, and the International Police of Aliens." *Citizenship Studies* 6 (3): 265–92.

Wasby, Stephen. 1995. *Race Relations Litigation in an Age of Complexity.* Charlottesville: University of Virginia Press.

Weil, Patrick. 2004. *La France et ses étrangers: L'aventure d'une politique de l'immigration, de 1938 à nos jours.* Paris: Calmann-Lévy.

Weisbrod, Burton. 1978. "Conceptual Perspective on the Public Interest: An Economic Analysis." In *Public Interest Law: An Economic and Institutional Analysis*, ed. Burton Weisbrod, 4–29. Berkeley: University of California Press.

White, Lucie. 1990. "Subordination, Rhetorical Survival Skills, and Sunday Shoes: Notes on the Hearing of Mrs. G." *Buffalo Law Review* 38 (1): 1–58.

Wiegand, Wolfgang. 1996. "Americanization of Law: Reception or Convergence." In *Legal Culture and the Legal Profession*, ed. Lawrence M. Friedman and Harry M. Scheiber, 137–51. Boulder, CO: Westview Press.

Wihtol de Wenden, Catherine. 1988. *Les immigrés et la politique.* Paris: Presses de la Fondation Nationale des Sciences Politiques.

Willemez, Laurent. 2003. "Quand les syndicats se saisissent du droit." *Sociétés Contemporaines* 4 (52): 17–38.

Zitouni, Benedikte. 2007. "Michel Foucault et le Groupe d'Information sur les Prisons." *Les Temps Modernes* 62 (645): 268–307.

Zolberg, Aristide R. 2006. *A Nation by Design: Immigration Policy in the Fashioning of America.* Cambridge, MA: Harvard University Press.

Index

CPSIA information can be obtained
at www.ICGtesting.com
Printed in the USA
LVOW03s2314110917
548301LV00010B/166/P